The Tribe
and its Successors

THE TRIBE
AND ITS SUCCESSORS

*An Account of African Traditional Life
and European Settlement in
Southern Rhodesia*

WILLIAM RAYNER

FREDERICK A. PRAEGER, *Publisher*

New York

BOOKS THAT MATTER

First published in mcmlxii
by Faber and Faber Limited
24 Russell Square London W.C.1
Printed in Great Britain by
Latimer Trend & Co Ltd Plymouth

Published in the United States of America in 1962
by Frederick A. Praeger, Inc., Publisher
64 University Place, New York 3, N.Y.

Library of Congress Catalog Card Number: 62–9462

FOR MY MOTHER AND FATHER

Contents

Contents

Illustrations

PLATES

Illustrations

MAPS

Illustrations 1, 2, 3, 4 and 6 are reproduced by permission of Dr. M. Gelfand, numbers 7, 8, 10, 11, 23, 13 and 14 are reproduced by permission from the Federal Archives of Rhodesia and Nysasaland; number 5 is reproduced by permission of African Newspapers Limited; and number 9 is reproduced by permission of the Radio Times Hulton Picture Library.

Preface

I have tried in this book to show the collision of two cultures, one born out of Bantu Africa, the other derived from Western Europe, and to give some indication of the ways in which they have reacted on each other. The setting is that part of Africa now called Southern Rhodesia.

The book attempts to give a picture of the old life of the Mashona tribes, and to set this picture beside that of the European occupation. In fact, the book is a deliberate hybrid, drawing from anthropology as well as history in the hope that one will illuminate the other. If this juxtaposition affords a new perspective, I shall have achieved what I wanted to do.

I have tried throughout to write for the general reader. This has led me, for example, to avoid using the Mashona plurals of words, which are formed by a change of prefix that I think might have been confusing. This is perhaps also my opportunity to point out that the words 'Mashona' and 'Shona' are used interchangeably: there is no difference of meaning between them.

In one sense, this is the story of what happened to a part of Central Africa as a result of its occupation by white colonists in the final phase of British imperialism. But it also provides an instance of a much more important general process: the transformation of the world by Western industrial culture. The pioneers did not merely take over a tract of land in Central Africa; they imposed their way of life on an existing society which, because of its material poverty, they dismissed as worthless and savage. Thus, the picture presented here, despite its markedly individual nature, may also serve as an example of what is perhaps the most characteristic phenomenon of the modern world.

W.R.

Acknowledgments

I should like to express my debt to the small group of people who have written on the Mashona, and particularly to Dr. Hollemann and Dr. Gelfand, whose work I have made great use of in the first part of this book both as a source of information and as a guide to my own enquiries. Any fault in the interpretation of this material must, of course, rest on me.

My thanks are due to a number of publishers and authors, from whose works I have quoted. The sources of these quotations have been separately acknowledged in the notes and list of books consulted.

I should particularly like to thank Dr. Gelfand for allowing me to use several photographs of Mashona customs which had previously appeared in his own books, *Medicine and Magic of the Mashona* and *Shona Ritual*, both published by Messrs. Juta of Cape Town. I should also like to thank the Federal Archives of Rhodesia and Nyasaland and African Newspapers Ltd., Salisbury, both of whom supplied me promptly with the photographs for which I asked.

Lastly, I should like to thank my wife for her interest and encouragement.

A map of Southern Rhodesia showing the places that are of importance
to the book

The maps above and overleaf are meant to be aids to the text, and the
information given on them has been restricted with that end in view.
Neither map is intended to provide an exhaustive topographical record.

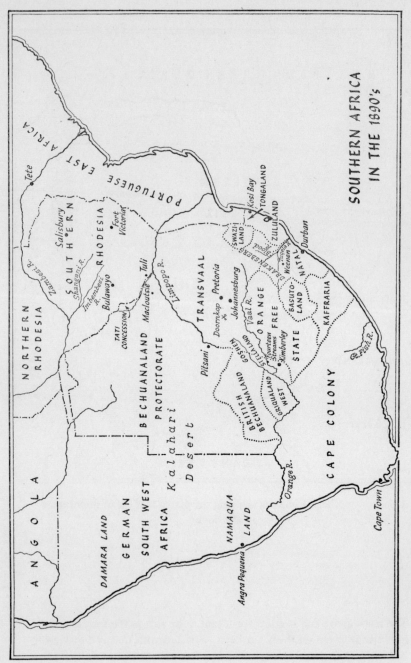

Note: Griqualand West had been annexed to the Cape Colony before this period, but its boundaries have been shown for the convenience of the reader.

SOUTHERN AFRICA
IN THE 1890's

PART ONE

The African Past

CHAPTER I

Bushman and Bantu

This part of Africa lies between the rivers Limpopo and Zambesi. It is bounded on the east by such mountains as the Vumba and Inyanga; on the west by a line that follows no distinctive natural feature but runs arbitrarily across parched scrub from the Limpopo in the south to the Zambesi in the north. Beyond the eastern mountains lies Portuguese East Africa; over the line drawn in the west, Bechuanaland begins.

The whole region is within the Tropics, but as part of the great interior plateau of Africa it is shielded by its altitude and does not suffer the enervating heat that afflicts tropical lowland. Only in those places that rise little over 2,000 feet is the heat ever really gross, and here also the threat of malaria is at its worst.

The most healthy and therefore the most coveted part of the country is the high veldt, an area 4,000–5,000 feet in elevation, running from north-east to south-west in a broad, central spine. Here you will find wide plains, often with a dry wind blowing over them that burns the skin of those who are unused to it. The wind makes the tall grass roll and sway round the humped shapes of the kopjes which rise like basking whales out of the plain—ponderous granite hills that go frail with distance as they stretch back to the horizon. Sometimes the open savannah gives way to bush and when such an area is entered, the horizon contracts: infinite numbers of little trees form a screen that moves with the traveller to the point of his stupefaction. Some of these trees have a spindling Chinese elegance. Others are stocky and covered with bland white thorns. Others, again, look like bunches of closely extended fingers, but ridged, spiny, and dull green, with some of their members dead and contorted by the withering sun. These last are the cacti.

There are parts of the country where the rock rears naked from the plains in bald domes or broken heaps, but more usually the hills have a covering of shrubs, whose leaves are dark green and glossy to combat the loss of moisture to the dry air. Every sort of vegetation here has had to evolve some solution to the problem of drought: for seven months of the year no water is provided. From April to November any rain that falls will be the result of a freak storm. The skies have a luminous Italian brilliance for weeks together and the soil crumbles into dust and is whipped into spouts by the high wind. Yet the country is far from being a desert.

It is so long since the Bantu first entered this region, drifting down over the Zambesi from the north, that they have kept little or no memory of the circumstances of their arrival. We know—though they do not—that their appearance here was one incident in a process of migration that must rank amongst the biggest and longest the world has ever seen. It is some two thousand years, more or less, since the Bantu started on their fumbling journey southward. Nobody can be more accurate than this for no records have been kept. The Bantu could not read nor write and unlettered peoples have no way of preserving their ancient history. Oral traditions may be kept alive amongst them for a time, but eventually they become so obscure, so encumbered with legendary additions, that in the end people can no longer make sense of them and they are forgotten.

But we do know, at least, that by the tenth century A.D. some of the Bantu were already established in the hinterland of Sofala, and perhaps even farther south. We get this information from the Arab writer, Massoudi, who went on a trip from Baghdad down the east coast of Africa at the time when most of it had fallen under the control of Islam. He wrote of a black people he called the *Zendj*, who, from his description, could only be the Bantu. He also referred to another race, one which will not be found there nowadays: a race of little yellow people whom the *Zendj* hated and despised and killed without compunction. The *Zendj* called them *Wak-wak* and thought them no better than baboons.

The *Wak-wak* can only have been the Bushmen, who seem to have been the original owners of much of Africa, including that part of it which lies between the Zambesi and the Limpopo. It seems certain that when the first bands of Bantu tribesmen crossed the Zambesi they found, living on the plains in primitive balance with the game, their ancient enemies, the Bushmen, whom they and their forefathers had already driven before them down much of Africa. No doubt the process went on, for to the Bantu, the Bushmen were both a pest and a danger.

20

They were particularly hated because they raided the Bantu herds, just as they were later to raid the cattle of the Boer stock farmers, and for this misdeed they were hunted to the point of extermination by both black and white men, their few survivors retreating farther and farther back into the wilderness until they reached the barren safety of the Kalahari, where they are now awaiting extinction.

The centuries of war fought between the Bushmen and the Bantu represent a clash between two levels of culture. The Bushmen were Stone Age hunters; the Bantu, herders of cattle and agriculturalists of a rough and ready sort. An even more decisive advantage lay with the Bantu, for they had entered the Iron Age and could forge knives and assegai blades as well as metal heads for their hoes. Between two such different groups there could be no peace, particularly as the Bushmen, despite their contact with the Bantu, never grasped the idea of taming and owning beasts. Cattle never became more to them than game-animals got with unusual ease.

The Bushmen roamed about the veld in small bands: they were essentially nomadic, following as they did in the wake of the herds of game they hunted. They never, at their most ambitious, built anything more than screens of brushwood to protect themselves from the weather; more commonly, they took advantage of caves or overhangs of rock, or of natural depressions in the ground. They did not wear any clothes, with the possible exception of a kaross when the wind was sharp or the nights cold; nor did they grow crops, any more than their rare descendants do today. They were still at the stage where the men hunted and the women supplemented the diet by digging up roots and bulbs out of the veld. They brought to this task one of the few inventions the Bushmen ever made: a digging-stick weighted by a pierced stone. Their only other dependable creation was the bow, a weapon which made them feared by the Bantu because of the poison they smeared on the bone tips of their flimsy reed arrows.

The Bushmen had one other skill, a most remarkable one: they could paint. Over much of Africa their pictures can still be seen, in such places as caves or rock overhangs where they are protected from the worst of the weather. It is strange to stumble across one of their old shelters, like finding a message from a past so distant and so alien that it defies the imagination. You might see zebra drawn there, heads up at the alert; or antelope bounding across a plain that the eye makes for them out of the unadorned rock. There might be elephants looming like cliffs over the little men who are hunting them; buffalo whose massive necks and shoulders are occasionally emphasized by use of the bulges and concavities in the rock surface.

These animals are drawn with a free grace that immediately brings to mind the work of the cave artists of prehistoric Europe. There is the same flowing ease of delineation and the same tenderness. It is usually surmised that the Bushmen, like the men of Altamira, drew their pictures for magical reasons. The subjects are almost always the animals they hunted—you do not see lions or leopards—and such men as appear are cursorily treated and look insignificant—if you ignore the bows and pointed sticks they carry in their hands.

Although the animals are beautifully drawn, once their images had been created they were not shown any great reverence: time and again an artist has painted over some earlier work, disfiguring it in the process of making his own. It looks very much as though a picture's function was fulfilled on its completion, so that a later artist could ignore it without feeling any sense of vandalism or sacrilege. All this certainly seems to suggest magic, and it may well be that the pictures represent an attempt at magical provisioning, that they were intended to ensure the presence of game when the hunters next went out. But this is not the only possibility. Savage peoples often feel the need to propitiate the spirits of the men or animals they kill; sometimes, indeed, they go further and beg the pardon of the streams they dam or the trees they fell. Bearing this in mind, it seems possible that the Bushmen may have made these paintings in an attempt at providing a new repository for the spirits of the animals they slaughtered. Amongst primitive races, a houseless spirit is usually regarded as a malignant one.

Whatever the original meaning of the paintings, you cannot doubt the aesthetic pleasure they gave to their artists. It rings out from the paintings, telling us in a more adequate way than perhaps the Bushmen's meagre implements ever could of his kinship with us, his claim on humanity. You can read there of his awe when faced with the turbulent fountain of life, of his understanding of the beasts he killed, and perhaps of his compassion for them.

These are the Bushmen's sole personal memorial; the only record we have of him that was not given by an enemy. In the past, both the black man and the white spoke insistently of his bestial nature with the authorized contempt of the victor. From their descriptions we must imagine him as a malevolent little pygmoid, a parody of humanity who got his living by preying on the herds of real men. He was a creature that smeared its body with rancid fat and slept in holes in the ground or on the open veld; an untameable, hideous dwarf with peppercorn hair, a prognathous mouth, a receding chin and a nose squashed flat against his cheeks. His women had a monstrous steatopygia of the buttocks, a condition the male also suffered to a less marked degree, and he was set apart from the rest of mankind by the possession of a penis that was always semi-erect and a language made up of ridiculous clicking sounds.

Many of the Bantu tribes refused to recognize him as human: they asserted that the Bushman had been put on the earth as the brother of the wild beasts, before the creation of the first true man. Although this story does, no doubt, reflect the condition in which the Bushman must have first appeared to the invading Bantu, it also offered a pretext for his destruction. It relieved the Bantu of the guilt that always comes with the killing of a man. The only members of the Bushman bands who stood any chance of being spared were the young, marriageable girls, who were sometimes taken as slave wives. It was they, and the Hottentot girls who are their racial cousins, who introduced the characteristic Bushman click into some of the Bantu languages. This mannerism is found most frequently amongst the Xhosa peoples, who were in the van of the Bantu migrations.

The European, too, seems to have doubted the humanity of the Bushmen. Certainly, they were hunted down like vermin because of their depredations on his stock. Boer farmers went so far as to organize drives, in which they hunted the Bushmen on horseback, flushing them from their 'forms' amongst the rocks and tall grass and killing them as they bolted. Only the children might be spared, sometimes, to rear up as 'apprentices'; adult Bushmen were considered untameable.

Even the early missionaries could find little that was good to say about the Bushmen. Here, in an extract from the Transactions of the Missionary Society for 1800, is the impression received by the first minister who tried to work amongst them:[1]

'Their way of living is very horrible. Their dwelling and resting place is between rocks, where they dig a round den about three feet deep in which they lie with their whole family. . . . They mostly lie down and sleep except when hunger greatly torments them; then they go a-hunting; but they live many days without food. When they find no wild beast, then they make shift with a sort of small wild onions and wild potatoes, which the women seek but never the men. They are content to eat snakes and mice. . . . They are total strangers to domestic happiness. The men have several wives but conjugal affection is little known. . . .

Their language is so very difficult that no one can spell or write the same. It consists mostly of clicking with the tongue.'

The passage goes on to describe such customs as the killing of infants amongst them who were born deformed or who could not be fed. The Bushmen would also kill any of their children who could not be carried away 'when they were obliged to flee from farmers and others'. It is a picture of a harried people living in the grip of extremity. Like some Siberian tribes who are faced with conditions of comparable harshness, the Bushmen used to abandon their old people once they had become too weak to keep up any longer with the band. They left them with 'a piece of meat and an ostrich egg' to die as best they could. Finally, the missionary reports: 'Many of these wild Hottentots (Bushmen) live by plunder and murder and are guilty of the most horrid and atrocious actions.'

In recent years, those Bushmen who still survive have been given sympathetic attention by European investigators. The solicitude of the anthropologist is easily explained: the Kalahari Bushmen are representatives of one of the most primitive races in the world, and one which is fast becoming extinct. They have still not changed their ways: they have made no attempt to compromise with the imported civilization of the European, as the Bantu have done. A few scattered bands of them still draw a bitterly hard existence from the gourds and roots and vigilant game of the Kalahari. They still hunt with poisoned arrows and sleep in the open, hunched round their fire, edging so close to it to escape the piercing cold of the desert nights that they often burn themselves in their sleep, as the scars on their bodies show.

But in one important respect their lives have changed: they no longer paint their pictures. Nowadays their only artistic pleasures seem to lie in the dance and in their 'mood-songs', which they sing to the accompaniment of the mouth-bow; songs that tell of the triumphs and humiliations of their lives.

These Bushmen are the last faint syllable of an old story. The present they live in is so fiercely demanding that it leaves them neither the time nor the ability to think much about the future. This is a final mercy, for like other primitive remnants such as the Australian Blackfellow, they have no future. All that will be salvaged of them is that part of their blood that has entered the vigorous Bantu stream by way of slave wives.

In the lands between the Zambesi and Limpopo there were no white men to help in the extermination of the Bushmen. It was carried out by the Bantu alone, and in the process, here as elsewhere, some Bushman blood doubtless entered the stream that flowed in the veins of their conquerors. If it did, such a strain would represent only one more infusion into a people who are fundamentally of mixed stock; for the Bantu are generally thought to have come into being as a result of the mingling of the true Negro, now found at his most pure in West Africa, with the people of Hamitic stock who have lived since before history in the lands north of the Sahara. From time to time, it is conjectured, bands of Hamites must have wandered far to the south, where they appear to have come in contact not only with the Negro but the Bushman, too. From the mingling of Negro with Hamite, the Bantu emerged. Some ethnologists have suggested that a similar cross-breeding between Hamite and Bushman is responsible for the Hottentots who preceded the Bantu in their southerly migration, and whose remnants are now found along the shores of Cape Province.

There is a wry genetical twist to this explanation of Bantu origins, for the Hamites are a branch of the Caucasian family of races, quite closely allied to the Semitic peoples, and ancient cousins of the white races of Europe. So, the Bantu, from their very creation, were the owners of a Caucasian strain—and one of ancient illustriousness. The Hamites can claim to be the founders of the civilization of Egypt, for then as now the people of the Nile valley were of Hamitic stock. Thus, if the idiotic game of genealogies is to be played, the Bantu hand has an unexpected strength. He might lead with the men who built Memphis and Thebes, as his distant ancestors, and it is hard to see what card the Dutch could play to beat that. If such speculation is foolish, it is no more so than the theories of racial purity and superiority which are still commonly offered in South Africa as the justification of white behaviour there.

By simply looking into the faces of any group of Bantu Africans you can see evidence of the racial strands woven into their identity. They vary in colour from light brown to deepest black and their profiles present a wide range of racial divergence: from the splayed, almost flat nose of the Bushman, or the heavily everted lips of the negro, to the thin mouth and aquiline nose of the Hamite. Amongst those tribes that have spent any time on the East Coast in the course of their migration, you can sometimes see a Semitic strain, transmitted direct from the Arab traders who have had footholds there since time immemorial. It is noticeable, for instance, in the Makaranga, who now live in Southern Rhodesia, hundreds of miles from the sea, but who still retain a marked Semitic cast of feature in some cases. The Makaranga, when first observed, were also found to practise customs which might well have been adopted from Arabs of the pre-Islamic period. The big sea-going dhows, 'the great birds from heaven', which made the monsoon passage to Calicut also brought Indians to such ports as Sofala, who added a tinge of Oriental blood to the mixed races there.

To this genetic confusion, the white man has been adding his quota, ever since he first arrived in Africa; he continues to do so today, despite the legal prohibitions set up in Southern Rhodesia and the Union of South Africa to check such behaviour. The Bantu, from whom he now seeks to protect himself, have already left their mark on the face of many a South African, particularly on those who are of Dutch descent. A good many of their forefathers indulged their sexual eclecticism to the full in a country that offered a whole range of 'inferior' women. Such racial purity as ever existed has been crumbling for a long time now, which is why it has been thought necessary to bring in legislation to enforce it.

But the Bantu themselves, despite the consciousness of race they now sometimes assume for political reasons, are the outcome of massive historical miscegenation. Even their name is not an indication of race, though it is often used in that sense. The word 'Bantu', as properly employed today, is a convenience of European scholars, intended to demarcate the members of one linguistic family. Here is Professor Seligmann's definition:

'The Bantu might be defined as all those "blacks" who use some form of the root *ntu* for *human being*; with the plural affix this becomes *ba-ntu* (Bantu) i.e. the men (of the tribe), whence the term under which the whole great group has passed into anthropological literature.'[2]

The Bantu migration, then, was made up of slow tides and surges of men, gradually flooding the major part of a continent. Some tribes appear to have been more volatile than others, but amongst them all there was wandering and raiding and a general drift, with many back-waters and eddies, towards the south. When people are asked to explain *why* the Bantu should have kept on the move for so long, they will usually point to such causes as the pressure of population on available land or the dislodgements created by war. No doubt these played a large part, but in addition, there are other, more spiritual qualities that nomadism gives birth to, and perhaps these also might be invoked. There was the wilderness itself, which offered a temptation that was constantly renewed as each horizon was succeeded by another. We know what happened to many of the solid burghers who settled originally at the Cape: Africa changed them into compulsive wanderers. The trek-Boer, like the Bantu, did not work the ground for long in any one place before he was overcome by the urge to move on. He became intolerant, too, even of the men of his own race, should they live near enough to him for their smoke to show on his horizon.

The trek-Boer brings to mind a similar phenomenon, created by the American wilderness: the Mountain Man, as he was sometimes called. He was a pioneer who had been captured by the forests and mountains, who had rejected the idea of a settled agricultural life in favour of the pleasures of nomadic hunting, living off buffalo meat beyond the line of the settled frontier. As that line advanced, so the Mountain Men retreated, until the frontier met the sea and there was nowhere left to go. There is an obvious parallel between the changes wrought on the trek-Boer and the Mountain Man by contact with the wilderness. Perhaps similar influences helped to motivate the Bantu, as they wandered through the gigantic emptiness of Africa.

CHAPTER 2

Chaka and Mizilikazi

As the Bantu moved down from the north, the Boers in the southern tip of Africa were fanning out from their original settlement at the Cape, and the two peoples first clashed in the neighbourhood of the Great Fish river. In order to establish some approximation to civil peace, the government at the Cape tried in 1778 to declare this river the boundary dividing white from black, but in the circumstances of the time such efforts were bound to fail. Quite apart from the raiding by both sides, the erection of a boundary was an affront to the new outlook that had developed amongst the Boers, and they ignored the instructions of their government. They had already gained a taste for wandering, and now they looked on the lands over the river as theirs for the taking. Young men did not want to live as dependants on their father's farm, particularly as, at his death, the lands would be divided amongst all his sons according to the terms of Roman-Dutch law. They could carve out great possessions for themselves beyond the frontier: they were infected already with the mental habit of gigantism, and its corollary, solitude.

Stock thefts and intrusions across the Great Fish river by both Boer and Xhosa led inevitably to more serious fighting. The first of the Kaffir wars had begun, and the Boer, equipped with the long musket he could use so well, had the advantage which time and again was to prove decisive. Yet even so, for a long time the Xhosa held stubbornly to the land east of the Great Fish river. But they could not move forward; indeed, gradually, they were being thrust back, and so the millenial southward flow of the Bantu was at last dammed. They recoiled upon themselves and southern Africa burst into the tumult of the *Mfecane*.

The *Mfecane* means the Breaking, the Crushing, and is the name given by the Bantu to the fierce wars which broke out amongst them in the early part of the nineteenth century. The customary flicker of war and raiding burst into a ravening fire; campaigns of expansion and extermination were fought; tribes fled headlong and fell upon other tribes in their retreat; whole regions were deserted and laid waste. This swirling acceleration in the movement of the tribes was produced by desperation and terror. It was a process which thrust some of them from Natal as far north again as Nyasaland and Northern Rhodesia.

In such a situation, a military dictator might be expected to emerge. One did appear amongst the Ama-Zulu, which was an obscure tribe linked for survival's sake to Dingiswayo and his powerful Ama-Tetwa. When Dingiswayo died, he was succeeded by Chaka, leader of the Ama-Zulu, who was to organize and direct the military power that carried the *Mfecane* to its bloody climax.

Chaka had inherited from Dingiswayo an army organized on the basis of the *impi*, or regiment. The warriors were under strong discipline. In this society, love was subordinated to war, and sexual passion channelled into martial ferocity. This was accomplished by enforcing celibacy on all young men. They were not allowed to marry until they had proved themselves for years in battle, and when the time finally came for them to take wives, a whole regiment would be granted the privilege together, and would be settled in one spot so that they still existed as a complete military unit. It was a nation geared to war. Chaka tightened discipline still further and used this military machine to devastate much of southern Africa. Zulu legend also attributes to Chaka the invention of the assegai with a truncated haft. All his armies were equipped with this weapon and it proved as deadly at close quarters as had the short sword of the Roman infantryman long before.

At this time among the Bantu, it had been customary to bring two spears into battle: a light javelin for throwing from a distance and a heavy assegai which was used when the two armies had engaged. Both were long in the handle, and the heavy spear was for this reason cumbrous and hard to manœuvre when in-fighting took place. Chaka seems to have dispensed with the light spear altogether, working on the assumption that the ox-hide shields his warriors carried would be enough to protect them from the spears thrown by the enemy. He shortened the haft and broadened the blade of the heavy assegai, which may not seem a very startling innovation, but in the conditions of warfare usual amongst the Bantu, was enough to give his men a devastating advantage, when combined with good discipline.[1]

In addition, Chaka perfected the attacking technique he had learnt from Dingiswayo. Before a battle, he would deploy his soldiers in a formation that resembled the head of a buffalo: a powerful body of men would be placed at the centre, representing the massive boss of the buffalo's forehead; and two crescents of men, one at either side, for the horns of the beast. His object was to throw out his flanking 'horns' and encircle the enemy, forcing them to an encounter at close quarters in which the short stabbing assegai his men carried could be used to full advantage. So long as his opponents chose to fight against him in the traditional way, he remained invincible. It was only when firearms or new evasive techniques were used against the Zulu that they failed to gain the victory. Or when, as happened with the Basuto, a group of shattered tribes were welded together and took up a strong defensive position in mountain fastnesses where they could not be brought to battle on terms that gave the Zulus their normal advantage.

Chaka did not tolerate defeat. If one of his generals came back from a campaign without the usual evidence of success in the form of captives and looted cattle, he was liable to be 'eaten up' as a punishment, the death sentence often being extended to include his whole kraal. There is one example that will be important in the course of this book of a Zulu leader who chose not to surrender himself to Chaka's displeasure. This was Mizilikazi, who had been at one time a favourite of the king, but had fallen into disgrace, some say over a personal quarrel, others because he had failed to bring an enemy successfully to battle. He was to become the founder of the Matabele nation by his decision to flee with his followers rather than accept the punishment of the king.

He was not the only one who was on the move. Defeated opponents of Chaka from amongst the Nguni peoples, such as Soshangane and Zwangendaba, were also streaming back with their supporters towards the north. One group was to settle in Gazaland in Portuguese East Africa, where they still go by the name of Shangaans in memory of their leader; the other horde was to travel even farther, settling at last in Nyasaland, where they are known as the Angoni (Nguni).

All of these military fugitives carried the devastation of the *Mfecane* into distant areas, but it is with Mizilikazi that we shall be concerned because he finally led his nation to the lands between Zambesi and Limpopo and settled them there.

When Mizilikazi played the renegade and marched his army away, he took with him his knowledge of the Zulu method of waging war. There were many tribes over the Drakensberg that might be plundered, and by carrying off wives and cattle, he could transform his army into a nation.

In 1835, the Matabele had made themselves masters of a large part of the western Transvaal, but they were not destined to stay there. They were to move again, this time across the deadly tsetse-fly belt of the Limpopo valley and into the high plateau country of what is now western Rhodesia. Mizilikazi did not make this further migration from choice; but because he had come up against an enemy he could not defeat: the Boers in the van of the Great Trek.

The Matabele were an arrogant nation, proud of their dominion over the land. By this time, they had come into contact with a few white men—hunters, traders and missionaries—but these men had come singly or in small numbers and had always been willing to make formal submission to Mizilikazi's authority by asking him for 'the road'—for his permission for them to travel through the lands he dominated. The Boers did no such thing. They came in ominously large numbers, bringing with them their wagons, stock, wives and children. Mizilikazi realized that they were challenging him for the land itself and so he tried to destroy them.

The Boers had two main methods of fighting, both of them effective against spearsmen provided there was enough time to put them properly into effect. If they were surprised on trek they would drag their wagons into a square and fill the spaces between the wheels with thorn-brush. From behind this barricade they could then direct a heavy fire on the enemy, who was forced to try to storm their position, or at least always did so, for the code of Bantu war enjoined a direct assault rather than a siege.

On the other hand, should the Boers be out on horseback, with no need to worry about their wives and children nor the safety of their possessions, they would adopt the tactics of the controlled retreat. On such occasions they acted like mounted infantrymen: getting down from their horses to fire and then going quickly back into the saddle in order to gallop away until a safe distance had been reached. They would then dismount and reload and as the *impis* neared them again the process would be repeated. They could go on doing this almost indefinitely in open country, raking the enemy with no losses to themselves except those caused by an unforeseen accident.

Mizilikazi's soldiers could find no answer to these elusive 'men riding on cattle': they could not be made to stand for a frontal attack, and they could do damage from an appalling distance. If they were surprised

whilst on trek with their wagons, they made a fort of them, and against
their murderous musket fire a direct assault was all but impossible. The
only way in which the Matabele might have swung the balance back in
their favour was by attacking in broken or heavily wooded country, by
setting ambushes or mounting surprise attacks at night. If, instead, they
continued to fight on the open plains of the Transvaal, their defeat was
assured. But Mizilikazi was no strategic innovator and the terrain did
not favour him.

For all that, the advantage seemed to lie at first with the Matabele.
They surprised the Liebenbergs on the north bank of the Vaal and
wiped them out. Potgieter, the Boer leader, managed to form laager
hurriedly against them at Vegkop, but had to endure the humiliation of
watching them drive away his cattle. But then, the Matabele allowed the
Boers to fight a running battle against them. Potgieter and Uys and 135
followers inflicted a heavy defeat on them in a nine-day fight along the
banks of the Marico river. The Boers did not lose a single man in the
engagement. The formidable nature of these mounted men armed with
their *roers* was decisively brought home to Mizilikazi; he decided to
withdraw his people out of their way across the Limpopo. It was either
that or submit to them.

Mizilikazi set up his new headquarters at Bulawayo and his *impis*
went out far and wide. They descended invincibly on the existing inhabitants of the region: the Mashona tribes, their close cousins, the
Makaranga, and the Batonka. For the next fifty years and more, all
these peoples were to suffer under Matabele raids and many of them
were to endure enslavement or vassalage under their harsh if somewhat
intermittent rule.

Right up to the end, when their power was destroyed by Jameson and
his invading column, the Matabele maintained their custom of the great
annual raid. After Mizilikazi's death, when his son, Lobengula, ruled in
his place, white men were quite often present at the Great Dance that
was the preliminary to the beginning of the raiding season. Indeed,
those who were staying at Bulawayo and were consequently Lobengula's
guests were expected to be present. They would squat beside the king as
he sat in the bath-chair he favoured in his later years, in front of the
royal cattle kraal, facing the great crescent of assembled warriors, perhaps 12,000 strong, who had gathered for the ceremony.

The time of the Great Dance was one of expiation, and also of thanksgiving. No blood might be shed then and no violence attempted; even
the wearing of a red ornament or article of clothing was forbidden. It

was also the time when the king performed a ritual declaring the direction of the big raid for that year. The dance took place in February,
when the main rains had come to an end, and was so arranged that it
followed immediately on the full moon. At the climax of the celebration,
the king danced alone before the nation and then threw the assegai that
would show in which way the *impis* were to go out. As the assegai struck
the earth, the warriors broke ranks, running forward to stab their own
spears into the ground where it had fallen in excited affirmation of their
loyalty and obedience to the king.

Afterwards, the raiders would set off to extort tribute in blood, ivory,
and cattle, and sometimes in young boys who could be bred up to follow
the Matabele military tradition. There were enough of such boys to
form a separate Estate, who though they were regarded as somewhat
inferior because of their birth, were nevertheless an accepted part of the
Matabele nation. They were called the Ama-Holi.

The Matabele were predators. Raiding underpinned their social system. They needed it, not only for the plunder it gave them, but for the
mystique it provided. Without the raid there would have seemed to
them no adequate way of proving their bravery and showing their
superiority over the tribes they despised and habitually tyrannized.
Indeed, there would have been no meaning left in the Matabele nation,
which was essentially a military machine geared to annual campaigns of
plunder. Like Froissart's medieval knight, the Matabele believed with
all their hearts that 'to rob and pill' was a good life. Their inability to
stop making punitive raids into areas where Europeans had settled was
to give Jameson his reason for the march on Bulawayo and was thus to
bring about the downfall of their system.

We might think of the Matabele as barbaric Spartans, living as they
did for the martial virtues, fed hugely on captured beef and sworn to
celibacy in their youth to keep them fierce. What about the tribes they
preyed upon? At first sight they seem merely feeble. Amongst the
Mashona and the Makaranga there does not seem to be the glimmer of
an Athenian quality that we might set against the bleak Matabele disciplines. It is true that these two peoples, nearly allied in origin, sank
into wretchedness under the Matabele persecution, but we should be
wrong to dismiss them merely because they could not defend themselves adequately. In fact, the Mashona had some remarkable attributes,
which they preserved as best they could, despite the harsh pressure of the
Matabele on their way of life. Not least striking is the scale of values they
managed to maintain. They rated civility and moderation above courage,

for instance, and do to this day. They were a gentler people, interested and absorbed in the complex network of human relationships they spun amongst themselves rather than in the pursuit of slaughter as an ideal. If they had wanted to oppose the Matabele, the only way they could have done so with any hope of success would have been to become like them in social and military organization. Such a profound change was quite beyond them, alien to their make-up and no doubt distasteful to them.

The Mashona were an old, settled people, in deep decline at this period. One senses their exhaustion in the means of defence they adopted against the Matabele. In the past, their forefathers had built strong and sometimes complex forts of dressed stone, which they had set on the tops of hills; the Mashona in decay seem to have kept just enough memory of their former powers to try to protect themselves in the way their ancestors had done: they flung up on the kopjes crude girdling walls of rough stone. But their old skills had been lost, and the optimism that prompts men to attempt elaborate works in stone had died in them. The hill refuges they built at this time are miserable relics. You can still find them huddled amongst the long grass on many kopjes, and though they have been deserted for a long time now, an air of ancient desperation still seems to cling to their roughly heaped stones and broken cooking-pots. To the imaginative observer, they suggest mournfully that cultures which have advanced some way can fall back again; that people can lose their nerve; and that perhaps men can be helped towards defeat by the dim memory of their own irrevocable past.

The ancestral forts seem to have been part of a co-ordinated system, but later Mashona chieftains refused to be drawn into any stable form of alliance. As a result, they suffered the fate of the disunited: they were harried, tribe by tribe. Many of them were butchered or were turned into vassals—the 'dogs' of the Matabele—with the task of herding the royal cattle or ostriches. Some fled out of the reach of the Matabele, but they had a long way to go to be safe, for the marauding *impis* would sometimes travel hundreds of miles from their starting point at Bulawayo in their search for prey. The Mashona never knew when some raiding party might not fall on them and 'let their assegais drink'; even those who were in official vassalage to the Matabele king might suffer the same fate in punishment for some slight misdemeanour. After enduring many years of this, the Mashona had become a thoroughly defeated people, so demoralized that they came to accept the Matabele contempt for them as justified. In their humiliation and self-disgust, they were prone to condemn themselves; as one chief was to put it, in later days, when

34

speaking with a white man: 'We are a slave people, descendants of slaves.'

The first Europeans to arrive in any number in the country, the 1890 Pioneers, were buccaneers by temperament and as a result were unlikely to be impressed by the cowed Mashona tribes, whom they took at the low valuation set on them by the Matabele.

The Pioneers intended to take the control of the country out of the hands of the black man, and the more thoughtful amongst them searched about for some ideology to justify their action to themselves. They found it, as did their instigator and financier, Cecil Rhodes, in the theories of Darwin. Here is Selous, who was employed as adviser to the Pioneer column, writing on the point in relation to the annexation of Matabeleland. The arguments could, of course, be made to apply against any of the Bantu peoples.

'Matabeleland is doomed by what seems a law of Nature to be ruled by the white man and the black man must go, or conform to the white man's laws, or die in resisting them. It seems a hard and cruel fate for the black man, but it is a destiny which the broadest philanthropy cannot avert, while the British colonist is but the irresponsible atom employed in carrying out a pre-ordained law—the law which has ruled this planet ever since, in the far-off misty depths of time, organic life first evolved on this earth—the inexorable law which Darwin has termed "The Survival of the Fittest".'[2]

The Matabele was the immediate competitor of the white man in this struggle, and for him he could feel an admiration perhaps in part compounded from guilt. The virtues of the Matabele warrior were such as could be easily recognized by other military freebooters. He went down with great courage and discipline before the Maxim guns of the Pioneers, who could refer any doubts they might feel at such slaughter to Darwin and Natural law.

The Mashona were a different matter. It was impossible to consider them as rivals for their failure seemed to have been already decided on in terms of evolution. They were cowed and negligible. Selous referred to them as: ' ... The various peoples known as Mashonas, whose principal characteristics are avarice, cowardice, and a complete callousness to the sufferings of others.'[3]

Yet the Mashona had another sort of virtue: they could hang on in times of adversity, and have done so with such success that today they make up the majority of the population of Southern Rhodesia. Those who know them—and who give them a chance to show it—will still find evidence of their polite gentleness of character. It has often been taken for servility; indeed, it has sometimes been forced to become that because of the demands of various masters, but it still appears, like evidence of their allegiance to their basic traditional attitudes.

The Mashona are interesting because they once exercised wide authority without ever feeling the need to discard the traditional Bantu way of living. Their ancestors appear to have been in control for several hundred years of a very big area, but they do not seem to have altered the nature of their society much in response to the demands of power. There is no evidence of them perverting the state into an armed camp; of the harsh disciplines of the Zulu and Matabele, the instilled ferocity and the regiments of celibates. Throughout their long period of domination in Central Africa they must have maintained the familial and clan structure common in Bantu society, for it is still alive today. To my mind, this makes them more interesting than such specialized predators as the Matabele, about whom the truest word was perhaps spoken by John Moffat in 1889. He wrote: 'The Matabele are a miserable people and have made myriads of other people miserable, too.'[4] But they were brave and dangerous; they carried the glittering aura that seems to surround the professional destroyers of men, and many white people were sufficiently fascinated by them to praise them. Accounts of their defeat sometimes take on an elegiac quality in the books of Europeans. The Mashona have not been served so well; but perhaps it is true to say that, when faced with an alien people, many men can only respect what they have some reason to fear. Mildness is often the subject of contempt. This has been true of the Mashona, in the past.

CHAPTER 3

A Few General Observations

For a long time the black man has held a special place in the popular imagination of Europe. He has been used, very often, to symbolize the idea of absolute savagery; his name has been used for centuries to evoke images of slaughter, rapine and cannibalism—the old joke of the missionary in the cooking-pot still appears almost every Sunday in the cartoon page of some newspaper or other. But perhaps we should turn to an older cartoon to gain a more general picture of the folk viewpoint: Gillray's satirical comment on the British government's policy of recruiting people to be settled in South Africa in 1820.

His drawing shows the colonists after their arrival. They are in a clearing surrounded by exotic, broad-leaved vegetation, and they are suffering an attack by Africans. The black men have frizzy hair, their teeth are filed to points, their big eyes are rolling with delight and their faces are split by maniacal grins. They are carrying off the women and threatening the men with spears. Balloons issuing from the mouths of the white colonists enclose words of regret and lamentation that they could ever have been so foolish as to leave England.

This cartoon depended for its effect on the existence of certain ideas already deeply rooted in the European mind. The black man was often felt to be more than merely savage, he was diabolic—an impression confirmed by the colour of his skin. He lived in heat and nakedness amongst the gross vegetation of a jungle. He filed his teeth so as to be able to tear more ferociously at his human victims. He was unregenerate man, given over to the powers of darkness: a bogy to children and a threatening or seductive archetype in the dreams of the adult.

Though this image has been consciously discarded by educated Europeans, it still seems to be alive amongst the ordinary people of England, for instance. It has been fed by a stream of 'adventure' literature and a number of films of a similar type. Mau Mau, with its deliberate perversion of customary practices, seemed to offer new evidence of its truth, and the débâcle in the Congo set it murmuring again in the minds of some of those who had been at pains to dismiss it. None of which is really surprising, for this view of the black man is of long standing and has gained the tenacity of myth over the years. Myths of such a kind are not easy to eradicate once they have struck deep root: they fix themselves in depths of the mind scarcely accessible to reason.

What connexion does this myth have with the reality? First, there are customs amongst many African peoples that must strike a European observer as strange, bizarre to the point of lunacy, or worthy of condemnation in terms of Christian practice; there are some which may be understandably repugnant to him, but none are the purposeless folly they have sometimes taken to be. Many early visitors to Africa reported instances of murder, mutilation and even cannibalism—a custom usually held in abhorrence by the Bantu. They saw tribe prey upon tribe in whirling anarchy and beastliness but—it seems hardly to need saying—this was not typical of Bantu life.

The very presence of the European implied extraordinary circumstances, and his demands upon the African were often of a kind to provoke the excesses he witnessed. This is clear from the nature of the first European intervention in Africa, that of the Portuguese in the fifteenth century. It was their appetite for slaves which led to the breakdown of the native kingdom of the Congo. Under Portuguese pressure, the interior was ransacked by African rulers, fearful that if they did not supply the needs of the white men from elsewhere, their own people would be taken. The process begun here was continued and extended for a very long time, and throughout the slaving period there was a progressive corruption of the Africans involved, a crumbling of native states, or their reorganization in merely predatory terms. Degenerative forces were unleashed that travelled deep into the interior of Africa. Nor were the Europeans the only marauders: whilst they operated on the West coast, because of its nearness to the American markets, a similar process was occurring on the East coast, where Arab slavers were at work. To gain what they wanted, the slavers used a mixture of bribery, in the form of beads and bales of cloth, and threats in the general shape of the musket. From the first, the gun was unanswerable: it was this which allowed a few men to disrupt a continent. Their chief aim, for a long time, was the forcible export of human beings.

The slavers of Bristol and Liverpool were later to play a large part in this trade. They worked mainly on the Guinea coast, though they did some business in the Congo, too. It was a rewarding way to employ capital: people could be bought cheap on the Slave Coast and sold dear in the constantly buoyant market of the Americas. The only risk lay in transportation. Under the conditions of the Atlantic trip, many Africans who had appeared sound when they were bought, died, taking their purchase price with them over the side of the ship. But such losses did not stop the slavers making heavy profits. One wonders how much English capital, now employed in more respectable forms of business, was originally amassed out of the slave trade. No doubt some of it has gone back to Africa to help finance the mines and factories that use the cheap labour of the new African proletariat.

Slaving could only be engaged in so long as the people bought and sold might be thought of as an inferior species. In his day, the Bantu had refused to acknowledge the humanity of the Bushman; now, in his turn, he found himself regarded as something less than human and treated like an object of trade. It is humiliating to think of the procedures of the slave market, where men, women and children were herded together and inspected by prospective purchasers as we might now examine cattle, but it is as well to force ourselves to remember these things because they were indulged in by our own quite recent ancestors. And surely no other of the systems of slavery known to history turned a man so completely into a commodity. The tale of mercantile expansion and the praise devoted to the enriching operations of commerce by European economists would have had a hollow ring to the African, could he have understood it all, as he waited on a wharf with many of his fellows, rated as perishable goods in transit, to be sold on arrival to the highest bidder in the open American market.

In 1482, when the Portuguese first touched at the mouth of the Congo, they began to debate amongst themselves whether the natives they found there were made in some approximation to the image of God; whether in fact they possessed immortal souls like themselves. The matter was investigated by the Church and the priests who visited the Congo gave a verdict for the Africans—though this did not make much difference to the way they were treated. It was their fate over a period of centuries to be disposed of for profit, until finally civilized opinion, notably in Great Britain, revolted against the monstrous assumptions that underlay the slave trade.

Whenever one racial or ideological group refuses to accept another as fully human, we have learnt to expect disgusting consequences. This should have been finally brought home to us by the conduct of the Nazis. The slave trade, though it did not show the purposeless malignity that attended the Nazi policy of exterminating the Jews, can be seen now as a historical indecency of similar scope. It festered on for centuries; is estimated to have been responsible for the destruction of more human life than even the death-camps can claim; and was probably the cause of more misery.

It is against a background of such events that we must weigh European descriptions of African savagery. There must also be added the theologically-inspired doctrines of slavery held by the Boer frontiersman. In his opinion, it was the natural destiny of the Bantu to serve as slaves; he rested his argument upon the Bible, identifying the black men with the children of Ham. It was a generous act of Divine Providence that provided them to labour for the *volk*. We have already touched on the pressures set up amongst the Bantu by Boer expansion from the Cape: they were a further great stimulus to disintegration whose effects were felt throughout Central and Southern Africa. The extraordinary nature of the *Mfecane*, with its military empires and fleeing hordes, must be kept in mind when we are considering the white man's judgement of the black.

We might well ask, How did the Bantu live in more normal circumstances? In the chapters that follow, I shall try to give an answer to that question, at least so far as the Mashona are concerned.

CHAPTER 4

The Mashona Past

As they appear today, the Mashona are a loose congerie of tribes, speaking variants of the same language, and closely allied to the Makaranga, who live beside them. They do not seem to have had any definitive name for themselves in the past. The word '*Mashona*' has been imposed on them. It is supposed to come from the contemptuous Matabele name for them, *Ama-Swina,* meaning *The Unwashed Ones*, though this derivation is uncertain. In the past they are said to have resented the name, but that is not true any longer. Today they have accepted it as a generic term suggesting their relatedness and use it to encourage a sense of solidarity more embracing than that inspired by the tribe.

These days, when they say they are one people, linked by ties of blood and language, they are doing no more than re-state the major historical fact about their past. There is little doubt that those tribes we call the Mashona had some part—to put their claim at its most modest—in the creation of a state that has left evidence of itself in the ruined stone forts found scattered in their hundreds over Rhodesia, and in more esoteric buildings such as the Great Enclosure at Zimbabwe.

The period of their rule can still only be tentatively stated. Wood which was found supporting a drain at the base of the main wall of the Great Enclosure at Zimbabwe has been carbon-dated and gives an answer of 800 to 1000 A.D. This seems to suggest that the main walls were begun about that time, but in fact the dates cannot be conclusively accepted because the tree from which the wood was taken, *tambootie*, has a poisonous bark. It is most unlikely that it was actually felled by the builders of Zimbabwe; indeed, after its death it may well have been left for a long time to dry out before it was brought into service. There is

41

another point to consider. *Tambootie* is a very hard, resistant wood and one which repels termites. To understand the value of such properties, you must imagine a country where a wooden stake cannot be left long in the ground without being eaten away; a country where even today such things as railway-sleepers, fencing-posts and telegraph-posts must all be made out of metal or concrete if they are to survive. In these conditions, it becomes quite feasible that the wood was precious enough to salvage from some older building and transfer to the drain at Zimbabwe. If this did happen, then of course the building of the main wall might have taken place at a time considerably more recent than the wood suggests. It would, in fact, approach more nearly the medieval date that most archaeologists favour. For our purposes, the dates do not matter; the important point is that for a long time, probably for centuries, the country that we now call Southern Rhodesia was under some form of unified control. The many stone ruins it has left testify to the energy and the unusual nature of that state, though perhaps the number of hill forts could be interpreted to mean that control was only held with difficulty. The threat to their builders may have come from outside: from such hordes as the Ama-Zimba and the Abambo who ravaged down the East Coast of Africa in the latter part of the sixteenth century, even sacking Mombasa and overwhelming the Portuguese settlement at Tete on the Zambesi; hordes set in motion by forces obscure to us. Alternatively, the forts may be seen as evidence of coercion. They may have been dominating islands in a hostile sea, the handiwork of a conquering minority, intended to keep a subject population cowed, rather like the Norman castles in England. But we have no reason to suppose they were the work of an alien élite, other than the existence of the forts themselves. In face of the large-scale gold mining that took place here, it is much more likely they were strongholds where gold was smelted and stored. Evidence of gold smelting has been found on the Acropolis at Zimbabwe and at other, similar sites.

Obviously, the forts could also be manned for defence in time of war, and no doubt were: functions tend to be diverse rather than exclusive in such matters. The bigger and more elaborate structures seem to carry the marks of prestige building; they may well have been intended to symbolize the power of their creators. Early Portuguese hearsay accounts certainly make this point: they talk of the majesty surrounding the *Monomatapa*, or ruler, of this inland kingdom; he was, they say, 'of great reverence and was served on bended knee.' But this reflects Portuguese hopes as much as anything. Not too much trust can be put in these reports, which are demonstrably confused about other matters relating to Zimbabwe.

In the sixteenth century Portuguese expeditions following the Zambesi far inland, claimed to have come up with an African ruler who went by the title of the *Monomatapa*, but he was not living in a stone dwelling. His hut, like those of his entourage, was made of the usual pole and wattle and daub. He explained his lack of pomp by saying that he had been driven from much of his kingdom by rebel chieftains. This may well have been true, for the Monomatapa's kingdom appears to have been gradually disintegrating at this period. Sometime earlier the Barozwi had already gained control of Zimbabwe. They are usually thought to have been a rebellious group from within the wide territories controlled by the Monomatapa, or from the Venda peoples to the south, who are in any case racially and culturally linked to the Mashona. They do not seem to have been absolute intruders, for they knew the techniques of building and went on putting up structures of dressed stone until at least as late as the eighteenth century. But they seem to have let the gold trade fall into decay—at least, very little of the legendary gold found its way any longer to the coast. This may have been due in part to the greed of the Captains-General of the Portuguese station at Sofala, who refused to allow the Arabs and coastal natives to carry on any longer their ancient role as agents and middle-men with the producers of the interior. The Portuguese complained bitterly about the mere trickle of gold dust that reached Sofala. Their reports sent back to the government in Portugal are full of such remarks as that the trade was 'a great expense for so little revenue and profit' and the Captains-General often angled for transfer to the dazzling station at Goa in India.

Yet there was a good deal of truth in the stories that had originally given rise to Portuguese hopes. Gold was certainly mined, and mined extensively, in the kingdom of the *Monomatapa*. Centuries later, when the white Pioneers occupied Southern Rhodesia to prospect for gold, they were to complain that 'the eyes had been picked out of the country' long before their arrival. They noticed, too, that this had not been the grubbing in shallow holes or washing of alluvial sand that is as far as Africans usually go in their search for gold. In this region, shafts had been sunk, some of them to a considerable depth; galleries had been driven from them and large amounts of gold extracted. About the end of the last century, its value was estimated by a white engineer to be somewhere near 90 million pounds sterling. A comment on the efficiency of the ancient miners can be found in the fact that, to this day, nearly all Southern Rhodesian gold mines are situated near old workings: the miners of the past had located all the major deposits. To the early Pioneers, it seemed impossible that such feats as these, or such achievements in stone as the buildings at Zimbabwe, could ever have been performed by the African. They quickly came up with the theory that this was ancient Ophir; that it was the handiwork of Phoenician or Sabaean colonists. They could not reconcile the possibility of its being a Bantu achievement with their own knowledge of the African, nor did they want to, because of the disturbing implications inherent in such a theory.

Things have swung recently to an opposite extreme. Some apologists for the African past have allowed themselves to read far too much into the stone ruins at Zimbabwe, Khami, Dhlo-dhlo, or Naletali. They point to them as evidence of an indigenous civilization, stimulated a little by trade with the coast, but owing little or nothing to outside influences beyond that. Their motives are generous: they want to raise the self-esteem of the emergent Bantu and equip him with a past that has its own achievements. This may be good for morale, but it seems to me to depart from the facts so far ascertained in favour of a philanthropic gesture.

To write (as Mr. Basil Davidson does) of the 'civilization' of Zimbabwe is to stretch that term to a point where it loses its usual meaning. Excavations at this site have not shown any evidence of civilization as it is normally understood. The stone fortifications and enclosures have invariably been associated with pottery and hut-debris that show little or no advance on the usual level of Bantu culture. It is true that objects have been found which testify to a link with the Orient via the east coast port of Sofala, but such objects are rare enough to suggest that the link was a very tenuous one. The presence of such things in Central Africa does bring a shock of amazement at first—beads from Persia, a fragment of Ming china—but they do not argue civilization amongst those who came to possess them any more than did, say, the presence of Roman trade goods amongst barbarians living far beyond the Imperial frontier. The extent and character of the mining operations show a fair level of technical ability, but if these are taken together with the stone buildings, we cannot say that they constitute evidence of a civilization. It might be more accurate to describe the kingdom of the Monomatapa and the Barozwi as an illiterate, barbaric realm. It reveals a culture that, though in advance of its neighbours in a few special skills, was very little different from them in the general, material level of its life.

The Mashona Past

It is certainly true to say that the architecture at Zimbabwe and similar places owes nothing to outside influence—as trained investigators such as Randall MacIver and Miss Caton-Thompson were quick to point out. Indeed, it looks as though it grew out of the round grass-huts and pole-and-straw enclosures that can be found in any kraal, so far as design is concerned. It is surmised that the workers in stone began to imitate these structures with their new material. The idea of working in stone would not be too difficult to hit upon in a country whose hills are generally composed of exfoliating granite that splits naturally into 'leaves'. All that remained was to dress them for building purposes, and this procedure would be forced on the builders by the irregularities of their material as they found it.

Gradually, the masons became more ambitious, but it is as well to keep their limitations in mind. For instance, they never learnt to measure accurately nor to keep a regular distance between two parallel walls, any more than they learnt to bond one wall into another. Again, they set sculptured stone birds up in parts of their building, and they carved stone dishes, but to take praise to extremes for this kind of achievement is really a form of patronage. The material in which they produced these things was soapstone, which is soft and cheesy in texture. They seem most likely to be the result of an extension of the wood-carving skill common to most African peoples by a group who had become very conscious of the possibility of doing things in stone. Soapstone is the nearest thing to wood that they could find in the mineral world.

I have no intention, in making these remarks, of belittling the achievements of the men who threw up such massive walls as those round the Great Enclosure, or created the cunning maze of fortifications on the Acropolis at Zimbabwe. I would say that these people showed striking advances on the usual level of Bantu culture in three directions: they built ambitiously in dry stone; they mined gold extensively; and they appear to have kept some form of control for a very long time over the wide areas in which their forts are scattered. They were barbarians, not primitives; and their achievements were great enough to make early white settlers reject with some heat the idea that they could ever have been created by the lazy sun-loving Kaffir.

Apparently provoked by the extravagant claims made for Zimbabwe 'civilization', some archaeologists have lately swung the pendulum a long way in the other direction. They say they can see no more in such a monumental work as the Great Enclosure than the results of a 'wall-building complex' that developed out of a desire, perhaps, to impress. I,

45

for one, am not at all sure what they mean to imply by this term. Surely there is a sense in which Westminster Abbey or Notre Dame could be described as the results of a similar complex? Presumably they mean that the Great Enclosure has no function that they can discover. It seems to be no more than a ponderous variation on more domestic structures, serving no point except that of megalomaniac fulfilment for some African ruler. It may be so, but would Notre Dame or Westminster Abbey be easily understood if they were found deserted and ruinous by someone of completely alien culture? If one of the aims of the builders was to create a sense of awe, then they were successful: Bullock writes of tales, common amongst the tribes in his day, telling of Barozwi attempts to build a scaffolding to the moon, and how they tried to move mountains and set them up again at Zimbabwe.[1]

But, to my mind, it seems unlikely that the Great Enclosure was the product of a mere obsession with the grandiose. Objects such as the conical towers which are found there seem to imply a ritual significance just because they have no understandable purpose. What are you to make of a thirty-foot conical tower, meticulously executed in some of the best masonry to be found in the ruins, a tower that is solid through and quite unscaleable, a tower, which was adorned near its summit with the chevron patterning that seems to have been used by these people to indicate things and places of particular importance, except to assume that it was a cult object?

Early European visitors to the Great Enclosure called it 'The Temple', and though this title has been rightly dropped for begging the question since there is no evidence of its use for religious purposes, their guess may have been right, for all that. African life in the past was so closely interwoven with ritual observances of various kinds that it seems unlikely, talking merely in terms of their psychology, that they did not make use of this imposing building in some part of their cults. There is other, indirect evidence. For a long time the Barozwi held the ascendancy at Zimbabwe. To this day, members of the Barozwi tribe have a high reputation amongst the Mashona for their skill as magicians and workers of wonders. The apex of traditional Shona ancestral religion rests in the august spirit of Chaminuka—and according to Mashona legends, Chaminuka first made his appearance at Zimbabwe, as we shall see. Even now, it is still customary for a Barozwi to act as 'priest' at the installation of a new Mashona chief. Keeping the religious significance of these survivals in mind, it seems probable that the Barozwi used enclosed areas such as the Great Enclosure for ritual purposes.

Whether or not this was so—and now it seems likely to remain permanently in the realm of speculation—there can be little doubt that the labyrinthine construction of the Enclosure and the ruins that stretch from it down into the valley were intended to impress the foreign visitor or the uninitiate. Yet perhaps even this is doubtful: the ruins are inscrutable and the local Africans deny any knowledge of their original purpose.

What does seem certain is that these ruins are the wreckage of the legendary 'Empire of Monomatapa' and of its Barozwi successors, which the Portuguese heard about almost as soon as they set foot on the shores of Mozambique, and whose accounts led European cartographers to give it a shadowy place on their maps of Africa for centuries afterwards. It is equally certain that the tribes who now go under the general name 'Mashona' played some part in that 'empire', though nowadays they disclaim any memory of it—at least when talking to white men.

CHAPTER 5

The Mashona Family:
An Alliance of Flesh and Spirit

The kingdoms of the Monomatapa and of the Barozwi are now part of the dead past. Barozwi rule seems to have been already in decline when a Swazi horde, set in motion by the *Mfecane*, broke all but the last shadow of its power about 130 years ago. According to legend, these invaders flayed alive the Mambo, or Great Chief of the Barozwi.

The people of the region must have found themselves in danger and bereft of government. They seem to have fallen back, naturally enough, on the family and clan allegiances from which any greater power that developed in the area must have originally sprung. The obscurity of this time is profound, but presumably the modern Shona tribal pattern emerged out of the chaos and dispersion that followed the Swazi invasions and the collapse of Barozwi rule.

In such circumstances, each group would have had to fend for itself as best it could. The history of the tribe as told by the old men who keep the verbal record reflects this state of affairs. It makes no mention of the Great Mambo—all memory of rule by such dignitaries seems to have been suppressed among the modern Mashona—but usually begins with the story of a settlement being founded by a group of related people in some defensible area called by them the *nyika*, or territory. Of course, it is just possible that these stories refer to the original entry of the tribes into this part of Africa, but in that case there is a broad gap in their history covering the centuries of rule by the Monomatapa and the Barozwi, and all their achievements in building and mining. It seems more probable that this period, with the shame of its destruction, has

48

2. The present medium of Chaminuka, the greatest *mhondoro* spirit. The medium is praying to Chaminuka shortly before becoming possessed by him at a public ceremony.

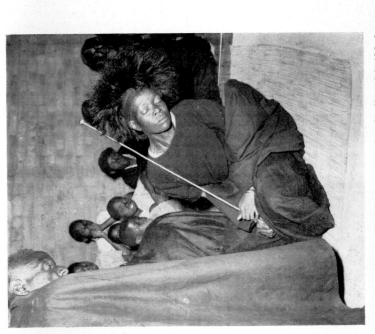

1. A woman medium possessed by her family spirit (*Mudzimu*).

3. An old Mashona praying to his grandfather's spirit (*Mudzimu*)

4. An *nganga* with some of his paraphernalia set out before him.

been thrust away out of memory and that their stories refer to more recent tribal dispositions.

However that may be, the *nyika* would be chosen to include a hill of refuge, which they might roughly fortify with stone walls, and would include mastery over a limited area of land. Similar groups of people would be lodged in the surrounding hills and the stories tell of 'wars' that ensued over grazing and cultivation rights. Though these tales loom large in the stories of the old historians they probably did not involve more than a score or two of men on either side, and the campaigns may have lasted no longer than a day.

If such a tribal nucleus established itself successfully, as the numbers of the people grew, it became necessary to send out colonists to ease the pressure of population on the lands of the *nyika*. They would go off, in all likelihood under a son of the chief, and try to find, or capture, a place that could furnish them with land and a hill of refuge of their own. But, even if they were successful, they would still look to the parent *nyika* as their heartland.

Such colonies were given the name of *dunhu*. As time went on, they might flourish and multiply, and in the process force the amalgamation of less successful groups, as well as attracting bands of unrelated people by the protection their strength afforded. The *dunhu* still exists today as a ward, or tribal division, though the Government has never paid much attention to it. To an African, it is important. The tribe as a whole has often become too big to have much emotional claim on the individual—though the significance of the original *nyika* is still kept in mind. It is his *dunhu* that a man remembers when he travels far away to the European cities or mines; it means to him the place where he grew up among his own kind; the villages of his childhood; the lands where as a herd boy he watched his father's cattle; the earth that holds the bones of his ancestors.

Thus, under the original chief there would be lesser chiefs or headmen, each in control of a *dunhu*. Within the *dunhu*, each village had its headman and each family its patriarch. If the villages were small, the headman and the patriarch would be the same person. This picture gives us the typical pattern of authority, the simple hierarchy common amongst the Mashona. It was a rash man who chose to wield dictatorially any powers granted him by the system. He was usually controlled by bonds of custom and by the knowledge that he had to keep and win the voluntary submission of the people to his authority. If they did not like him, they were at liberty to break away and sue to join some

D   49

other group. The headman was called 'Father' by those he governed, and he in turn addressed the tribal chief as 'Father'. These titles reflect the familial beginnings of the tribe.

The family was the vital unit in Mashona society, but it was a larger family than we recognize in England and one with closer duties and ties. In it, for instance, the son of a brother would be regarded as a son, and called by that name; all the cousins would call each other 'brother' and 'sister'. A more extensive network of relationships was generally observed, and the obligations of one member of a family towards another were much more closely defined by custom than has been the case in modern Europe.

The family was a group bound powerfully together. The allegiance its members felt for one another extended beyond the living to include the dead, whose spirits were believed to watch over the people of their blood and exercise a powerful and intimate influence in all affairs concerning the family. Indeed, to the Mashona way of thinking, it was both the living and the dead together who made up the family, which was regarded as an entity that lived and grew through successive generations. Both the living and the dead were concerned, above everything else, with the continuation and strengthening of the group—which meant in practice the birth of as many children to it as possible. If babies did not come plentifully, then their *rudzwi*, their kind, was threatened. They could envisage no worse catastrophe.

In a way, the dead were dependent on the living. Should the family die out, the dead members of it would be damned to oblivion: if there was no one to remember them, they would drown in the obscurity of their fate. The living gave purpose and meaning to the spiritual existence of the dead and provided the fleshly instruments through whom they could make their influence felt. The ancestral spirit, or *mudzimu*, must be thought of as existing in a kind of symbiosis with living flesh and blood. Without that relationship, the spirits might linger on for a while but their existence would be pointless; they might as well not exist, which to an African meant that they did not exist, not in any terms that he could imagine. But if the ancestral spirits were dependent on the living, they in their turn considered themselves to be under the tutelage and protection of the spirits. The two groups worked together, both of them determined that their blood and the corporate 'entity' enshrined in it, the *rudzwi*, should not be allowed to die out. Both rejoiced at every child born to them.

According to some of the Mashona, the link between the child and the *mudzimu* might be even more strong. They believed that sometimes the spark of life that entered a child in the womb might, in fact, be the *mudzimu* of one of its paternal ancestors, who wanted to be born again. This did not mean that the child had no spirit of its own, but only that during its lifetime it would be the spirit of its ancestor which remained active in it. At the moment of death, its own spirit would wake out of its dormancy and go to join the ranks of its forebears. But this positive belief in the possibility of reincarnation was not held by the majority of the Mashona.

Enough has been said already to make it clear that the Mashona, like most of the Bantu, had a reverence for life and fecundity that was closely bound up with, and directed towards, a reverence for the dead. Fertility was given powerful religious sanction. It was because the ancestral spirits did all they could to help the welfare of the family that they were so loved and respected by the living—and, on occasion, so feared by them.

In these circumstances, it is not surprising to find that a *mudzimu* did not always confine himself to protecting his own; he would also punish them, if he thought fit. Anyone who jeopardized the safety of the group by his unlawful acts, or anyone who slighted the dignity of the *mudzimu* by omission of the customary rituals, could expect spiritual retaliation. The towering figure of the old father dominated this scene: the dead grandfather, who was regarded as the most powerful of the ancestral spirits because the nearest and most attached to the living. Indeed, he would be remembered parentally by the older members of the group, who would still bear him in mind as the patriarch he had been when alive. But death had granted him powers much more far-reaching than any he had wielded as a living man. In his new authority, he could send sickness or misfortune on the guilty; as punishment for some crucial misdemeanour he might strike dead a member of his family. Such acts as these would be utterly condemned in a living man: it was the mark of the witch alone, amongst the living, to cause sickness or seek deliberately to bring about death.

In the past, some anthropologists have noticed this fear that is attached to the spirits of the dead by primitive races and have chosen to describe it as 'the transformation of the soul into a demon at death'. Freud used such statements to support his theories on the underlying tensions in the family.[1] He suggested that the fear which such spirits evoked in the living was due to the element of suppressed hatred to be found in their past love-relationship with the deceased. The hidden antagonisms showed themselves as pleasure, felt inescapably by the survivors at the death of the man, and this secret and shameful impulse of pleasure led to a sense of guilt and a desire to punish themselves for their wickedness. The wish to punish was then projected in the guise of the vengeful spirit of the dead man, who appeared to wish to do them harm. Their only defence lay in ritual propitiation of such a spirit.

The psychological mechanism described here to explain the belief in spirits of a dangerous kind seems plausible, but it does not really fit the facts so far as the Mashona were concerned. Though they may have feared the *mudzimu* in some of his aspects, and certainly felt the need to propitiate him ritually, their prevailing attitude seems to have been one of awed reverence. He and they were really in alliance against the many dangers, physical and mystical, that threatened the prosperity of the group. He would not punish them unless they were guilty of some offence, and though he might sometimes appear jealous and severe, they knew that, in the last resort, they were his children and he loved them and wanted them to flourish.

This did not mean there was no ambivalency in the relationship. Some of the actions of the living recognized that, in a sense, they had usurped their ancestor and his generation. For instance, when the crops were ripe in the past, the first fruits might be taken by the head of the family and lodged in the fork of a tree sacred to the ancestral spirits. The patriarch would then say: 'Look, grandfather, here is maize. Here is pumpkin. You can see now that you have not been displaced and forgotten by your children.' In the same way, if a member of the family had died and the diviner had declared the death to be due to an angry *mudzimu* spirit, the family would carry out the ritual act of expiation suggested by the diviner—usually it would be the sacrifice of a bull— and then the leader of them would say: 'Now we have done what you required of us. Now please let us be, grandfather. Let us live out our lives in peace with you.'

But even if sickness should be caused by a *mudzimu*—and other things could be responsible for it in their eyes—it was not always a sign of anger; they might interpret it rather as a timely reminder of some important act they had omitted to perform; or it might be a mark of distinction. This last explanation applied when the person who had fallen ill was being given a sign that the *mudzimu* wanted to 'come out' through them; wanted to use them as a spirit-medium, in fact. A person singled out by a *mudzimu* for this honour was traditionally informed of the spirit's wishes in this way. The cause of the sickness had to be confirmed by a diviner, though the *mudzimu* might well have appeared in dreams already to the person he had chosen and explained what he wanted. As soon as the person accepted the spirit, the sickness would go away.

Many families—though not all—had such a medium amongst their number, whose mouth was always ready to be put at the service of the spirit. Through this agency, the *mudzimu* would advise the family on all matters of importance: it would talk to them about their crops, their cattle, or the provisions they should make for the future; if a journey had to be undertaken, it would discuss with them the best time to begin it; if witchcraft was feared in the neighbourhood, it would offer its advice.

Today it is a common complaint amongst Shona converts to Christianity that their new religion does not offer them any direct contact with the spiritual world. There is no warm, personal tutelage, such as could be had from the *mudzimu*: God and the saints maintain a perpetual silence.

When a medium was coming under possession by the spirit, he would grunt and roar and his whole body might heave about; when the spirit was leaving him, his limbs would be seen to shiver and quake. This sounds rather like the behaviour of mediums at séances in Europe, and indeed the whole conception is not dissimilar to that held by members of the Spiritualist sect. But the Mashona beliefs were far more meaningful, and the operation of the spirits was an integrated part of their lives, not a series of random and aimless communications. The *mudzimu* was part of the pattern of their existence. As we shall see, the Mashona believed themselves to be involved with other spirits, too, but the *mudzimu* held an honoured place in the hierarchy of the dead.

CHAPTER 6

Marriage and the Barren Wife

We have seen that when the *mudzimu* 'came out' he was trying to ensure the prosperity of the family, and that ultimately this depended on the number of children born to it. As you might expect, marriage was a very important institution amongst the Mashona because it provided children, and this was seen as its only important object. Love might develop between a man and his wife, but it was incidental, and many successful marriages flourished without it. There was no trace of a tradition of romantic love, such as that which has run so powerfully through European societies since the time of the troubadours. The Bantu, generally, regarded marriage as an arrangement, and the affection born between partners was more likely to spring from satisfaction at the way each had played the role allotted to them by society rather than from any more passionate cause.

But to be satisfactory, a woman had to conceive. If she proved barren, she was regarded by her husband as a broken instrument, and he might go to her father and claim her younger sister to bear children for him as 'the raiser of seed'. The position of a barren woman in African society was usually one of deep humiliation. Her failure was so fundamental and profound that there seemed no way in which she could restore herself to public esteem and the favour of her husband.

Livingstone describes how he once cured a barren woman of a complaint and, in consequence of this, she managed to bear her husband a son:

'Her husband having previously reproached her for being barren, she sent me a handsome present, and proclaimed all over the country that I possessed a medicine for the cure of sterility. The consequence was that I was teased with applications from husbands and wives from all parts

54

Marriage and the Barren Wife

of the country. Some came upwards of two hundred miles to purchase the great boon, and it was in vain for me to explain that I had only cured the disease of the other case. The more I denied, the higher their offers rose; they would give any money for the "child-medicine"; and it was really heart-rending to hear the earnest entreaty, and see the tearful eye, which spoke the intense desire for offspring.'[1]

This incident took place among the Bechuanas, but it reflects a state of mind common to almost all the Bantu, and would apply equally well to the Mashona.

In connexion with marriage amongst the Mashona, one has to remember that originally all members of a clan were thought to bear a relationship to each other that prohibited sexual union. A man should never take a woman from amongst his own clan or he would be committing incest. The deep horror of incest is shown in the Mashona belief that any such liasion would blast the crops and bring down disaster on the whole community.

The common identity of the clan was symbolized by their possession of a totem object, or *mutupo*, and originally, marriage was forbidden between two people of the same totem. But as the clans grew and spread, a subordinate division was introduced within the clan, which went by the name of *chidawo*. The *chidawo* was not itself of totemic origin, it was a device for marking off patrilineal families and sub-clans when the original totem group had grown too numerous to be any guide in the practical arrangement of an exogamic marriage. Only in the case of two people with a totem and a *chidawo* in common would marriage then be forbidden.

The *mutupo*, or totem, was often an animal, though other things could serve as totem objects. A clan felt some form of mystical identification with its totem, and there was consequently a strong prohibition— usually found in connexion with this mysterious belief—against harming the animal or plant concerned, and particularly against using it for food. But in this part of Africa the taboo had been relaxed with the passage of time and in the period we are concerned with only one part or organ of the totem was likely to be forbidden. Some clans even seem to have introduced an element of fraud into their relations with their totem: Bullock writes of one sly group of the elephant totem that had forbidden itself to eat the tusks, and there were others who would not allow themselves to eat the bones of their animal! But, on the whole, *mutupo* and *chidawo* were taken seriously. A man inherited them from his father, and revered them as the distinguishing marks of his people;

in later times it was the *chidawo* that received most respect because it made a more precise and personal definition.[2]

When a man married, he would take his wife from another totem or *chidawo* group in order to avoid the danger of incest. But although she came to live at her husband's village amongst his family, she never relinquished her own totem and *chidawo*. Spiritually speaking, she remained a member of her own group and when she died, her spirit was thought to go to join those of her own paternal ancestors. So it was that each new generation of children was born into a family by women who were not themselves really members of it. They were, so to speak, loaned by one family to another so that the consequences of incest might be averted.

In compensation for the life-long use of this woman by an outside group, her father would expect a payment. Traditionally this would be made in cattle—they had no money—and would allow the girl's family to make a similar 'borrowing' of a bride for one of their own young men. But it was always a 'borrowing of the womb', and not the degrading, outright purchase of a chattel that many Europeans have imagined it to be. A woman gained in marriage by this payment, known as *lobola* or *rovoro*, did not become the absolute property of her husband and his kin, by any means. She was never part of their spiritual unity, though her children were born into it. When she died only a member of her own group, a blood relation—or her son, who shared some of her blood—was allowed by custom to cut her waist-string in the symbolic act that freed her from the ties of life and assisted her spirit to leave the corpse to go to join those of her paternal ancestors. This ritual deed was forbidden to her husband.

We can see by now, I think, that the payment of cattle for a bride was not a degradation of woman. Without the *lobola* the girl provided, her brother might not be able to find the number of cattle necessary to ensure him a wife. A woman would often refer proudly to her brother's wife as 'the wife of my cattle'. In fact, a girl's contribution to the welfare of her family was to go outside it and provide by her marriage the wealth with which another woman might be 'borrowed' for it.

Despite the hostility of missionaries and the past disapproval of government officials, *lobola* is, to this day, almost always paid over at a marriage. It makes the contract solemn, acts as an assurance of good treatment for the wife, and helps to bind together the members of a family in mutual obligations. A man should have his father's consent, and would need his help, in order to marry; the *lobola* he required would have been provided for him by his sister and given to him by his father. Such things increased a man's respect for his father and his sister. In token of the important part she played in such a transaction, the sister was given certain customary rights over her brother and his wife, including the right to act as judge in any arguments or disputes they might have with each other.

In the past, if a poor man had several sons but no daughters, help would have had to be found for him in the matter of *lobola* amongst the wider branches of the kin. Nowadays this problem does not arise so acutely as there are new ways of earning money for *lobola* open to young men: they can travel to the cities and work in factories and mines for a time. If all else failed in the past, a young man might enter into a rather inferior kind of marriage in which he went to live with the family of his wife and carried out various services for them in lieu of paying *lobola*. But this was an act of desperation and happened only rarely. It upset the usual system because it did not bring cattle to the girl's family—and the work of the groom would not breed beasts for her brothers. As a result, such a marriage was only likely to be acceptable to a family who already owned a good many cattle.

There was also a more extreme kind of service-marriage amongst the Mashona. A poor man—often a destitute stranger who had wandered into the area and asked permission to settle—might sometimes bind himself for life as a bondsman to the family of the girl he married. Occasionally, chiefs made use of this method in the past to provide themselves with dependent retainers, but it was never at all common and has fallen completely out of use today, when the conditions which bred it no longer exist.

Now and then, a girl might be reserved from birth for a certain man. This was only done by the girl's family when the man had done them some exceedingly valuable service, or put them in some other form of deep debt to him that they could not repay in any other fashion. But, again, such arranged marriages were a deviation from the normal system of marriage by *lobola*; they were the rare result of special circumstances.

In the past, *lobola* seems to have been usually set at about four head of cattle; nowadays it may be as many as fifteen, sometimes with a cash payment as well. This rise in the payment has led white officials to conclude that under modern conditions, the *lobola* system is being abused. but *lobola* was always high. In the past, many fewer cattle were kept, and it was as hard to raise four head of them then as it is to raise fifteen today. Modern conditions offer opportunities for earning money that were simply not there in the past.

It was always essential that the payment asked for a bride should be high in relation to the wealth of the community. It gave to the institution of marriage a dignity that was a true reflection of its fundamental importance in the life of the group. It also acted as a safeguard to the wife against the cruelty or neglect of her husband. If a wife left her husband, alleging that he was treating her badly, her own family, to whom she would have returned, would be most anxious to settle the quarrel amicably, if only because otherwise they might have to give back to him some of the *lobola* they had received for their daughter. But should they become convinced that the husband was guilty and seemed likely to repeat his actions if the daughter went back, they might well encourage her in her desertion, give her shelter, and flatly refuse to return any of the *lobola*—and their decision would probably be upheld in the chief's court.

In a case such as this, divorce was impossible, and the woman would continue to be regarded as the man's wife. It would be a galling and frustrating situation for him: he had lost his *lobola* and gained nothing for it, no wife to cook, bear children, or work in the fields. His obvious course, once his anger had cooled, was to try to bring about a reconciliation with his wife—and this would involve a promise of better treatment for her in the future. Thus, *lobola* dissuaded men from bullying or other forms of cruelty and encouraged the stability of marriages.

Divorce did occur amongst the Mashona by mutual agreement, but it was always difficult to arrange because of the readjustments in *lobola* that had to be made. If a pair had separated, the usual aim of their families would be to bring them together again and try to get a pledge that the acts which had caused grievances between them would not be pursued any longer.

When a new wife came into her husband's family, she was treated with great respect. As was so often the case in Mashona society, the situation was ritualized. The bride was led bashfully to her husband's kraal, lured on by little presents whenever her feet stumbled, as she made sure they did, over pebbles or bits of wood on the path. When she arrived, she would be shy and reticent and the members of the family would offer her gifts or tokens to 'see her face'. There would be polite clapping of hands in greeting and much attention paid to the girl, who was assumed to be still reluctant at the idea of leaving her parents. But her social position would wane if she did not fall pregnant fairly quickly.

As time passed, and no sign of a child appeared, she and her husband would begin to cast round for a possible reason. The Mashona believed that, besides being sterile because of some physical defect, a woman might be unable to conceive because witchcraft had been set to work against her, or because an angry *mudzimu* spirit had decided to interfere with the course of nature.

The married pair would go to consult a diviner on the matter, who would advise them what to do. If he diagnosed the trouble as the result of a *mudzimu* he would tell them what sacrifices might be expected to placate it. If he thought it due to spells set upon the wife by a witch he would do his best to cancel the power of her evil medicines by devices or concoctions of his own. There remained a third possibility: the woman might have been struck barren by the acts of some former lover of hers who was jealous of the marriage. If a young couple liked each other and could see no clan or family reason to stop them marrying eventually, they would often exchange pledges with each other. The token offered by the girl had little in common with Western romantic notions—it was often a piece of her pubic skin with hair on it, or a bit of material that had been in contact with her genitals—but it did suggest in plain terms the rights she intended to grant her lover. Nowadays, the token is more likely to be something bought from a shop, such as a hat or shirt, but the intention behind the gift is the same.

If the couple quarrelled afterwards or family wishes forbade their association, the girl, if she were wise, would try to get her pledge back. If her ex-lover kept it, he could use it to perform acts essentially the same in kind as those a witch might commit. For instance, he might hang the token on a twig or plant near enough to a waterfall to be kept in constant motion by the currents of spray and air. According to the sort of reasoning employed in sympathetic magic of this kind, the swaying would be reproduced in her womb and would make it impossible for a child to form there. He might gain the same result by employing the services of a 'black' diviner, or—a rather more modern instance—he might bury the token under the floor of a stable where mules were kept, in which case the woman would be as barren as the mules.

But what if neither offerings to the *mudzimu* nor medicines against witchcraft had made any effect on her, nor was there a past token she had not recovered? The Mashona knew that a woman might be naturally sterile and that the condition was often incurable, but before they came to that bleak conclusion, the husband and wife might well explore one last alternative, which would be a degree less grievous to them if it proved to be the cause: that the husband was the infertile partner.

If the husband thought this might be so, he would secretly approach another man in the family and ask him to try to make his wife pregnant. Such an arrangement was known as *kupindira* or 'entering on behalf of' and was kept a strict secret amongst the three people concerned. If any word of the agreement were to leak out the husband would feel badly humiliated. Dr. Gelfand[3] gives an example of the ritual speech by which a member of the Manyika tribe informed a 'brother' that he wanted him to conduct *kupindira* with his wife. The husband said: 'I give you this arrow.' To which the correct reply was: 'I accept the arrow. If you find me with your wife, kill me with it.' Once the agreement had been made, the husband would take himself out of the way for a week or two, having explained to his wife that if the 'brother' came to her discreetly she was to allow him to make love to her.

In some tribes, instead of the giving of the arrow, a compact was made amongst the three people concerned, and its nature solemnized by the carving of a *shashi* mark on some tree deep in the bush: great importance was given by the Mashona to any such physical symbol of agreement. Then, after the husband had gone away, the 'brother' would make his dangerous love to the wife. The mystical threat would be too great for him to take much pleasure in the act; he would do it largely out of a sense of duty and kinship, to 'keep the seed within the family'. The spirits might be angry at this apparent adultery and punish him or his family as a result. Nevertheless, out of affection, and in his anxiety that the *rudzwi* should be fruitful in all its branches, he would brave the possible dangers of the act. The wife would co-operate for similar reasons.

If the wife still did not fall pregnant, the husband would probably despair of her. He might then ask for the return of some of his *lobola*, which had been paid on the understanding that the wife would bear children, or he might claim her younger sister to 'raise seed' for him.

The position of the wife declined, in such circumstances, and became one of permanent humiliation.

CHAPTER 7

Pregnancy and Birth

If, as usually happened, the wife became pregnant soon after her marriage, she entered a time in which she could be mystically dangerous to others. The Mashona shared that belief in the spiritual potency of women, particularly at menstruation or during pregnancy, which is common to many peoples of the world.

When the wife realized she had entered this new condition, she knew that she had two duties to keep in mind. During the coming months she had to shield the child inside her from any sort of harm, and she had to prevent the spiritual charge temporarily present in her body from injuring those about her. Gestation, like death, was regarded as a breaking of the pattern of everyday events. The mystical current it generated had to be deflected by taboos from harming other people or animals, or the land itself.

This is what lay behind the forbidding of pregnant women from entering fields where certain types of crop were growing. She had to keep well clear of the cattle kraals for the same sort of reason. Other men than her husband would be reluctant to approach her. They said: 'We do not know whether she will deliver a child or a monster.'

The woman had also to take care to guard against creating some deformity in her unborn child. Hence, she might not eat the flesh of the tortoise or of anything sour. She should not carry a winnowing-sieve on her head for fear the child's fontanelle might be enlarged. In a more recent addition to the lore, she is not supposed to look at a man in braces in case she might prepare for herself an obstructed labour in which the child's cord would be twisted like the braces.

Such prohibitions as these are the common stuff of folk-lore, and things like them can be found all over the world. Indeed, many beliefs of a similar sort still linger in the twilight region of European consciousness. There was no real difference of intention between the action of an English midwife who slipped a pair of scissors under the mattress of a woman in labour and, say, the Makaranga who knocked a hole in the back wall of the delivery-hut when a birth was taking place. In both cases the mode of thinking was the same: the behaviour of both was aimed to cut pain and make the birth easy. Both were essays in magic.

In the past, the Mashona woman was thought to have become so potently charged that by the eighth month even her husband could no longer visit her. She would go to a special hut, which would have been built ready for her, and it was there that the child would be born. Nowadays, the same hut is used as the woman has been living in, but after the birth it must be purified before the husband may safely enter it.

Some time before the child was due to be born, arrangements would have been made with the midwife who was to attend the delivery. She would be sent for as soon as pains began and, as the contractions got faster, she would tell the woman in labour to strip herself naked and put herself in a sitting position, with her back against a drum or grinding-mortar—which is why, among the Mashona, they will sometimes describe a woman in childbirth as 'at the drum'. The woman's legs would be placed wide apart and bent, and she would be told to grip the insides of her thighs and exert pressure in that way. No men were allowed near the hut during the labour, but women would often come to watch or help at the birth.

It has always been an article of Shona belief that if a birth is hard and protracted, it must be due to the unconfessed adultery of the mother. At first, if the labour showed signs of being a difficult one, the midwife might do her best to help by applying herbal medicines, but if these did not work, both she and any other women in the hut would begin to suspect that the mother must be an adulteress. They believed that, in such a case, the womb would not let go of the child until the mother had named her illicit lover. So they would try to persuade her to mention the name of any man other than her husband who had slept with her. If the woman was obstinate and her condition was growing worse, they might even resort to torture in their desperation. This was not done to punish the woman, but because of their fear that if they did not get her to speak, both she and the baby would die. Leather thongs might be tightened round her head or wrists; or a stave, split part of the way down, might be forced apart and put on her temples. In these appalling circumstances, the woman often admitted that she had committed adultery—and the womb then opened. She had to give the name of the man (or men) concerned, and later he would be fined a number of cattle. No further action seems to have been taken against the woman, and the child, of course, was gladly accepted as her husband's.

If, in spite of being tortured, the woman insisted that she was virtuous, the relatives would take the case quickly to a diviner, who would be given the task of deciding whether she was telling the truth or not. If he found her innocent of adultery, then the relatives knew that the obstructed birth must have been caused by an angry *mudzimu* for some other reason, or that the woman was a victim of witchcraft. In either case, they would hasten to take what steps they could to help.

What happened in the end, of course, was a satisfactory conclusion to the labour, or death. But whichever of these two events occurred, a purely physical explanation of how it had happened would not have seemed adequate to the Mashona. They would ask *why* this woman's labour had been abnormal; if you were able to point to some physical defect in the woman, they would still want to know how it had got there and who was responsible for its presence. They looked for evidence of conscious intervention in many matters that we in Europe nowadays, are willing to dismiss as the action of blind chance. To their minds, the fall of a sparrow was not merely marked—it was engineered. Nature was meaningful, and they strove hard to find the logic of its events. As we shall see, this attitude towards the world played a great part in their beliefs in witchcraft.

But usually the birth would go off well and the husband would be informed by the ritual calls of the midwife that all had happened as it should. He would also be able to tell from the number of cries she gave what the sex of the baby was. The husband might begin the rejoicings then, but he himself would not be allowed into the hut to see the child until the cord had dropped off. Meanwhile, the baby would have been smeared with strength-giving ointments, and sometimes with the mother's milk, as soon as it came into her breasts; particularly on the genitals, in the hope that the application of milk would encourage fecundity in adult life.

But the child was not yet regarded as fully human. If he died at this stage, there would be no proper burial for him nor any of the usual funeral rites. It would be thought enough to bury his body in the damp earth at the bank of a river or to throw it into the water 'to cool the spirit'. A baby did not become a real person until he had cut his first teeth, and even here there was a danger, for if he showed himself unnatural by cutting his bottom teeth before his top, he would be called 'crocodile' and might be killed as a potential witch.

This refusal to recognize the small infant as fully human can perhaps be explained in psychological terms by pointing to the high rate of mortality amongst babies. The loss was less severe if the child were not yet recognized as being of full human status. Even so, many traditional Shona names, coined by parents for their children, ring with the grief of past loss: *Taruberekera*—We have given birth for death's sake; *Mhute*—Mist, the fleeting one; *Tichivangani*—How many of us are left?; *Mabwazara*—The caves are all full; *Pururai*—Strip us off (as leaves from a branch); *Chinyama*—A little piece of meat (that will be consumed by the witches); *Imbayevu*—House of clay; *Sarai*—Good-bye; or simply, *Rufu*—Death.

This refusal to acknowledge the infant as human before it reached a certain stage of development may also explain how a people so passionately fond of children could kill those who were deformed or who happened to be born twins—a twin birth, being unusual, was feared to be monstrous. But in this context it is as well to remember the Classical Greek custom of exposing deformed or unwanted children, or the infanticide practised in Imperial China. Such actions were by no means confined to Africa, and though obnoxious, are not the exclusive mark of savagery.

Before the Mashona husband came in to see the child, the floor of the hut had to be treated with medicines or sealed afresh with the mixture of earth and cow dung that is the normal material put down in African huts. If this were not done, the husband would be vulnerable to the mystical properties inherent in the process of birth, and might suffer from swellings and crippling pains in the legs.

Throughout this account, it is necessary to have kept in mind the peculiar nature of gestation and birth as the Mashona saw it: the process was abnormal, mysterious, and dangerous, particularly in the case of a woman who was having her first child.

The child would grow up in the village amongst his kin, and gradually he would learn of the bonds that tied him to his *rudzwi* and his ancestors. Like his fathers before him, he would come to understand that he was one totem and one community with both the living and the dead. The belief would be inculcated in a thousand ways that when he grew up his first duty was to assist in the welfare of his own kind, though beyond them he would recognize the large alliance of groups that made up the tribe, with their chief, like the father of them all, at the head of it.

5. Young educated Mashona stage the 'death' of Chaminuka at the hands of the Matabele. The photograph was taken at Nharira school, Salisbury, in 1960.

6. A man dancing, possessed by a Matabele *shavé*. He has rigged himself up as best he can to look like a Matabele warrior. (See Plate 8.) This is done to please his *shavé* and induce it to enter him.

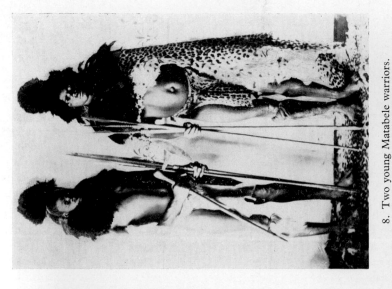

8. Two young Matabele warriors.

7. The Conical Tower and some of the main wall as seen from within the Great Enclosure at Zimbabwe. The photograph was taken in 1903, but by this time European gold-seekers had done much damage to the ruins. It will be noticed that the top has been knocked off the Conical Tower. This was done to see whether it was hollow, in which case it might have contained

CHAPTER 8

Death and Obsequies

The Mashona did not accept the death of a man as a natural thing. They wanted to know *why* one man should be struck down and another man spared and, as with an obstructed birth, they felt there must be some conscious agency at work: an angry *mudzimu* spirit or perhaps a witch.

It was usual to make enquiries into the reasons for a death so as to counteract or propitiate the agent, if necessary; but before they did this the relatives would arrange for the burial to be completed with full ceremony. They reasoned that if they did not do it that way, they might offend the newly dead man, and they did not want that to happen because he was now invested with the powers of the *mudzimu*. So, in order to confine misfortune to its existing dimensions, they would first arrange the interment.

The corpse would be laid out in his own hut and all the women would weep and wail, joining noisily in the mourning. Some did so from genuine grief, some to satisfy custom, but there were others who wailed, despite their indifference, for fear that they might otherwise be thought to welcome the death of a relative. This keening went on until the corpse had been taken to the grave—an act that could never be delayed very long in a hot country. The men of the family would file into the hut, each dropping a small offering into a bowl that had been placed near the head of the corpse. This was their *chema*, their ritual token, given as a mark of respect for the dead man. Mourning would go on overnight and people would refresh themselves with the food brought especially by the women to meet the needs of those gathered there.

Meanwhile, some of the men would have prepared a grave at a place not far from the village. In the past, caves were often used as natural sepulchres, their mouths being sealed by boulders after the corpse had

E

been deposited inside, but more recently graves have been dug. There was a customary positioning of the corpse at burial that differed from tribe to tribe, but whatever the posture prescribed, the male relatives who received the body would take pains to follow it. If they were careless, the spirit might not be able to find rest and in those circumstances would be justified if he punished them for their slackness. When the grave had been filled in, the brother of the dead man would call on the ancestral spirits—mentioning by name all those he could remember to show that he kept them in mind—and would ask them to welcome their kinsman who had come to join them. Then, a goat might be killed and a ritual meal eaten by the graveside.

After all this was finished, everyone who had been at the funeral would go down to the river and bathe there in order to wash away their association with death. In the old days, it was thought proper for men who had actually handled the corpse or arranged it in the grave to undergo a purification ceremony, but this seems to have fallen out of use now. Meanwhile, among the women back at the huts, steps would have been taken to perform a similar cleansing of the dead man's hut by sprinkling it with herbs, or sometimes by smearing the floor with cow dung and earth.

Later, an ox would be killed, and that evening the mourners would feast. Some tribes allowed dances of death to be performed, often lasting all night. Then the drums would beat, the men would sound their ox-horns, and the women chant and shake their rattles. Other tribes seem to have forbidden such dancing.

Between a week and a month after the burial, it was usual for a deputation to set off to consult a diviner about the death of their kinsman. Out of the various 'doctors' they naturally chose one who had the reputation of an expert at divining the causes of death. Preferably, he would be a man who lived far enough away to be a stranger to them: they knew quite well that a diviner might sometimes cheat and so did not want one whose decisions might be influenced by local knowledge. They would make a point of giving no information about themselves to the diviner, their argument being that as he was a powerful seer, he ought to be able to find out their trouble without any help from them.

The diviner would make his enquiries in the spirit world and give them his decision. If they were satisfied with it, the mourners would return home. There, beer would have been brewed for their homecoming. The dead man's brother would address the spirit, saying that beer had been brewed in his honour and that now they were going to

kill a beast to do him reverence. If the diviner had told them that his
death had been caused by an angry spirit this, too, would have to be
placated by beer and sacrifice, after which they would plead with it to
recognize their penitence for any oversights they might have committed and ask it 'not to kill any more'. If a witch had been cited, they
might try to find out with the help of a diviner whether anyone in their
village was responsible.

There was another chapter in the story of a man's death: the carrying
out of his obsequies, which were usually performed at some time between six months and a year after burial. There were two parts to this
ceremonial: the bringing back of the spirit to the village, and the
appointment of his successor, together with the distribution of his wives
and personal property.

What took place was, in fact, a ritual presentation of the continuity of
the family, summarized in one act, that brought the dead back to the
living and appointed the heir who would take over the responsibilities
of the deceased. The heir would be formally given the name of the dead
man and would go by it in future, so that it should not die out of the
mouths of the living.

The ceremony might take this form: First, beer would be brewed
and there would be a dance on the night before the spirit was to be
drawn back to his home. The dancing could take several forms: one
group of women might be giving a last dance of mourning, whilst others
nearby were enjoying a spirited, even lascivious dance, to celebrate the
forthcoming return of the spirit to his home and people. Next morning,
the relatives would go to the grave and set about tending it with a show
of ostentatious, loving care. They would tear out any weeds that had
grown on it and sweep the earth smooth and neat to show their solicitude. Then they would pour beer to the spirit, either on to the grave or
under a nearby tree, calling on the spirit by name whilst they did so and
reassuring him in every way they could think of that their intentions
towards him were beneficient. Next, they would pause to drink some
more beer they had brought with them in a separate calabash.

By these means, the shy spirit was encouraged to enter the nearby
tree. When the relatives assumed that it had done so, a man would
climb the tree and cut off a slender branch that the spirit was taken to
have occupied. He would cover the branch quickly with a cloth, so that
there was no chance of the spirit becoming separated from it by accident, and then the party would make its way back to the village, dragging
the branch along the ground and pausing every now and then in its slow

procession to make sure that the spirit did not become tired with the journey. Once back there, the branch might be installed under the eaves of the dead man's house, or in some similar place, and celebrations would break out again.

Late on the night that the spirit had been drawn back, his heir—who would probably be his eldest son—would be informed officially that in future he was to take his father's name and accept the responsibilities that had been his father's. In a sense, he would *become* his father. Next morning the heir would be ritually washed and anointed and praises would be sung to him about his father's virtues. Then he would sit down in the yard in readiness to accept publicly his father's battle-axe or knobkerry, and with them his duties and position.

The wives of the dead man would be offered new husbands from within the group. The heir's own mother would usually be taken by the brother of the dead man, whilst the heir himself might take any of his stepmothers. But a woman was always given the chance to refuse any man offered to her. She could, if she liked, go back to her father's kraal. When this matter had been arranged, the heir would give out the dead man's personal possessions as he thought fit. He himself would keep the dead man's cattle, but he had to care for any children left by the deceased as if they had been his own. After the distribution, a feast would be held at which the heir would be offered gifts and saluted in the dead man's name, and with that the ceremony came to an end.

Again, it seems to me, this ritual was intended to emphasize the unity of the living with the dead, and to ensure that the family lived on in peace under a recognized authority.

CHAPTER 9

Mhondoro

Because the forms of Mashona society grew out of the family, we might expect to see the relation between the living and the dead repeat itself with similar manifestations at the higher level of the tribe. We should not be disappointed. The tribe did look to ancestral spirits that concerned themselves with the welfare of the whole people. They were sometimes, though by no means always, the spirits of tribal progenitors, original chieftains, who had 'come out' for generations through different living mediums.

The role of the *mhondoro*, or tribal spirit, was rather similar to that of the *mudzimu*, except that, of course, he worked in a wider field and was a more potent figure than a 'grandfather' could ever be. Some of the reverence in which he was held became reflected on to his human medium, who often rivalled or surpassed the chief in importance as a result.

The tribal spirit and his medium both went by the name of *mhondoro*, which means 'lion'. The association of chiefs and great men with the lion in Mashona society needs no explanation—the sense of power and dignity intended is obvious. Certain tribes made a more literal connexion between their chiefs and the lion. There were some of them who believed that, at a chief's death, his spirit might wish to enter a lion. They catered for the chief's convenience in this respect by leaving open a vertical shaft in his grave to ease his passage back and forth between lion and corpse. At first, in the early days after his burial, it was assumed that he would come back quite often to his corpse but as time went on, he was thought to return less and less frequently; when they thought the spirit had finally deserted his decayed corpse, the mourners would seal the shaft.

To emphasize the honour and dignity of his calling, a *mhondoro*

69

medium wore a distinctive form of dress, and it was forbidden for ordinary people to approach him directly. Those who wished to speak to him, and the spirit he represented, had to do so through his assistant, or *nechombo*. It was this man who put the questions to him when he was in a state of possession, always speaking to him with the greatest deference and clapping his hands gently together in a show of formal, Mashona politeness.

The *mhondoro* spirit was concerned with tribal welfare. His powers were great; he was thought to be able to advise on, and sometimes to intervene in, such matters as rain-making, war, invasion, the fruitfulness of the soil, the social harmony in which people should live and the epidemic diseases that might break out amongst them. It was he, too, who proclaimed the *chisi* days—the days of rest—that the tribe should keep. But like the *mudzimu*, he could afflict men for their sins as well as help them in their struggle against nature or human enemies. He shared the jealousy of the *mudzimu* towards any slur on his honour, and particularly towards any crime that might bring about a division amongst the people. If the *mhondoro* were seriously angered, he might withhold the rain, or he might send clouds of little seed-eating birds on to the crops; he might even let loose smallpox amongst his people. But it must be stressed that such acts were exceptional; in normal circumstances the *mhondoro* was benevolent. Indeed, he was a primal 'grandfather' and his people looked to him for guidance and assistance. His anger, when it appeared, was an effect of his love, meted out to prevent the occurrence of worse disaster. It was a warning as much as punishment.

Just as there was a simple hierarchy in Mashona society rising from the family patriarch through the village headman to the sub-chief or *dunhu* headman and from him to the tribal chieftain, so in death there was a pattern of increasing power. The family *mudzimu* gave way to the lesser *mhondoro* and they to *mhondoro* of greater stature, until finally the illustrious few were reached whose names had a more than tribal dignity. At the apex of this structure was the most powerful *mhondoro* known amongst them, the great spirit of Chaminuka, whose name is still revered amongst the Mashona today. The spirit has 'come out' again in a human medium and is active in Rhodesia at the moment.

Chaminuka possessed all the usual attributes of the *mhondoro*, but he had them to an enhanced extent. He was the master to whom all other *mhondoro* spirits would appeal if a matter 'overcame' them by its scope. Yet he must not be thought of as a god. The Mashona, like most other Bantu peoples, believed in the existence of a primal creator, a Great

Spirit or Fashioner who had made the fabric of the world and all the creatures in it. They called him *Mwari*. Unlike Chaminuka, *Mwari* had never been a man and felt no special kinship with mankind. He seems to have been thought of as a Spirit remote from the objects of his creation and indifferent to them. The prayers of living men could never hope to sway him: people depended on the *mudzimu* and *mhondoro* for protection and for the more local manipulations of Nature. But in a time of great catastrophe, many people believed that an august spirit like Chaminuka had some hope of interceding for mankind to the High God.

Many legends gathered round the name of Chaminuka. In some of them, he appears as a culture-hero: the man who first taught the people how to cultivate certain crops; how to make beer and mealie-meal porridge; how to extract iron from certain 'stones on a big mountain'. Before ever he 'came out' through a human medium he was sometimes said to have spoken from the air at Zimbabwe. As Zimbabwe was the headquarters of the Barozwi power, this last story must be taken together with many others referring to the special religious gifts of the Barozwi. They were supposed to be able to hear the voice of the High God himself, and hear it direct, without need of an intermediary, issuing out of mountain caves or forest groves. It is interesting—and perhaps significant—that this ability is now confined to a dissident group who left the Zimbabwe area long ago and travelled a hundred or so miles to the west, where they settled amongst the Matopos hills. It seems possible that they might have left Zimbabwe as a protest, when they saw their newer, purer *Mwari* worship being recaptured by the old religion of tutelary ancestral spirits. The *Mwari* cult of the Matopos has kept alive in an esoteric form to this day, particularly at the Njelele Cave. It appears to be oracular, with the god speaking through his chief officer, who goes by the name *Mulumo*, or Mouth. He has also been reported to speak directly on occasion, from the dark interior of caverns.

In the mechanics of communication, the two forms of religion are not dissimilar, and some link seems to have been retained between the oracular priesthood of the Matopos and the *mhondoro* of Mashonaland. At least, when the *Mulumo* gave it as the advice of his god that the Matabele should rebel in 1896, the *mhondoro* further east joined with him and helped raise the Mashona tribes. It should be explained that the Matabele, on their arrival in the Matopos area of Matabeleland, were impressed by the *Mwari* cult and adopted it. Lobengula, chief of

the Matabele, son of Mizilikazi, was a minor official of the cult in his
day. The Matabele called the cult after the name of its chief officer,
Mulumo or *Mlimo* and this name was taken by European pioneers to be
the designation of the god himself. When the *Mulumo* called for rebellion, he was echoed by the *mhondoro* mediums, but the extreme nature of
the call here, the burning hope of driving out the white usurpers, was
probably enough to draw *Mulumo* and *mhondoro* into an alliance that
disguised their differences in belief.

In both forms of religion, it is worth noting, the spirit world used
human mediums to contact the living. And perhaps it is significant that
Chaminuka was supposed to have spoken first from the air, as the High
God of the Matopos may still sometimes do today. It seems possible that
old memories of oracular pronouncements by *Mwari* at Zimbabwe may
have been grafted on to traditions concerning Chaminuka. Perhaps the
Barozwi had developed the concept of a High God to whom there was
direct access, but had later to abandon it as a political sacrifice, to appease
the majority of their people. If, as seems probable, the other Shona
tribes found the idea of direct communication with *Mwari* unacceptable,
then their Barozwi leaders, all but the most zealous of them, may have
found it expedient to re-emphasize the power of the *mhondoro* by way of
Chaminuka. They may, for that matter, have been seduced from their
more austere cult by the religious notions of the majority of the tribes.
There would be no novelty to the Barozwi in the idea of ancestral worship. It is a belief almost universal amongst the Bantu in one form or
another and would certainly have preceded the idea of praying direct to
Mwari amongst them.

The followers of *Mwari* associated the divine name with the idea of a
wind; they used a religious calendar based on the phases of the moon;
and they showed a decided preference for worshipping on hills and in
mountain caves. This evidence, together with the monotheistic nature
of the cult, has led some investigators to suppose that the concept of
Mwari, the one High God, was originally borrowed from Semites
trading on the East Coast. This may have been so, but the whole subject of origins and theological intention is very obscure. All we can say
for certain is that the two forms of religious observance existed (and
still exist); that their ritual, with its dependence on mediums, is similar,
though the subjects of worship are not the same; and that the religion
centred on the *mhondoro*, with Chaminuka at its head, was much
stronger in terms of adherents.

Although the Barozwi had been broken by Swazi raiders in about

1830, they held on to a shadow of their former power until the warriors of Mizilikazi completed their dispossession. There is a tradition amongst the Mashona that explains the ultimate downfall of their Barozwi leaders in terms of a punishment sent by Chaminuka. The great *mhondoro*, they say, ordered them to abandon their old custom of sacrificing a man—usually a near relation—at the death of a chief. The Barozwi were truculent and turned on the medium of Chaminuka, intending to make a bodily attack on him, but he evaded them and disappeared from their sight. Then they heard the angry voice of the great spirit calling to them out of the long grass and warning them that if they persisted in their disobedience, they must expect to suffer defeat at the hands of the Matabele. Furious with disbelief, they set fire to the grass from which the voice had issued, but immediately they heard the voice again, rebuking them out of a grove of trees. In their maddened state, they chopped down the trees and burnt them, but again the voice moved, speaking to them this time out of the rock itself. It told them it would make good its threat. Another ominous sign of the *mhondoro's* displeasure was revealed to them; they had just dismembered a bull in sacrifice; now they saw its limbs come together again and the animal stood before them whole. After a moment, it charged away. Then the people understood that the bull was the symbol of Chaminuka, who was deserting them because of their defiance and leaving them at the mercy of the Matabele, who would be his instruments of punishment.

This is a typical Mashona way of interpreting events. In this story they have given a mythical rendering of the reasons for the destruction of the Barozwi power: because of their disobedience and irreverence, their spiritual protector had forsaken them. However, Chaminuka returned later, when his punishment had been exacted.

The Mashona tell another story about Chaminuka and the Matabele, one in which we may perhaps glimpse the faith of a subject people that their conquerors will not be able to destroy them. According to this legend, Chaminuka prophesied that the Matabele would come to his medium, Pasipamire, and try to kill him. Soon afterwards the Matabele did come and all but four of the people ran away in terror. The Matabele were quick to kill the four faithful men, but when they turned on Pasipamire, they could not hurt him no matter how fiercely they thrust and stabbed with their assegais. Finally, the voice of Chaminuka came from Pasipamire's mouth and told the Matabele to give a spear to a little boy who was standing nearby. Chaminuka then allowed the boy to do what all the Matabele warriors had failed to accomplish: the boy was told to make a thrust with the spear and when he did so, it pierced the body of Pasipamire, who fell down on the ground. However, the medium was still not dead, for his body kept rolling about in the dust. The Matabele were infuriated by what had happened. They seized the bodies of Pasipamire and his followers and skinned them all, but still the flayed body of Pasipamire rolled about as though alive. The Matabele cut out his heart and put it in a grain bin, but next day when they came to look at it, they found the heart still beating, with several snakes coiled near it protectively. In a frenzy of fear and hatred, they ran to cut firewood to burn the palpitating heart, but every branch they touched turned into a snake. When, in the end, they went back, defeated, to the place where they had left the bodies lying, they found that all five of them had vanished. And as they stood gaping, they heard the voice of Chaminuka speak to them out of the air. It prophesied the defeat of Lobengula at the hands of a white race who would attack him from the east. It was even supposed to have said that a great city would be built by the new invaders at Harari, which is the Mashona name for the district where Salisbury now stands. But these look like recent additions to the original story.

Quite apart from the obvious defiance of the Matabele which informs the story, and the implication that in Chaminuka they had a spiritual power stronger than Matabele force, there are some odd elements in this Mashona legend. If you consider the voluntary death of Pasipamire at the hands of a young boy, his subsequent skinning and the placing of his heart in a corn bin where snakes were kept, the suspicion may well come to you that perhaps you are being given a glimpse of some older ritual. Embedded in the story there may be fragments of a rite of fertility, of death and resurrection. Snakes are often sacred and, because they slough off their skins, are obvious symbols of rebirth. It is not impossible that the memory of such a rite should have been refurbished to express the terms of Shona defiance of the Matabele. As we shall see, ritual killing was not unknown amongst the Mashona in the past.

The respect given to Chaminuka as the greatest *mhondoro* is still noticeable amongst many of the Mashona. His name is liable to occur in rather improbable contexts. I, myself, have heard an ordained Mashona priest link the name of Chaminuka with that of Jesus Christ, in a sermon given to Africans. His point was that both were great prophets and miracle workers and both the sons of God, through whom intercession might be made. This, of course, is to turn Christ into something very near a *mhondoro*; a mental transformation that appears to be quite common amongst African converts to Christianity. Thus, the old beliefs have a hidden strength, even amongst those who seem to have discarded them. But their willingness to see Christ as a *mhondoro* gives eloquent testimony to the high place the *mhondoro* held in their lives, and to the usual nature of his influence.

Three big festivals were held each year—and in country districts go on being held—in honour of the tribal spirits. Two of them were ceremonies of thanksgiving, the least important occurring in January, when the *mhondoro* spirits were thanked for providing a crop of green leaves and relishes. Nobody was supposed to eat such things until this formal offering of the people's gratitude had been made.

The next most important festival took place in April, and was similar in form. This time, the people thanked the spirits for the millet they used in brewing beer and in some kinds of porridge.

The biggest of the ceremonies occurred in September. This had a dual purpose. In part, it, too, was a harvest festival, this time for all the crops of the preceding year. But it was also the time when the *mhondoro* spirits were asked to send good rains in the coming season and when the seeds were blessed. The spirits were shown particular honour during the course of this festival. It was at this time that first-fruits and other gifts were offered to each of them by the *nechombo* on behalf of the people. The *nechombo* would address the spirit in words like these: 'See what we have brought you. Here is the cloth we know you like. Here is beer and grain.' The cloth would then be draped over the body of the recumbent medium. It would be a black cloth—the colour of power and holiness—and of a kind known to be favoured by the spirits. 'Keep us all well,' the *nechombo* would continue. 'Send us good pumpkin, mealies, nuts and millet.' He would hold out the pots of seed which were to be blessed. 'Please give us these things.'

The medium would stretch out his hands and dip them into the pots of seed, letting the grains run through his fingers and charging them in this way with his benevolent power. It was thought that every family should have a few such seeds to mix with the others they intended to sow in the coming season and so pass on their magical qualities.

When the pots of seed had all been blessed, they would be handed over to the chiefs and headmen for distribution to the heads of families. Then the *mhondoro* would give his opinion on the crucial matter of rainfall in the coming year. He would advise them what to expect and what crops they should therefore rely on. Drumming and dancing would bring the ceremony to an end.

In this way, the harvest festival and the blessing of the seed for the next year were brought together in one ceremony that affirmed the continuing power of the *mhondoro* spirits over their people.

CHAPTER 10

The Mashona System of Law

Perhaps you might think that with ancestral guidance so intimate a part of Mashona life, it would have acted as a clog on the development of more mundane systems of government and justice. Certainly it was always the wish of the chief and his people that they should obey custom and give honour to their mighty dead, and this tended to create a very conservative outlook, giving established forms a strong religious sanction. In such a society, the innovator was suspect, and might well find himself open to accusations of impiety or even witchcraft. It was a climate of mind that goes a long way to explaining the static and allegedly primitive nature of many African societies.

But, of course, no group of people could live together without finding the need for some method by which they might settle their disputes. The Mashona knew well enough that they could not rely on interventions from the spirit world to solve their everyday differences, and so, long ago, they developed their own system of law.

There were three levels at which a dispute might be heard, and these reflected the levels of authority in Shona society. If the case had been brought because of an injury done by one member of a family to another, then it would come before the village headman, who would act as arbitrator rather than judge. His role was essentially that of the father who tried to reconcile opposing factions within his own family. No fees were paid to him for his work. He would sit round with the rest of the village and try to reach with them a joint solution of the problem.

But if the matter were too serious to fall within his jurisdiction, he would refer it, after a preliminary examination, to the *dunhu* headman. This was not his only link with the *dunhu* court. He also acted as its officer when any of the people from his village had got into a dispute with someone from outside: it was his duty to see that the summons to the *dunhu* court was obeyed in such circumstances. He would often represent any of his villagers at the higher court, though he did not take personal responsibility for the payment of fines unless the wrong-doer were a close member of his family. Even so, he was expected to exert his authority on any man under his care who was slow in paying a fine. If a member of his village had been wronged, the headman would act as the formal complainant at the higher courts. His presence there at such times was demanded by his people, because, 'He is like a father to anyone living in his village, and a father ought to know what his child is doing.'[1]

As we have already seen, the next step from the village court led to that of the *dunhu* headman, where proceedings were carried on with rather more formality and small fees had to be paid. The *dunhu* head-man had to try to balance the interests of all the villages within his area, and it was before him that the important matter of land-disputes between villages was brought.

The appeal from a decision arrived at in a *dunhu* court went to the court of the tribal chief. As a result, the *dunhu* headman would not give a judgement unless he felt sure both parties would agree to it. Issues so small that, in theory, they should have been well within the head-man's jurisdiction, might well be sent up to the chief's court on appeal, as well as those serious cases such as stock-theft, homicide, or witch-craft, which had to go on.

A tribal court was held before a chief, helped by two or three assessors. It usually took place in an atmosphere where ritual formality and unrestrained excitement were curiously combined. The Mashona took a very different view of the function of a court from that familiar to us in Western Europe. They did not see it as a place where men bowed them-selves before the impartial majesty of the law, nor one confined to highly trained specialists. To them, it was more like a place of democratic assembly, where any man might air his views if he chose. Nor did they feel that evidence should be given only on the matter in dispute: in their opinion, the whole environment of a dispute, including past quarrels and enmities, had to be taken into account: they would have thought it inadequate and irresponsible to judge a case in isolation.

The Mashona outlook did not have our Western regard for a judge-ment that is academically correct—reached by a dispassionate sifting of the evidence and measured against similar rulings given in the past. Their aim at a legal hearing was neither so rigid nor so 'scientific'. What they were really seeking at such a time was a judgement that was roughly fair and that both parties would accept, a judgement which promised to heal the breach that had opened up between different members of their community. That is why, if a man were clearly at fault and yet refused to admit guilt and pay compensation, the Mashona would not think it enough merely to order him to do so. The court would tend to assume that the guilty man was refusing to come to an agreement because some deeper source of enmity between him and the complainant had not been revealed by the procedure of the court. They would set about to discover it, in the knowledge that grievances which are allowed to fester are a growing danger to the community. One man after another among the spectators might rise to his feet to 'seek clearness' in the matter. They would argue, plead, exhort, mock, or even threaten, but always in the hope of laying bare the hidden grudge. Eventually, under this kind of public pressure, some sort of agreement would be arrived at.

You will have realized that the Mashona tribal court was concerned as much with persuasion as with judgement. Friendship had to be restored amongst the people. That is why, when a man agreed that he had done wrong, the court required him to get up before the people present and admit his guilt in so many words, and make a public promise of compensation. Often he had to show his 'guilt' to the court in the form of a pebble or some other small object that he held in his hand; one of those physical tokens that seemed so important to the Mashona mind. It was all part of the expiation that came as a necessary preliminary to reconciliation, which was the real aim of the court.

When anger had been stirred by the case, or hatred revealed amongst the disputants, the chief might ask them to make a formal act of friendship when it was over. They might share snuff-tobacco or eat a fowl or a goat together—acts no man would consent to do with an enemy. By this means, they pledged their renewed brotherhood before the assembly. Often everybody present, including the chief himself, would receive a pinch of snuff or a scrap of meat in token of their common brotherhood.

In order to get a glimpse of the mode of procedure in a chief's court, we might take an example of a simple kind of case that could be brought. Moyo, let us suppose, has charged Rabeka with wilfully allowing his cattle to wander on his lands and damage his crops.

The hearing would begin when the 'messenger' told the chief and his assessors that the parties in dispute were present at the court. To show the dignity of his office, the chief would be sitting on a rock or stool that elevated him physically above anyone else in the assembly. His assessors sat below and beside him. In the front of the court, well away from each other, one to the right of the chief and one to the left would squat the two disputants, with their supporters crowding behind them. Their marked separation from each other signified their antagonism. By court procedure, they might not talk directly to each other; they had to go through an official intermediary, whom they must also use when they wished to address the court. They were, so to speak, shut off from direct contact with the court or each other, in a kind of moral quarantine that would last until their case was decided.

Moyo would begin to speak. When he did so, he moved forward until he was squatting right in front of the chief, though he was still addressing the intermediary, as he must. Before the actual speech began he would clap politely and perhaps call out some of the praise-names of the chief. Then he would give his view of the matter. His aim would be to offer the court as convincing and dramatic a performance as he could; he would act out again all the feelings of loss and outrage that he had suffered when he first saw Rabeka's cattle destroying his crops, and perhaps he would allow himself the implication that Rabeka had deliberately let them stray there because of an old grudge he bore him. At the end of Moyo's speech, the intermediary would repeat a shortened version of it, though of course, the entire court would have heard Moyo's words.

Rabeka would be just as eloquent in his turn, and he too might go beyond the bounds of the present dispute to explain why Moyo had seen fit to bring this case. He would try to suggest, if he possibly could, that the accusation made against him had been motivated, in part, at least, by ill-will. Any such assertions would be welcomed by the court in the hope that they would clear the air of hostility. No evidence was inadmissible. When Rabeka had finished, his speech would receive the same treatment as Moyo's had done from the official intermediary, and then the witnesses would be called.

The 'witnesses' would perhaps be better described as supporters. From the experience of living in close communities, the Mashona had learnt not to expect the statements of witnesses to be impartial. They recognized that it was only natural for sides to have been taken already and made no demand for the whole and absolute truth, being under no illusion that they would get it from a party who had already interested himself in the matter.

The witnesses, too, would employ all the arts of rhetoric they could command in order to influence the court. In a society that set a high value on public speaking, the skill of some of them might be considerable. After they had all given their evidence, the case would be thrown open for general discussion. One man after another might get up to question the disputants. At this stage of proceedings, the excitement mounted and the audience might lapse from time to time into noisy wrangling. If the hubbub became too great, the court would be called to order by one of the assessors, not in an attempt to restrict anyone's right to speak, but merely to maintain the minimum of decorum without which the case could not be heard.

At the end of all this, the chief and his assessors would sum up the case as they saw it, and refer to any precedents in public memory, though they did not have to follow them unless they wanted to. They would have taken a look at Moyo's lands already and so would know to what extent he had exaggerated the damage in his claim. It would then be up to them to get the defendant to admit his guilt. Agreement would also have to be reached about the amount of compensation.

If Rabeka refused to accept his guilt, even though he had been shown to be in the wrong, the case would go on with more probing and persuasion until he could be swayed. If it was at all possible, there had to be voluntary submission to the verdict of the court. Even if he admitted his negligence or wrongdoing, Rabeka might jib at the amount of compensation he was asked to pay. Here, again, there would be discussion. If the people thought the fine too heavy, they would soon let the chief know with cries like 'Aiee, do you want to kill this man?' and the chief, whose authority always rested on consent, would no doubt quietly reconsider. Once agreement was reached, the disputants would make their formal act of friendship and the case would close.

It is easy for a European to criticize this system as cumbrous or unworkable, but the first thing to remember is that though the procedure may seem long and unneccessarily complex, to the African time was not important. He felt no sense of waste when time was expended. He did not divide it into areas nor allot it under priorities. He felt free to give it with lavish generosity to any trifle that might catch his attention and suffered no sense of deprivation or incongruity afterwards, as we might. Secondly, he liked to attend court sessions, which were a form of pleasure to him—the nearest thing to drama to be found in his society. Here the play was one in which he might take part and try to give a display of that oratorical skill that he and his fellows all tried to cultivate. A polished speech would bring a storm of applause and lift him high in the estimation of his fellows.

It is possible to argue that the man found guilty could sabotage the court by refusing to accept his guilt. It was most unlikely to happen, however, if the decision come to by the chief and his assessors was generally considered reasonable. Overwhelming public pressure would be brought to bear on the guilty man, pressure that his whole social training would prompt him not to resist. He knew that if he went on being stubborn, the whole community would blame him for deepening the quarrel: it would look as though he were bent wilfully on the disruption of social harmony. Few Africans could stand up to disapproval of that kind from their fellows, even if they wanted to. If the man did remain obdurate, however, the chief would have had to impose his decision, though with reluctance, for that kind of end settled nothing. Nowadays, he would refer the case in desperation to the court of the Native Commissioner.

Perhaps the last word on African customary law should lie with Livingstone. He describes how, whenever his bearers fell into a dispute, they came to him as their 'father' and he would hear cases in the manner he had learnt from them. He did this once before some Portuguese, who 'complimented me on the success of my teaching them how to act in litigation; but I could not take any credit to myself for the system I had found ready to my hands.'[2] Livingstone's bearers were Makololo, from the north side of the Zambesi, but this evidence of the existence of a system of indigenous law could have been applied equally well to the Mashona—or to other African peoples.

CHAPTER 11

The Witch

What we have seen so far of the Mashona has shown us a people whose lives were closely bound up with each other, and with those of their dead ancestors. As the ancestral spirits were well disposed towards their children, indeed were in active alliance with them except when angered by their offences, such spirits could never be used to explain the arrival of evils on people without reason. The Mashona asked why it was that his child had died when the children of other men went on living. Why it was that his crops failed when the crops of others flourished. If there were no guilt on his part to expiate, and consequently no anger on the part of the *mudzimu*, how was it that such terrible thing could come about?

Working from a knowledge of the envy and malice that live in the human mind, the Mashona attempted to answer such questions in terms of the witch, the *muroi*. It was a conceptual leap in the dark, but one that has been taken by most of the peoples of the world when faced by this dilemma. The fabric of creation appears to have unmistakeable strands of evil woven into it. How are they to be explained? The problem is one that has taxed the ingenuity of Christian theologians. Within the Christian sphere, stubborn and widespread sects such as the Gnostics and their descendants have held that the physical world can only be a creation of the Demi-urge, the Devil, its basis is so evil. In the East, Buddhism regarded the physical world as an illusion, a manifestation of 'error', or evil. These doctrines were formed as answers to the same question that the Mashona answered with the witch.

In modern times, Western man has learnt to dismiss apparent evil as an accident, to attribute it to the workings of blind chance, but he has come no nearer to solving the moral problem at the heart of the question. At the most, he is spared the grievously false assumptions of witchcraft that disfigure the thought of the Mashona and that of many other races.

The basic definition of a witch, in Mashona eyes, would be a person who has a settled desire to do evil; someone who takes pleasure in killing men and livestock or blasting crops. The psychological foundation on which the belief in witches has been built is not difficult to discover: it can be found in everybody alive. We are all of us aware, surely, of the atavistic side of human nature: the greedy, lustful, covetous *id* that would happily disrupt society to gain its own ends. In most people, this brutish part is held reasonably well in check, but all of us are made forcibly aware of its existence from time to time. The saints themselves, by their own accounts, were no strangers to it. It is small wonder, then, that so many races should have imagined the apparently malicious strokes of Fortune to be the work of people who had surrendered to their evil impulses and come to find pleasure in destroying the lives or well-being of others.

The beliefs of the Azande are illuminating in this respect. They are an African people living far to the north of the Mashona—the Sudan is their home—but like all Africans they are deeply involved in witch-craft. Evans-Pritchard's investigation of them brought facts to light that help to make clear the connexion between the witch and the recognition of gratuitous evil among Africans. They are as aware of the threat of inborn evil as the Christian is of Original Sin.

Among the Azande, this awareness has led to the belief in a physical witch-substance, something present in the body that dissection can reveal. Most people amongst them are thought to possess this substance, but only in some does it become 'hot', or active. In the majority, it remains inert, though there is no guarantee that it will always do so. This seems to be a recognition of the fact that most of us are potential witches, that the evil desires which characterize the witch are present in a suppressed state in the majority of mankind. Like the witch-substance, such desires are born with a person, as part of their psychical inheri-tance. Nor is it always a question of personal choice whether or not they remain inert. The Azande are often filled with anxiety at the idea of becoming witches unawares. Although a person may work evil through deliberate choice, very often the conversion into a witch is involuntary in the first instance, though the state may be consciously embraced as the delight in evil deepens. It begins, if you like, as a cancerous quicken-ing of the witch-substance; a rebellion in the depths of the psyche.

Recent history should have left Western man with no doubt that such moral collapse can occur, and that it may plumb terrible and ingenious depths of spiritual degradation. We have had to learn again that the psychopath and the criminal lunatic have a terrifying potential for evil and that they are always with us. We were in danger of forgetting because of the efficiency of those arrangements by whose means we can thrust such people out of sight with the same smooth dispatch that we dispose of our dead. It was only in the fantastic circumstances of the second quarter of this century, when such men had been granted political power and had made themselves irremoveable, that we in the West were forced into prolonged contemplation of them and their motives. But in simpler societies, there are no asylums and no jails.

The Mashona believed—as did the Azande—in hereditary and captured witches, as well as in voluntary ones. The real defect in their thinking arose, not in the recognition of the evil impulses that may afflict men, but in the further belief that those impulses are supported by more than human powers. Yet they had no alternative to this conclusion, once they had accepted the idea of the witch as the source of unwarranted misfortune. How else could the witch perform deeds which they knew by experience to be beyond ordinary men?

As we might expect from a people who attributed so much power and influence to the spirits of the dead, the Mashona explained the extraordinary powers of the witch in terms of her possession by the spirit of a dead relative who had been a witch in her day. This witch-*mudzimu* would 'come out' in a living member of the family, often a little girl of about seven years old. The spirit might declare its wish to possess her by making her fall sick—often the opening gambit of the communicative dead—or it might be noticed that she went out of the hut at night, in her sleep, which was taken to mean that her spirit was being called to a meeting of witches in the bush.

Witches, of course, have always been creatures of the dark. They were thought to slip away naked at dead of night to attend unholy, sometimes cannibalistic, feasts and to plan campaigns of evil. They would often come to their meeting-place riding on their beasts, the pig or the hyena, and perched on their fist might be their messenger of death, the owl. If an owl were seen to alight on a man's hut, it was often taken to announced the coming death of some member of his family, and so to discourage the bird from landing there, the peaks of many Mashona roofs were crowned with a tripod of stiff, twisted straw. The owl could be more than a messenger: it might, on occasion, be an embodiment of the witch herself. It was sometimes held that, after death, the spirit of a witch might take up residence in the owl, rather as a chief's spirit might enter a lion. The otter was another magical beast amongst the Mashona and witches were believed to value its bones, which they crushed and rubbed into incisions in their skins, after the normal manner of administering an interior medicine amongst Africans. This was supposed to increase their powers.

Most witches were women. There is no certain explanation of why this should be so, but in this context it may be relevant to call to mind the mystical potency with which even ordinary women are endowed by many races: the charge in woman's menstrual blood, the power that enters her at pregnancy. She seems to be regarded as more dangerous in her very nature than is man. Fragments of similar belief can be found to this day embedded in the folk-lore of England, for instance. We have most of us heard that a woman in her menses cannot bring the butter into a churn; that if she handles flowers at that time they will quickly wilt in the vase; that she can harm the child she is carrying by seeing or eating the wrong things. There is no medical reason why men abstain from intercourse with them during menstruation, but there are deep emotional ones: the aversion is too strong and of too ancient a lineage to be adequately explained in terms of hygiene.

In Europe, too, most witches were women. Jakob Sprenger makes the point in his *Malleus Maleficarum* and supplies reasons—of a kind— why this should be so. Sprenger was a noted member of the Inquisition; a man who seems to have possessed to a marked degree those psychological attributes that have led men to believe in witches. As a leading churchman, he felt obliged to confine his explanations to crude interpretations of the Scriptures. Women were more often witches, he alleged, because of the innate moral weakness of the sex; they had a propensity for sin bequeathed them by their first mother, Eve. Such arguments as these seem no more, nowadays, than a gloss Sprenger was making on impulses he felt within himself, impulses rising from a far older, deeper, and less reputable source in the bottom layers of his consciousness.

Both Sprenger and the Mashona would have agreed that a man, too, might be a witch, but he would become one from a conscious striving after evil, an act of the will, not as the result of innate defect or involuntary possession.

If the parents of a little girl noticed ominous symptoms in her, such as the tendency to walk in her sleep, they might become concerned enough to consult a diviner. If he decided that the girl's somnambulations were caused by a witch, he would try to make contact with the spirit and persuade it by medicines or sacrifice to leave the child alone. Sometimes the diviner might try another stratagem: he would attempt to transfer the witch-spirit from the girl into a fowl which he would then carry into the bush and set free. Anyone who took the apparently ownerless fowl was thought to be accepting the witch-spirit which would perhaps turn its attention to them. But, for all that, most diviners maintained that the cure of a witch was so difficult and hazardous as to be beyond them.

The family might have to accept the possession of their daughter. Their aim in such circumstances would be to keep the witch-spirit as 'inert' as possible. But in many cases of possession, it was believed, no symptoms were observed, or if they were, they were wrongly attributed to some other cause. Thus, as the witch-spirit was a *mudzimu*, the tendency to witchcraft might be defined as a taint of heredity. Of course, if the mother was herself a witch, she would give her daughter every encouragement, in secret. There was another, less powerful, category of witches who were recruited by placing medicines in their food; and thirdly, there was the voluntary witch, who deliberately sought out instruction in the black arts. These witches were considered to be less dangerous than those possessed by an ancestral spirit: they had not been given the advantage of tuition in dreams by the *mudzimu*. Their families may well have been innocent of taint up to their time; though one imagines that at the death of the captured or voluntary witch, her spirit might well try to 'come out' in some living descendant —that with her, in fact, we see the moment of a family's contamination.

A person could also behave like a witch in one respect, without turning into one altogether. A man might buy a *gona* horn filled with magical substances. Such a horn would ensure riches or success for the man— nowadays it might bring him into high favour with his white master— but it only did so at the cost of the life of some member of his family. There would be no murder, but it was understood that someone must die. When he procured his good fortune in this way, a man consciously agreed to the magical destruction of another person, and that was the act of a witch.

Amongst the forms of witchcraft believed in by the Mashona, there was a curiously benevolent one, which they called *chikwambo*. It was really more like a talent, a special ability to find lost or stolen property. The only threatening aspect of this gift was that the recovery of the property, so it was thought, was often followed by the death of the thief.

The African Past

Chikwambo can be met in surprising places. For instance, I knew a woman, a rich widow, who lived alone in a town flat and was waited on by a single house-boy. One morning, she drew a large sum of money in notes from her bank and took it home with her. She was called out unexpectedly a little later, and when she got back she found the money had gone. She and the servant gave the flat a thorough search but they could not find the money, so she decided to call in the C.I.D. They also searched the flat—without success—and then interrogated the servant, on whom suspicion naturally fell. He protested indignantly that he had not seen the money, and what was more, he hadn't had the slightest idea there was so much money in the room. There were no clues and the matter seemed to have reached deadlock. Then an African assistant to one of the white C.I.D. officers suggested that they bring in another man. They did so. He, too, was an African, and he asked to be left alone in the room for five minutes. Everyone else left, and within the five minutes, he was out again and had joined the others in the corridor, holding in his hand the wad of money that had been lost. He had found it pushed under a pile of letters and papers in the letter-rack, where the widow now recalled that she had put it for safety.

Apart from showing how maddening absent-minded people must be to the police, this story serves as an illustration of *chikwambo* in action—and pressed into service in a surprising quarter. A white C.I.D. man explained that they had often used this African to discover property that had been stolen and hidden away, and undoubtedly he had a 'sixth sense' about such things. 'He says he smells it,' he remarked, with an apologetic grin.

The witch could work her evil on others either directly by poison or by magical methods often involving the use of 'medicines'. The very word for 'witch' in Chishona, *muroi*, seems to be derived from *uroi*, meaning 'medicine'. If a witch used poison, she was thought to hide a small amount of it under a finger-nail, from where she could release it secretly into her victim's food or beer. There seems little doubt that such poisonings took place. Often they might be carried out by unscrupulous diviners rather than true witches, though any such division is a hazy one: a person deliberately setting evil to work *was* a witch. The diviners or *nganga* had the knowledge of a wide pharmacopeia, and although they were supposed to be the chief enemies of the witch, some of them would betray their profession if the fees were high enough, and employ their drugs for 'black' ends.

But it seems likely that magic was used more often than poison. If it

88

were employed correctly, it was considered to be as effective, and whilst there was an element of risk involved in trying to sprinkle poison into food or drink, there was none in working by the more devious methods of magic. Perhaps I should point out here, though, that the distinction I have drawn between magic and physical poisons would not have seemed a valid one to the Mashona. To them, it was only in conjunction with magical power that poison became active: they believed there were circumstances when a substance might be inert, and others when it might be deadly.

If a witch decided to work by using magic, she would act in secrecy, by night, in the traditional manner of her kind. A common way of doing harm was to smear a thorn with medicines and thrust it into a fragment of the victim's clothing, or, if they could be got, a twist of his hair or a bit of nail from his toes or fingers. The thorn would be buried together with these things under some path that the victim was known to use; the first time he walked over it, the thorn was thought to recognize him and penetrate his foot magically, and from then on he would sicken.

This form of witchcraft was practised throughout Africa, from the Azande of the Sudan to the Zulu of Natal. The Mashona called it *chitsinga*. It gave them an explanation for many wasting forms of sickness, and particularly for the pangs of rheumatism and arthritis, that occur without any apparent cause.

The witch was also believed to have the Evil Eye and the Evil Touch. She could shoot 'arrows' of witchcraft into the bodies of her victims, and so, in effecting a cure, the *nganga* might have to remove them. In the treatment of any kind of sickness it was as well to be able to show some physical object that had been causing the trouble. The *nganga* would put his mouth to the affected part and suck. After a good deal of exertion, he would take out of his mouth the foreign bodies responsible for the sickness. These might be anything from bits of bone to dead worms or spiders. Of course, he was a charlatan, working by sleight of hand, but the psychological effect on the patient confronted by these objects was often enough to bring about an immediate cure. Such tricks were an almost invariable part of the repertoire of the witch-doctor and could be found throughout black Africa. If an *nganga* was pressed hard enough, he might admit that in his case fraud had been employed, but he would remain convinced that greater 'doctors' than himself had mastered the technique. Not for a moment would he be likely to admit that his own trickery invalidated the general principle of such treatment.

By their use of medicines, witches were thought to be able to pass through locked doors and to put people inside into a deep sleep. Such sleepers would become so stubbornly unconscious that even if the witch rolled them about on the ground or pummelled their bodies, they would not wake up. Next morning, they would find themselves stiff and bruised and would know that a witch had been practising on them, bowling them about the floor in malignant levity whilst they slept. Beliefs like these can be compared with the old English notion of being hag-ridden in sleep; and with the Hand of Glory, which had the power of inducing deep coma; or for that matter with the belief that if a horseshoe or some similarly potent object were thrown over the roof of a house, everyone within the magical arc it described would fall into a drugged slumber.

The Hand of Glory was that of a dead man. African witches had a predeliction for corpses, too, and would rifle graves if they were given the chance. Human flesh was reputed to make the most potent magic and a medicine-horn which included that amongst its contents would be very strong indeed. In order to frustrate the witches, it was usual for Shona graves to be guarded for the first few nights after a funeral. The young men set there were fierce with nervousness and if some lost stranger were to wander in the neighbourhood of the grave at night, they were likely to kill him as a witch before he had time to give an explanation. A witch could also work evil by putting medicines on the grave in the hope of discomfiting the dead man and making his spirit strike at his family in anger for their negligence towards him.

Human flesh is still sought. In 1960, at Gwelo in Southern Rhodesia, a witch went so far as to approach the attendant at the African mortuary with a request to buy the fingers of the dead for use in medicines. In this instance, the attendant informed his white superiors.

Medicine horns containing human flesh have sometimes been used in Africa for more official purposes. They were (and are) most notorious in Basutoland where, at the command of the chief's diviners, ritual murder was performed in a terrible fashion. It was a requisite in these killings that parts should be cut from the body of a living victim if full potency was to be assured. The flesh gained in this way was incorporated with other medicines and sealed in a horn that was given to the chief. It was supposed to confirm him in his power.

This practice cannot be described as witchcraft because it had the consent of the leader of society and his advisers. It was magic, supposedly performed for the maintenance rather than the disruption of the social order. According to Theal, human flesh was used officially in some African societies at the initiation ceremonies when boys were formally inducted into manhood:

'The rites of initiation were kept as secret as possible, but certain horrible customs connected with them are known. One of these was the infusion of courage, intelligence and other qualities. Whenever an enemy who had acted bravely was killed, his liver, which was considered the seat of the intelligence, the skin of his forehead, which was considered the seat of perseverance, and other members, each of which was supposed to be the seat of some desirable quality, were cut from the body and baked to cinders. The ashes were preserved in the horn of a bull and during the circumcision ceremonies were mixed with other ingredients into a kind of paste and administered by the tribal priests to the youth.'[1]

This custom, though it was horrible, as Theal says, was far less sickening than the Basuto rites because the cutting was performed on the body of a man already dead.

But the Mashona did not have initiation ceremonies—the festivals for the *mhondoro* spirits may have acted as a more gentle equivalent—and no case of ritual murder has ever been brought to court amongst them since the European occupation. However, there is a strong tradition alive that in the past such murders did sometimes occur, and that the victims were children, taken when the grass was high and choked with dry, sharp grass seeds before their bodies were mutilated. The men who made these killings were called *Mapakatsine* or *Nyamusenga*, names that can still strike terror into country Mashona. Bullock says the ordinary people looked on such killers as 'ogres', creatures less than human. Dr. Holleman was made so uneasy by stories about the *Mapakatsine* when he was engaged in field-work amongst the tribal Mashona in the Reserves that he ordered his own children to be kept near the camp when the grass was high. A Shona child can be quietened by mention of the dreaded names, rather as an English child might be by the threat of 'the bogeyman' coming.

After many years of white occupation, there is still no evidence of the activities of these ritual killers, yet the legend persists. One wonders what gave rise to it. The *Mapakatsine* might have been ritual murderers employed by the chiefs, as in Basutoland, but from what we know of Mashona society this seems unlikely; they might have been a secret society of witches, analogous with the Leopard Men of the Congo. There is a third alternative: it is just possible that the *Mapakatsine* were never more than imaginary horrors—after all, Europe has its vampires and werewolves.

Before we leave the subject of the witch for her opponent, the *nganga*, it is worth while, I think, to try to put the Mashona beliefs in witch-craft into perspective. They were the most serious blemish on what was in many ways a humane society, but they were not a wilful surrender to evil. We have seen some of the reasons that may have brought them to birth: they seem to have been formulated in an attempt to explain the evil found generally in the fabric of Nature. And though such beliefs were part of the climate of Mashona thinking, they did not dominate it. The fear of the witch was closely bound up with the fear of natural misfortune, and most of the time men cannot afford to have their lives inhibited because of what *might* happen. It would be a mistake to think of the Mashona cringing perpetually in terror of the witch, any more than our lives are shrivelled by fear of being involved in a traffic accident. The rate of incidence of both these phenomena was somewhat similar. All but the most neurotic people were sure they were not witches, and when they needed protection they turned to the witch-doctor, the *nganga*. It was his revelations that must have struck fear and disbelief into individuals when they were pointed out as witches, although such charges comforted the rest of the community. That was where the moment of horror lay: in the baseless accusation.

CHAPTER 12

The *Nganga*, or Diviner

Like witches all over the world, the Mashona witch did not have to strike at a man directly. She might choose, instead, to blast his crops with disease or drought, or make his cattle sicken and die. But whether it was himself that was afflicted, or his family, his beasts or his crops, a man would naturally turn in such circumstances to the source of help traditionally provided to combat the menace of the witch. He would go to the *nganga*, the expert in healing and exorcism, whose work for the good of society was held in such high esteem by Africans.

The *nganga*, or diviner, was a secondary postulate from the original one of the witch. If you believed misfortune was the creation of evil persons working by magic, then it was natural to assume that there might be other men with more than usual powers who were willing to use them on behalf of society rather than for its destruction.

The Mashona believed there to be three ways in which a man might become a diviner, just as there were three ways in which a person might become a witch. The most powerful type of diviner gained his skill—as with the most potent witch—by the tutelage of an ancestral spirit. The *mudzimu* concerned would have been a diviner himself whilst on earth and would now be anxious to pass on his knowledge to his descendant, whom he would teach in dreams. Diviners who had been given their training by spirits were particularly honoured amongst the Mashona. A diviner could also be granted skill in healing by an alien spirit, one with which his family had no connexion; it was usually thought of as the spirit of a stranger who had died far from his own land. The third way of becoming a diviner was the obvious one of going through an apprenticeship with a practising *nganga*. But, strange as it may seem to us, such a man would be under a handicap; the public would not think so much of him because his skill was only derived from a living man, who might well have kept his deepest secrets to himself. The third kind of diviner would find it hardest to establish his reputation.

It was the job of the *nganga* to diagnose and, if possible, to cure the ills of individual men and of society in general. He was also expected to deal in preventive magic—a part of his trade that has grown in importance since European law forbade the punishment of witches. He had to know how to prepare charms and prophylactics to cover a multitude of possible dangers. Some of these were intended for the individual, who would wear them on a string round his neck or waist; others were hung up under the eaves of huts to keep danger away; others, again, were intended to protect the paths into the village, and would be buried under them rather in the manner of *chitsinga* medicines; there was a last group that was used to immunize the perimeters of whole villages against witchcraft. A diviner might make a good reputation for himself in any one branch of his art and become a specialist in it.

If the headman of a village thought his people were being troubled by witchcraft, he would go and consult a diviner about it. The first task of the diviner was to find out whether the misfortune was due to witchcraft or whether there was some other cause such as an angry *mudzimu* at work. Most diviners used the bones to probe into the world of the spirit. There were four bones in a set, each of them carved with symbols on their sides; some diviners used more than one set, however. The diviner would throw the bones, after a formal sweeping clear of the dust in the yard, and read what they told him. In the preliminary investigation, he would be looking to see whether the bone called 'crocodile' turned up, for this was the sign of witchcraft.

The interpretation of the bones was complicated, depending on a whole series of readings taken from the combination of signs that appeared. If the diviner established that witchcraft had taken place, his next task was to try to identify the witch. The people of the village, or those of them the headman had reason to suspect, would be standing before him. Gradually, under the eyes of the village, he would narrow the field of his enquiry until finally the witch would be named.

It is clear that the *nganga* had to be a man who was intuitively sensitive to the feelings of the crowd and the suspects. If he were not, his findings might be rejected—this was by no means unknown—and he himself discredited. As a matter of fact, he quite often had the gratification of hearing his accusation supported by the woman he had pointed out. Confessions were not uncommon in answer to an accusation, just as they were not uncommon in the European witch-trials of earlier centuries. What this meant, no doubt, was that the judgement of the *nganga* settled on the abnormal, the hysterically inclined, those who were odd or unbalanced.

Not all diviners used the bones. Some were able to enquire into occult matters by staring at a piece of polished metal (or glass nowadays) and inducing a state of auto-hypnosis in which the matter was made clear to them. Others used the psychologically interesting device of the basket which, as it proved, the innocent could lift easily but the guilty one could not budge from the ground.

Although confessions did occur, many people who were denounced as witches denied their guilt, in which case they had to go for trial. The accused had the choice of a trial at the court of the chief or a trial by ordeal. Strange as it may sound at first hearing, most of the accused chose to be tried by ordeal. They seem to have felt that, by doing so, they were escaping the fallibility of human judgement.

There were three common types of ordeal, any one of which might be undergone. In the first of them, the accused was given a drink that contained poison. It was generally believed that the body of an innocent person would reject the poison, that he would vomit it with no harm to himself. The stomach of the guilty man, on the other hand, would accept the poison and activate it, and he would die from its effects.

Sometimes, poisoned drinks were administered on a large scale, when a specialist *nganga* was asked to purge a certain area that had been troubled by witches. At such a time, people would travel miles to offer themselves voluntarily to the poison ordeal, hoping in this way to establish their innocence in the eyes of their fellows. Such communal cleansing operations usually ended with the death by poison of several people; many others took the poison and vomited it out again successfully. The last big purge of this kind known to the authorities in Southern Rhodesia occurred within the last decade. Operations of this kind are illegal, of course, but they still happen sometimes because the rural African of the older generation still believes in their efficacy. Sometimes, nowadays, because of the stringency of the law prohibiting ordeals, poison is offered to a fowl instead of a man and the case is judged according to how it reacts.

The second ordeal was to plunge one's hand for a moment into a pot of boiling water to which medicines had been added. It was held that the guilty would be scalded and the innocent remain unharmed.

The third ordeal was to lick the metal blade of a hoe that had been heated in a fire. If you were innocent, your tongue did not blister.

If these ordeals seem to reflect the reasoning of lunacy, we must cast our minds back to the similar modes of thought that occupied our own ancestors. To envisage the region of the mind inhabited by the Mashona, we have to imagine a world directed by spirits, forces, magical emanations. As we have seen, to them nothing ever happened by chance. They would consider such a term a mere evasion. There were two reasons why things happened: each event had a physical *and* a mystical explanation. They believed in the power of thought and desire, allied to certain formulae, to manipulate material Nature. Stuff was clearly inert in itself, and so they felt it must respond to the dynamic power that could be exerted by the mind or spirit, a power they had experienced to a limited extent in their own heads.

We might define the belief in witchcraft as, first, a projection of repressed anarchic desires in men. They then made use of this projection to explain the malignant disposition the natural world sometimes seemed to reveal to them. The Mashona belief in witchcraft was part of a world-view in which spirit had been raised to a qualified paramountcy over Nature. They interpreted the world in this way because of their wish to understand: it was their attempt to explain the enigma of man's place in a blind universe. Certainly, their vision of the world was one in which man was engaged in a perpetual fight against spiritual evil, but it was also one in which he might glimpse the logic of events, and, witchcraft apart, might expect to receive treatment that corresponded with his own behaviour. We cannot regard this delusive mode of thought as alien or foolish: surely we can recognize there the craving for order and understanding that has echoed down history whenever men have faced the bleak chaos of the natural world.

Witchcraft had to be countered in terms similar to those in which it made its threat: it was fought by men preternaturally attuned to spiritual forces, by words and gestures of power, by objects made potent by the use of formulae. All this did not make the world more threatening, but infinitely less so. It conjured a fairly benevolent meaning out of the menace of the cosmic void. It calls to mind, inevitably, the intricate barrier of defences set up by the neurotic to control a dangerous world.

We in Europe pride ourselves on having discarded such conventions of thought, but it is doubtful how far we have succeeded. The fragility of our success is shown, perhaps, by the incidence of neurosis in the

modern world. Increase the strain on a man sufficiently and he often
slips back into a position where magic is invoked out of desperation.
Nobody claims that the neurotic is the intellectual inferior of the
balanced man—often his mind is sharper. His obsessive rituals are invented to help domesticate a threatening world; they are an attempt to
impose some recognizable order on the relations between the outside
world and himself; to attain some correspondence between what he
does and what is done to him.

Men are not driven into this position by lack of logic; they arrive at it
by demanding too much of the brute phenomena of the world. They
think they need only construct some defensive pattern to explain its
meaning to themselves, when in fact they need to master it and change
it by their understanding. They are men who have demanded to know
why without creating the necessary apparatus of investigation. Lacking
all empirical basis, their conclusions are at the mercy of the winds of
logic, which have driven men to fantastic regions of thought, but driven
them with a fearful uniformity, whether they lived in medieval Europe,
ancient Egypt, the Mexico of the Aztecs, or modern Africa.

Among the Mashona, the decision of a single diviner was often thought
insufficient, and an accused witch might not be committed for trial
unless her guilt was confirmed by a second or even a third diviner.
Mashona reverence for the powers of the *nganga* was shot through with
worldly doubt. They knew that an *nganga* could be wrong; that his
diagnosis might be perverted by superior powers of evil; that he himself
might be a trickster. They would have no more claimed that all their
'doctors' were free from fraud than a Christian would claim saintliness
for every man in Orders. But they never questioned the mode of action
by which the diviner proceeded. It was the man they might suspect of
inadequacy, not the theory which governed his actions. To people involved in this kind of thinking, it is impossible to move beyond the
possibility of individual fraud to a challenge of the general hypothesis.

If the chief or headman was satisfied by the reports of the *nganga*, the
accused person would go to trial by one of the methods already described.
But, even if found guilty, a witch was not usually condemned to suffer
capital punishment on her first appearance. It was more likely that she
would be warned and an attempt would be made to persuade her to
restrain her witch-spirit. She might well be given a severe beating, too.
If she was found guilty again, later, on the same sort of charge, she would
either be banished from the tribe and thus forced into an outlaw existence in one of the colonies of wizards and witches that could be found

in the land, or she would be killed. In the old days such persons were not killed outright: a wooden peg was driven into the skull and then they were chased into the bush. Within a few days they would be dead. Such a lingering form of execution was not adopted out of cruelty, but in the hope of escaping direct responsibility for the act.

These methods of combating witchcraft are, of course, forbidden under European law, but there is occasional evidence that they go on. Perhaps people no longer have wooden pegs driven into their skulls, but in 1960 at least one group of villagers was brought to court in Southern Rhodesia charged with causing the death of a woman who had been pointed out as a witch. They had stripped her naked and chased her for many miles through the bush, beating her with sticks until at last she fell unconscious. She died later, where she had fallen, of injury, shock, exposure—and, no doubt, despair.

It is tempting merely to turn away in angry repudiation of such behaviour, but it is not enough to do so: we must try to recognize the roots from which it has grown. We must condemn it, but we should also acknowledge its relation to yearnings and fears common to all humanity. It was the hunger for understanding, the desire to find meaning and justice in the operations of the natural world, that provided the soil out of which this misshapen hypothesis has sprung. There should be compassion mingled with our loathing: in its twisted way, the belief in witchcraft was a proof of humanity, not of bestiality. It shows the terrible pitfalls that awaited the enquiries of the wakening mind.

CHAPTER 13

Shavé

The Mashona recognized one more important manifestation of the spirit world and built a cult upon it. They gave it the name of *shavé*, with the meaning of a foreign spirit, one from far away. *Shavé* seems to have been an extension of their belief in possession by ancestral spirits. Once again, it was employed to answer the baffled 'Why?' that rose to men's lips when they saw the inequalities of Fortune.

The Mashona found it hard to understand why people should be unequal. Their whole way of life had been arranged to imbue them with a sense of democratic amity. They wished to be as little different as possible from others: to be unusual or odd excited suspicion, and might even be disastrous. Also, in a society where a man owned little beyond his hoe and his weapons and a woman little more than her cooking-pots, the more flamboyant possibilities of individual character had nothing to sustain or develop them. One of the things that private property does is to feed a man's sense of individualism and, if he holds it in large enough amounts, to breed in him an often arrogant awareness of his difference from his fellows. It has been, one might say, from the earliest historical times, the plain man's symbol of his own uniqueness; the one resounding affirmation of the self for men of unexceptional qualities. *104 303*

But the Mashona had no private property to speak of. Their lands did not belong to any one of them, not even to the chief, who was only regarded as the steward of the tribal domain. It was the chief who shared out the land amongst the people for cultivation, but that did not imply any ownership over the land on his part. The land was considered to be the possession of the entire community, but even they only held it in trust, lodging upon it in their day and then seeing it pass to the next generation. People did not work the same piece of land for any length of time, and shifting agriculture can hardly be expected to bring about love

99

for any one plot of earth, nor the exclusiveness that follows it. A man could not accumulate money, for there was no money. The Mashona herded cattle, it is true, and used them for ritual purposes and to 'buy' brides, but here again it was unwise to be noticeably richer than one's fellows: a man's undue prosperity might be set down to witchcraft or to the *gona* horn that threatened other members of the group.

Nor could men differentiate themselves in terms of their architecture. There was a way of building established by custom, and in any case, little evidence of personal nobility can be created out of materials like mud and straw. The houses were not even meant to be permanent: after the passing of a few seasons, during which the soil in their gardens had become 'weak', the people would move on, abandoning their village. A site would be chosen in the next area allotted to them and they would put up new huts. But a man did not even erect his hut by his own exclusive labour: the village was built by the joint efforts of the whole community at a big beer-and-work party, or *nhimbe*. This was an admirable institution in some ways, but not one likely to induce a sense of personal pride at a man's individual accomplishment.

For all these reasons, the Mashona had less understanding of the inequalities that exist in society than has Western man. Their way of life seems to have been arranged to discourage the growth of that European climate of thought in which a man assumes that if he is to gratify his personal identity it must be by setting himself at odds with the rest of society. Yet for all that, the natural differences in capacity between one man and another showed themselves amongst the Mashona, and could not be ignored. The Mashona were forced to try to give some explanation of them, and the answer they hit on seems to have been the *shavé*, or wandering spirit.

One can guess at the way they arrived at this conclusion. They seem to have argued that, as all of them were born alike and all were of one people, there should be no differences of importance between them. Yet as boys grew into men, they were forced to acknowledge that some developed gifts that others seemed to lack. One man became a brilliant hunter; another was unequalled at searching out wild honey; a third was a healer, though he had undergone no training and could not claim to have the tutelage of a *mudzimu*; a fourth was a man of unusual courage, a brave man in battle; a fifth was outstanding at the dance or the drum. These things could only have happened because something had entered such men from outside; some form of spiritual tuition must have been given them that arose outside the family or tribe.

Shavé

In that way, perhaps, was born the belief in the alien, wandering spirit, the *shavé*, who alighted on some men and granted them special gifts. Of course, the man had to repay the bounty of the spirit by trying to please it. A *shavé* was supposed to demand from its medium one or more types of reward, and these had become defined by custom over the many years that the belief had been established. Some *shavé* spirits required special foods, such as the liver of bulls or the blood of fowls. (The latter was commonly drunk amongst the Mashona to induce a state of possession.) Other spirits longed for distinctive kinds of ornament; others again insisted that their hosts should wear clothes indicating the origins of the spirit. For instance, a Matabele *shavé*, which was taken to be that of a Matabele warrior who had died far from his home, perhaps whilst on a raid—wanted its medium to dress like a man of the Matabele nation, particularly in the dances that members of a *shavé* group held to bring on a state of communal possession. In the same way, later, there was a white-man *shavé* which demanded that its host dress and eat like a European.

The *shavé* was orthodox in its method of approaching the living: it would first show its wish to enter a person by making them ill. When, at the recommendation of a diviner, the person accepted the spirit, he would become well again, but from then on he would adopt the special habits that suggested themselves to him. A man was not possessed by his *shavé* all the time, any more than was the medium of a *mudzimu* or *mhondoro* permanently inhabited by his spirit. But a man could call on his *shavé* to help him. The spirit would only 'come out' if it felt so inclined, but drumming and dancing seem often to have helped to persuade it. If a man did not treat his *shavé* with reverence, it might desert him; on the other hand, what was usually a privilege might become a burden, for occasionally a man might be fastened on by several *shavé* spirits who made his life a burden with their conflicting demands. A man possessed by his *shavé* was believed to be able to speak in the language of his spirit, or sometimes in a tongue understood only by those who shared his situation. This occult language went by the name of *Chishavé*. Such practices are strangely similar to some performed by European Spiritualist mediums.

Although the function of *shavé* seems to have been to explain special gifts in the individual, the Mashona would not have accepted such a description. To them, *shavé* appeared as a gratuitous event; it was not the explanation of anything, it simply *was*. The complications of belief that occur in *shavé* seem to cloud it further. For instance, the Mashona included the spirits of certain animals amongst those that could possess them, animals that were associated with certain types of skill, for example, a man in the grip of a baboon *shavé* would act like the animal when possessed at the dance, but the spirit was supposed to confer the gift of healing on him. The connexion between animal and skill seems obscure, but perhaps a clue may be found in totem. According to Shona legend, the *Shoko* (Baboon) clan is the oldest in the present area of settlement. Also, *Mulumo*, the Mouth, chief officer of *Mwari* in the Matopos cult is to this day hereditarily a member of the *Shoko* clan. This makes the connexion between the baboon and the gift of healing seem less of a wilful improbability, though it is still by no means really clear. However, it never seems to have given any trouble to the Shona mind.

Shavé has been used to explain other forms of oddity. The Mashona tribes living over the border in Portuguese East Africa believe that madness may be due to the visitation of a kind of *shavé*, whilst some Rhodesian tribes say that certain forms of witchcraft can be attributed to it.

CHAPTER 14

A General View

Mashona society had its foundations in the village, or *musha*. This was the home of the patriarchal family, out of which all larger associations amongst the Mashona seem to have grown. In its simplest and most ancient form, the village would accommodate only the near members of a single family group. Typically, it might be made up of a father, who would be the headman; his wives and children; a couple of his adult sons with their wives and families; and perhaps a few other relatives such as the headman's sister, or his father's sister. Sometimes there might also be representatives of maternal kin. This was the fundamental social arrangement out of which all the larger groupings developed.

Eventually, some of the married sons might feel the desire for independence and leave their father's village to set up one of their own. This was quite usual, and acceptable to Mashona custom. The intending founder of a village would go to the *dunhu* headman of his area and ask his permission. Normally, this official would not offer any objection; it was he who would show the new village-head where to build and what land he might work. The *dunhu* headman ratified this grant by ritually driving a peg into the earth on the site for the hut of the new headman's chief wife. A *dunhu* would extend its hospitality in the same way to strangers who wanted to settle amongst them, though if the man making the request were foreign to the tribe, the *dunhu* headman had first to gain the permission of the chief.

When a new village was set up, several huts and enclosures had to be built. This work was usually carried out with the help of people from the neighbouring villages. Collective labour, such as this, was important in customary Shona life. Men worked together, not just at the founding of a new village, but in all the big agricultural tasks that faced them throughout the year. Ploughing, planting, weeding, and harvesting were all tackled in the same way.

When a call for co-operation was made, it took the form, traditionally, of an invitation to a beer-and-work party, a *nhimbe*. Those people who came from the surrounding villages did so on the understanding that they were to give their labour. Their reward would be plenty of beer, a chance to meet and mingle with all their neighbours, and a dance in the evening when the work was over. They would be sure to come, not only for these pleasures, but because they themselves would be expecting to throw a similar party when they needed the help of others at different times during the year. Such parties were an important feature in the Mashona economy. By means of them, people tried to mingle work with pleasure. Perhaps to the eyes of, say, a Western industrialist they might seem slow, inefficient, convivial affairs, but their economic dubiety was redeemed—at least in Shona eyes—by their socially rewarding nature. The work got done, and people enjoyed themselves, both whilst they were doing it and afterwards, when drinking and dancing would go on late into the night.

When the huts were up, before anybody was allowed to settle into the village, the headman and his chief wife would dedicate the spot to its new domestic role by a ritual act of intercourse. This symbolized the part the village was to play as a place where the family would find shelter and be able to increase. Then the village headman would allocate gardens to all those members of his little community who were eligible to receive them. If there were married men amongst them who had more than a single wife, they were expected to divide the responsibility for the cultivation of their land equally between each of their wives. All wives would also get a patch of land they could put to their own uses. Young, single men would be given fields big enough to allow them to build up a store of grain against their marriage. Single girls were given a corner of their mother's fields to work for themselves.

As we have seen, the land was held collectively. The headman had only the right of apportionment. Land did not belong in perpetuity to any man. It was regarded as a part of Nature, no more to be alienated than was the air or the rain. Men worked the land and then abandoned it; they did not own it. The whole Mashona way of life denied the idea of private accumulation in such a fundamental resource. To take the land away from a man would have seemed like depriving him of the right to breathe or drink water from the river. It would have been the act of a witch—an enemy of mankind.

On the other hand, the things a man produced by his labour were his own, to do with as he pleased. This right extended to each wife: what she grew on her own plot of ground—as distinct from her husband's—was her own. Her husband had no legal right to call on it.

Of course, in a polygamous society, husbands had to be very careful to treat their wives with absolute equality if they wanted to avoid feuds and enmity within the marriage. As a result, most men seem to have slept with their wives on a rota system. They might choose to visit the hut of a different wife every night, or they might spend a week with each of them, but there had to be demonstrably equal conduct towards them all if trouble were to be avoided. Each wife would have her own granary, which she used for herself and her children, and should the husband have to offer one of his wives grain because she had exhausted her supply, he would have to make a similar offer to each of his other wives by custom, even though their granaries might be overflowing. If he failed to do so, accusations of favouritism would be levelled against him.

There was no formal division of work according to sex amongst the Mashona. All the people of a village would help in the fields, men and women labouring side by side. Even so, it was customary for the men to take on the heavier work. They were the ones to clear new ground and do the ploughing—which was performed laboriously by hand with the heavy African hoe, or *badza*. If new huts had to be built, it was the men who cut the poles and rafters and set up the skeleton of the structure for the women to proof with grass and mud. If wells were to be sunk, the men would do the digging. Men, too, were the ones who worked in wood and metal; it was they who hunted, or fished with nets and traps, or prepared the skins of wild animals for domestic use. Women did the cooking, helped to tend the crops, and looked after the little children. They also made pots from baked mud, and they plaited mats and bags from rush and other natural fibres. The boys would be out most of the day, herding their fathers' cattle. The girls helped their mothers, learning how to cook and manage domestically in preparation against the day when they would be married women themselves.

Amongst the Mashona, girls were expected to be virgins when they married, and to ensure that a girl had not allowed herself to be seduced by any of the young men from the neighbouring villages, she would have to submit to periodic examination by one of the old women of the family. If, on marriage, a girl was found by her husband not to be intact, he would send her family a hoe, with its metal blade pierced by a nail to symbolize her imperfect maidenhood. The receipt of such a token usually led to the return of some of the *lobola* paid for her.

Periodic examination was not the only way of prohibiting fornication employed by the Mashona. To the beliefs about the mystical potency of the female, to those powers that were acknowledged to operate in her at menstruation and pregnancy, was added the belief that if a girl slept with a man before she were married, she was threatening her parents with pain and sickness. Her father's crops might also suffer and the whole family be brought near to starvation. In face of threats like this, breaches of chastity were probably rare.

Adultery was an offence in Shona law. In practice, however, a wife could not bring an action against her husband unless she could prove that he was neglecting her lawful sexual demands because of his adulterous relationship. If a man brought a case against his wife, he might, if he won it, either accept the damages declared payable, which had to be found by the other man, or else divorce her. But if he chose to divorce her, he did not receive any damages. It is from this arrangement that we get the Shona proverb of the complaisant cuckold: 'An adulterous wife makes me rich.'

But the most powerful sanctions against adultery were not legal but religious. By his actions, an adulterous man endangered his children, who might be struck down by a *mudzimu*, enraged by his wickedness. The paramount value set on children by the Mashona is apparent here: the *mudzimu* struck at the most valuable possession of the father and his family group. The most sinister and dangerous cases of adultery were those a man committed with the wife of a kinsman. This, as they said, was like wishing for the death of the husband; it was incestuous and witch-like and threatened spiritual disaster to the whole of the community, which might be punished by epidemic or the failure of the crops.

Marriages were arranged in Mashona society. That, at least, was the theory of the matter, but in fact many elopements took place. So long as there was no kind of totem ban on the partner—and this would be most unlikely—the father would usually end by accepting the *fait accompli*— and the *lobola* which followed his agreement. But though young couples sometimes ran away together, there was no place of importance in Mashona society for the theories of romantic love. There might be love in a marriage; there was more likely to be respect. The circumstances of Mashona life discouraged the forming of strong emotional attachments between husband and wife. The husband lived much of his life apart from his wife, he even ate apart from her, and his emotions were directed more on to the group loyalties of his kin—of whom his wife would never be one. If a man showed himself uxorious, the rest of his family were more likely to attribute it derisively to witchcraft on the part of the wife than to any more passionate motive. Polygamy was also a strong dampener to romantic ardour. Romantic love carries with it, however provisionally, the assumption of uniqueness: the lovers suppose themselves fated for each other; theirs is a fierce, exclusive attachment. This illusion can hardly be prolonged by a polygamous husband. If a man did act in that way, he would fail to gain the respect of society; he was more likely, instead, to receive the denigrating explanation that witchcraft had been used against him. The Shona custom by which a dead man's wife would be taken over by his brother so as to keep her reproductive capacity in action for the good of the kin gives a clear indication of the kind of reason for which a wife was taken.

As we have seen earlier, marriage was essentially a 'borrowing of the womb' but this must not be taken to mean that no affection was given to a wife. Nor must it be inferred that Mashona women were unhappy with the arrangement: they had an honourable and respected place in the community, and though men wielded direct authority, their wives could often influence them successfully. Like all married women, they had their means of persuasion.

If we try to imagine a Shona village as it must once have been, we should perhaps begin with a cluster of huts, their conical roofs shaggy with straw, their single-room interiors floored with dung and earth, and cool with darkness. They would be set in the red or yellow soil of the African veld, in ground trampled to dust by the pad of bare feet. Nearby would be the kraals for their animals. The cattle would be out grazing, but the village would have lean fowls scratching round it and perhaps a goat or two.

In the middle of the cluster of huts would be the open space, the *dare*, where the men talked together and where the headman heard any complaints or grievances that had been brought. We must remember that neither he nor those who wielded authority at higher levels could afford to be autocratic. They governed by consent, and if their people did not like them or their methods, they were free to move away. They should be imagined rather as mediators and persuaders, men whose job it was to prevent the growth of faction or disunity, welders and reconcilers who worked, in the bigger villages, with a council of the older men. Beyond the immediate vicinity of the village, the tall grass would stretch, lolling in the wind, bending and swaying to the foot of the granite kopjes that rose out of the plain. Among the grass and the twisted trees, the young boys would be herding the cattle; somewhere there, the gardens of the families would be laid out. Not far away there would be other villages, linked with them by the bonds of kinship or friendship, the perennial sharing of work and pleasure, the 'borrowing' of wives.

Their lives were simple and not very arduous. Their pleasures lay in beer, the dance, the *dagga* pipes in which they liked to smoke Indian hemp, the oratory they admired, the cases in law they loved to attend, in the stories and riddles they swapped round the night-fire. Some of these riddles give a glimpse of the metaphorical vigour of their language. For instance, the riddler might say: 'Flame on the mountain', to which the correct answer would be 'Leopard'. He might say: 'Blood of the lion on which no fly settles,' to which the answer would be 'Fire'. He might say: 'A soft stick among thick trees,' which needs the answer 'Snake'. In a different mood, he might say, 'It has made even the chief move from the *dare*,' to which the correct guess would be 'Excrement', or 'Good on both sides,' which should be answered, 'A shilling'. Or, on more serious topics: 'Sweep, so that I may dance,' with the answer, 'Divining bones', and 'Youths who can dance the *mande shavé*', to which the answer is 'Reeds'. Again, 'The medicine-horn is burnt but the dipping-stick remains,' to which the surprising answer is 'A path', giving an example of the kind of riddle whose allusions seem obscure to the European mind.[1]

In this society, men regulated their lives by a web of custom. They strove to prevent the growth of enmity amongst themselves by prescribing the correct form that conduct should take in response to a very wide range of situations. Custom was fortified by spiritual powers: the ancestral spirits were as real as the living, as interested as the headmen in the welfare of the people, and much more powerful than the chief. Through their mediums, they were in direct, practical communication with their descendants. They were powerful allies in life—so long as men were virtuous. But despite the strength of *mudzimu* and *mhondoro*, evil still managed to flourish; its hand could be seen in the misfortunes that afflicted men. Thus the witch was known to be at large amongst them. One of the members of the village might be a diviner, an *nganga*, whose special powers were dedicated to the eradication of evil and the prevention of misfortune. But though there was this fear of the witch, lying like a shadow in the bold sunlight that warmed the huts and the meeting-place, it must not be exaggerated. Dread of the witch was part of the Shona psyche but it did not prevent men from living and multiplying and taking their pleasures. It was not the all-pervasive horror that some European writers have made it: it did not carry the defeating, sterile obsessiveness that we associate with the idea of deep neurosis, though it did allow much cruelty. We must remember that the Mashona saw witchcraft as the explanation of a situation whose mystery, without it, would have been much more alarming; one in which evil might have had to be seen as an integral part of reality rather than a distortion of it. And they had their defences against the witch: their amulets and protective magic, and above all, their *nganga*. The fear of the witch was real, but so was 'the loud laughter of joy' that Livingstone spoke of when describing the character of the African.

Mashona society must seem particularly alien to Western minds because its objectives were so different from those current in Europe. Briefly, it aimed at a limited perfection. Needless to say, that perfection was never reached, but the tendency of Shona society was to maintain a communal life in which the roles of all members had been fully worked out in the past. Change could only appear as a threat in these circumstances.

The society of the Mashona was one in which equality was guarded by material poverty. Men had specialized their labour very little. All of them were peasants; even the guilds of smiths and diviners followed this occupation most of the time. The chief or headman could not separate himself from the people by enforcing differences in the quality of his life: he ate the same food as all the others, drank the same beer, slept in the same sort of hut. He could not assume the *persona* of royalty through his wardrobe and possessions, nor could he trick himself out in the cultural attributes of divinity. He could not afford to be tyrannical: his people would strip him of authority by the simple expedient of deserting him and putting themselves under the protection of a more reasonable man.

There was no money in this community and so far as machines were concerned, there was not even the wheel. Men worked long enough to ensure their subsistence, and after that they stopped. Little in the way of surplus was accumulated, and this little usually only by the chiefs, part of whose duties included the support of those who had suffered misfortune. The Shona chief, like the Germanic 'ring-lord' of ancient times, was expected to be generous to his followers, so his granaries had to be bigger than most. He had the right to ask for a certain amount of labour from his people, as had the headman, to recompense him for the time he spent administering the law and indulging in public business. In the past, leaders of the Shona—or whoever it was organized the building of the old stone forts and enclosures—possibly developed the scope of this traditional right of labour to provide the men needed for such operations. But such a novel disposition of labour, which might have led to a more complex society with marked differentiation of status, does not, in fact, seem ever to have done so. The debris of occupation examined at the ancient sites has not shown archaeologists any remains that are significantly higher than the recent level of Shona culture.

It seems there were stubborn traditional forces at work amongst the dwellers in and near the forts, which is what we might expect from the Mashona, who aimed at a social equilibrium within a charted world. Innovation was discouraged, not only by custom but by the ancestral spirits who brooded over the scene. It was always likely to be levelled against those who advocated change or became noticeably richer than their fellows, that they were acting impiously or by witchcraft.

Wealth here must be understood in terms of cattle. Though the persistent seeking of profit, as we understand it, had no part in Mashona society, they did value their herds and try to increase them because cattle played a central part in the ritual organization of their lives. Without cattle for *lobola* no marriages might be contracted, and hence no children born to the kin group. Cattle, too, were the usual sacrifice for the ancestral spirits. Without them, a man could not show due reverence to his forefathers. Cattle were wealth, then, but in a different way from that in which we are accustomed to think of it. They were not coveted for their own sake, as money often is with us; nor even for their meat, which was only eaten after a ritual slaughter.

What few material possessions the Mashona had they wove into the fabric of their lives. Beer provides a good example of the significance any product was made to assume amongst them. They enjoyed beer for its own sake, of course, and made good use of its recreational gifts, but they did not think of it in isolation. The *nhimbe*, or beer-and-work party, associated it with building and with agricultural labours performed together. Beer was also used in libations to the ancestral spirits. Amongst the cattle given as *lobola* it was usual to include a bull, which could be expected to breed with the cows and provide natural increase but which was primarily intended for dedication to the *mudzimu*. This animal went by the name of 'the bull of the herd'. When the father wanted to tell the *mudzimu* any news about the family's life, he would talk to this bull and pour beer over its head in libation. Sooner or later, the animal would be sacrificed to the *mudzimu*. There would be ritual drinking of beer at that ceremony, as there was at all the major celebrations of the Mashona, whether they were concerned with birth, death, harvest or religious worship.

The Mashona had no belief in hard work as an independent virtue. Their way of life granted them considerable leisure. As might be expected, they were a people who could discuss matters at length and with delicacy of motive and of delivery; they might dance and drink for days on end. Their emotional and religious life was rich; their customs elaborate. They appear as people who flinched from all the more daring and dangerous choices open to developing humanity. Because their society was based on material poverty it gained an approximation to equality and a freedom from many of the corruptions that overtake richer and more enterprising races. Their chief concerns appear to have been the maintenance of ritual, the exploration of personal relationships, and the pursuit of simple pleasures. They seem to have had no impulse towards exploiting the material world, beyond a very weak one; there was none of the violent energy that is the most significant characteristic of modern industrial society in the West. Their 'choice' appears gentle to the point of timidity and, by our standards, stifling. It brought its own penalties: the belief in witchcraft that could never be escaped because the material world was never explored nor its secrets discovered; the helplessness in face of disease; the voluntary deprivation of the mind from such towering intellectual achievements as both the West and the East have attained to. It was a society satisfied and complete at its own level, like material so saturated that its only reaction can be a refusal to absorb. But this refusal would only operate so long as the society was strong enough to keep out novelties of thought and behaviour. By its very nature it was vulnerable to any culture more materially aggressive than its own.

When the extremities of the *Mfecane* and the mind of Chaka had between them fashioned out of normal Bantu life a murderous military machine, and when Mizilikazi fled with his disciplined Zulu *impis* to the lands of the Mashona, it was certain that they would be helpless against him. To defend themselves effectually, they would have had to jettison their traditional way of life and themselves adopt a system of military dictatorship. This they would not, or could not, do.

Then, after the Matabele, came infinitely stronger invaders, who offered material blandishments as well as force: the white men of the Pioneer column. With their arrival, the history of this part of Africa takes a completely new turn.

PART TWO

Conquest and Settlement

CHAPTER 1

Trekkers and Missionaries

By the early years of the nineteenth century, migratory Boer farmers had spread far beyond the confines of the old Cape settlement, and had turned the Bantu flood back upon itself in the tumult of the *Mfecane*. Before the Boer farmers had gone hunters and traders, and above all, the missionaries, most of them English, who often acted as unofficial emissaries at the kraals of Bantu chiefs for the coming power of the white man.

In the 1830s, the situation altered. Instead of the slow erosion of the frontier with the Bantu, a sudden lunge, like a great spear thrust, was made into the tormented body of the African interior. It was in these years that the Boers mounted the Great Trek and drove in a few seasons through vast areas of wilderness, opening up territories from the Transvaal to Natal and teaching defiant African chieftains the lesson of the gun.

Equipped with their *roers*, the Boers were invincible in the open country of the interior plateau, and those tribes who did not want to become their vassals could only move away, as Mizilikazi did, crossing the wide fly-belt of the Limpopo valley. Mizilikazi took with him the knowledge he had earned harshly on the banks of the Marico river, that at all costs war with the white man should be avoided, at least until the Matabele were equipped with firearms of their own. He was not the only Bantu chieftain to realize where the superiority of the whites lay: the Basuto, for instance, spent the next few decades trying to lay their hands on as many guns as they could, and Dingaan, the Zulu king, was very anxious to have his armies trained in the use of firearms.

The Trekkers who crossed the Orange river in 1835 did so, as they saw it, in defence of their way of life. Government restrictions and failure to support the frontiersmen, combined with stubborn Xhosa resistance, had led them to look to the north rather than any longer to the east. They were migratory farmers; the number of their young men was increasing; they had to have more land. Pressure was growing on the available territory and young Boers were finding themselves landless—an intolerable situation for these wandering stockmen. This was not the only provocation goading them into the Trek. Not only did the British government at the Cape refuse to understand their needs, and demand their submission to the law without offering them reasonable protection; in 1832, it had done a far graver thing by emancipating the slaves; an act which seemed to the Boers to strike a blow at the social and religious foundations of their nation.

The Boer was patriarchal in temper, governing his people with pious severity and including within the natural scope of his authority the servants and slaves amongst whom God had been pleased to set him down. There was no question in his mind that the black men were the children of Ham, destined to serve him as hewers of wood and drawers of water. This was no mere political arrangement that might be adjusted but part of the revealed wisdom of God. Indeed, it seems to have been the legal equality set up between the races that was resented more than the actual emancipation of the slaves. Anna Steenkampf, sister of Retief, spoke for her race when she declared the concept of equality between black and white to be 'ungodly'. 'We withdraw', she said, 'in order thus to preserve our doctrines in purity.'

As the Boers saw it, then, they trekked for two reasons: to gain new land and to safeguard their liberties—and that these should include the right to enslave others of inferior race seemed to them beyond dispute. This hunger for a liberty that remains sectarian can be seen again and again in the bitter comedy of South African politics.

Yet amongst themselves, they acted with all the headstrong democracy that might be expected from Protestants ultimately responsible to nobody but their God. When they came together in republican assembly, the burghers established the law and chose its officers by debate and the vote. They were reluctant to admit the authority of anybody, even their own elected leaders, and right to the end, the customs of their state allowed them a staggering freedom to disagree with the government and withold their support from it if they saw fit. Even in the crucial business of war, where, if anywhere, discipline is to be expected, they allowed themselves a surprising latitude of behaviour. They had to be convinced before they would obey. This characteristic can be seen as late as the time of the South African War, when Britain was putting vast

Imperial forces into the field against them. Even then, their army continued to be run on voluntary and democratic lines. The only order the Boers were forced to answer was the general call for conscription in defence of their homeland; beyond that, there was little or no pressure the government could put upon them. No disciplinary system could be imposed within the army: if the burghers had been subjected to such coercion they would have refused to fight. Their dislike for authority extended even to their military commanders. Officers were chosen by ballot amongst the men—the only army that I can think of to operate in this way in modern times, with the exception of the Red Army in the early days of the Revolution—and military decisions were come to in the same way. A man did not even have to abide by the majority vote. If he found that he could not, in good conscience, agree with the decisions arrived at, he could, and often did, refuse to take part in the operations that followed. He might merely hold back from that battle or he might, if he chose, take his horse and ride home. Similarly, if a man did not like his officer or section-corporal, he was at liberty to change to another section or even another commando. Every military decision, no matter how trivial, had to be made by a council of war, or *krygsraad*, in which the commandant, his officers, and the section-corporals discussed the matter together. The power of the men in these councils was indirect but great: it was they who elected their corporal and they who could dismiss him, so he was always careful to consult them before offering his opinions at the *krygsraad*.

All this might be taken to be independence run mad; individualism pushed to an extreme where it threatened the immediate disintegration of the state. Yet it took the British army nearly three years of war to subdue the Boer commandos and strip their Republics of the right to govern themselves. We can see, in all this, that the Boers were individualists of a heroic order. Their concern with personal liberty was profound and immediate; closely associated in their minds with the land itself. Yet the state they created was an exclusive one: it could tolerate no other race except as menials, and there was certainly no place in its pastoral economy for subjects like the *Uitlanders*, the employees of industrial capitalism, who were to invade it and burst its simple social arrangements wide apart.

When the Trekkers pushed into the wilderness, there were already a few white men amongst the tribes. Hunters and traders roamed the interior, but more significant than these were the missionaries. There was hardly an important tribe in whose lands a mission station had not

117

been established. Even the Matabele had received American missionaries whilst they were still in the Transvaal, though these men abandoned their intransigent flock in despair when the Matabele withdrew over the Limpopo. Mizilikazi was a personal friend of Moffat, the great Bechuanaland missionary, though neither he nor his tribe showed any interest in Christianity itself.

The failure of the missionaries to convert the Matabele is an example of a common situation. The chiefs rarely looked to white men for religious guidance; it was quite another kind of instruction they often demanded from them. The dilemma in which the missionary sometimes found himself is illustrated by the experiences of Francis Owen, who had been recruited by Captain Gardiner to help him in his evangelical work amongst the Zulu. At this time, the Zulu nation was under the rule of Dingaan, who had succeeded to the throne after killing Chaka, his half-brother, and who had gone on to secure himself in power by the execution of two more of his brothers.

Gardiner had preached before Dingaan in 1835, and made no religious impact whatever, though he did get an invitation to stay on at the Zulu court as an instructor in musketry. He returned to Port Natal and set up a station on the Berea there, but in 1837, he sent Francis Owen to re-establish contact with Dingaan. As we can see from Owen's diaries, Dingaan and his followers allowed Owen to preach, but their attitude to the word of the Gospel was humorously derisive. They were much more interested in the cloth Owen had brought as a gift, and in items of his personal clothing. These exerted such a fascination that, as Owen reports, one of the wives of Dingaan actually stole the ribbon out of his hat whilst he was preaching to the king's harem. The Zulus were also enthralled by his gloves, and fascinated by a piece of mirror he had brought; they begged Owen to let them share his toothbrush and to shave them with his razor.

This catalogue is not merely funny, nor is it mentioned to illustrate the childishness of the Zulu—though this is how Owen seems to have interpreted the behaviour of the tribesmen. It reveals a fundamental paradox in the position of the missionary. He thought of himself as a poor and dedicated man, inspired by God to try to save heathen souls. In his own eyes, and those of his countrymen, he was someone who had voluntarily embraced poverty, hardship and exile; he was a dweller in humility, a bringer of the Word.

That is not at all how he was seen by the Bantu. He seemed to them a person of great material wealth, a man able to dispose of all manner of precious objects. The marks of opulence were there in his wagon, his oxen, his clothes, all his personal accessories, even the glittering instruments in his black surgeon's bag—if, as was so often the case, he had taken medical training in the hope of curing men's bodies as well as saving their souls. What could it mean when such a man told them with a great show of gravity that Christ had advised his followers to give all they had to the poor, and maintained that it was harder for a camel to pass through the eye of a needle than it was for a rich man to enter heaven? What, anyway, *was* a camel or a needle? Here was a white man with trappings greater than those of a chief, a man swimming in riches, enjoining them to holy poverty.

We can see, now, that such a situation is an impasse, the result of the collision of two levels of culture. What was poverty for the European was dazzling affluence to the Bantu. In circumstances such as these, it is not surprising that the Bantu remained sceptical of the odd doctrines the missionary preached; but they respected him as an estimable, prosperous man, full of exotic knowledge, who seemed, moreover, to be of a peaceable disposition. They particularly respected this man of peace because, like other Europeans, he had a gun and knew how to use it.

Dingaan managed to get some gunpowder out of Owen before the missionary had learnt better, but when he realized his mistake and refused to supply any more, Dingaan became sullen. He next tried to borrow Owen's bullet mould. When Owen refused to lend it to him, Dingaan argued, as Owen notes, 'that the white people were not one with him. They granted him some things but other things they withheld (alluding to the gunpowder): yet he was ready to do all the white people asked of him: first one teacher asked to instruct his people, then another, and he granted all! Yet he could not have his wants supplied in return. He said, moreover, that I was like the rest: that I was one with the white people; for when he asked me only to *lend* him a bullet mould, I refused. He said it was of no use for me to "twist myself out of the charge" that he brought against the white people, for it was evident that I opposed him having firearms as much as they did.'[1]

Not long afterwards, Dingaan gave Owen a dreadful example of the uses he was likely to put firearms to, when he massacred Piet Retief and his Boer delegation before the eyes of the missionary. The Trekkers had come down into Natal over the peaks of the Drakensberg, looking for land, and Dingaan had lured Retief to his kraal with the promise that he would 'give him a country'. He offered the Boers all the land between the Tugela and the Umzimbuvu rivers, but when they came to negotiate the agreement, he had the delegation killed on the Hill of Slaughter near his kraal.

Whilst this was going on, Dingaan went to some trouble to assure Owen that he meant no harm to come to him. This was typical of the conduct extended to most missionaries by the leaders of even the military Bantu nations. They came as single men and asked the king for 'the road'; they were docile and interesting; they offered the king information and goods; sometimes they acted as intermediaries between him and white governments. They presented no threat to the independence of the Bantu, and so, according to the rules of African hospitality, they were allowed to travel through the chief's domain or settle in it amongst his people.

The truth of this can be seen, perhaps most decisively, in the career of Dr. Livingstone, who wandered the length of Central Africa, struck up a deep friendship with Sebituane and his warlike Makololo, and reported that he never met any insolence or molestation except in those territories where the Arabs and Portuguese had debauched the natives by trading with them in slaves. Livingstone wrote that: 'Every headman would be proud of a European visitor or resident in his territory, and there is perfect security for life and property in all the interior country.'[2]

But the Boers were a different matter. They came in tribes, not singly, bringing large numbers of wives and children with them. They spread out over the land: they were invaders, who obviously intended to wrench the territory out of the hands of its present owners. Dingaan tried to explain this distinction between the missionary and the Trekkers. Owen wrote down his words as follows: 'He said it was not his intention to kill either me or the other missionaries, for we had come into his country by *fews* and *fews*: he could live in peace with us, for we were his people.'[3] However, Dingaan went on, all the *armies* that came into his country would be killed.

Owen was not reassured by such arguments and went back hastily to Port Natal. The Boers took their revenge for the Zulu treachery towards Retief, and the sacking of the Dutch settlement at Weenen that had followed, by the massive slaughter they made amongst Dingaan's armies at the battle of Blood River. The Zulu regiments were broken and the complete superiority afforded by the gun was once again demonstrated.

From his point of view as an African ruler, Dingaan had interpreted the situation correctly: when the Boers moved in they intended to conquer and enslave. They came in an army and so they must be defeated in battle or they would take the land. Yet he knew that unless he could get hold of muskets and have his warriors instructed in their use, the Boers would always beat him. Nor, when he spoke of the missionaries as his people, was he merely indulging in extravagant metaphor. The Mashona were not alone in receiving strangers and giving them a place to live once they had been accepted by the chief. As Dingaan saw it, no doubt, he could make claims on the missionaries in all justice, for they owed him allegiance as his subjects and, according to custom, should have helped him against his enemies, because they lived on his land at his permission.

The same pattern can be seen repeating itself later in Matabeleland, where Lobengula welcomed traders and missionaries, and defended them as his guests, even in the most provocative situations. But he had the same fear of being invaded by a usurping 'army' of white men and the same keen appetite for firearms as the only effective means of defence. His armies were destined to meet a fate similar to that of Dingaan's at Blood River, though by that time white fire-power had been made even more devastating by the introduction of the Maxim gun.

There is an indirect link between missionary endeavour in Africa and the Maxim guns of Jameson's column. During the latter half of the nineteenth century much of public opinion in Britain was converted from its earlier attitude towards colonial expansion. In the past, experience had led successive British governments to the conclusion that extensions of imperial responsibility led to great expense for no profit. Gladstone kept this view and was to express it later when he said to Rhodes, concerning colonial expansion, 'Our burden is too great,' and went on to ask what the British government could hope to gain by a policy of imperial aggrandisement: 'Apart from increasing our obligations in every part of the world, what advantage do you see to the English race in the acquisition of new territory?'

Rhodes had his answers ready, as we shall see, but the question I wish to confine myself to at the moment is, What part, if any, did the missionaries play in converting public opinion in England to a policy of colonial expansion in Africa? The key figure in this context is Dr. Livingstone. His journeys through the interior of Central Africa stirred the imagination of Victorian England and his books on the subject created a sensation. Intelligence and sincerity were manifest in his writings. He was, in fact, a brilliant journalist—in the true sense of the word—and a man of deep piety. His good faith was not in question on any topic on which he wrote.

Livingstone set down his opinions in sharp, outspoken prose, and when he uttered a condemnation he gave it a memorable ring. One of the early targets for his disapproval was the Transvaal Boers, whom he denounced for their outrageous filibustering in Bechuanaland, where they came to raid for cattle and slaves. The Boers, for their part, had little time for missionaries, whom they regarded as mischievous intruders, men who worked to pervert the Kaffir by talk about his equality with all other races in the eyes of God. It was Livingstone who reported tartly the Bechuana saying that the Boers 'killed their enemies and enslaved their friends'. His antagonism to them can only have been increased by the raid they made, in his absence, on his mission station at Kolobeng, when they wantonly destroyed much of his property, including the library he valued so much. Livingstone knew that the Boers would like to seal off the interior by taking control of the Missionaries' Road that ran through eastern Bechuanaland on its way to the north. He wrote, in his *Missionary Travels* that: 'The Boers resolved to shut up the interior and I determined to open the country; and we shall see who have been most successful in resolution, they or I.'

In defence of the Boers, it must be said that since their original conquest of the Transvaal, they had always claimed that their western borderland included the Missionaries' Road and the Bechuana tribes who straddled across it. They saw it as part of their natural sphere of influence, and were determined to have control over the native chiefs there. This is what led them to such high-handed acts as telling Moffat that he must get the consent of their government before he could travel to the headquarters of his mission in Bechuanaland.

The Boers did not trade with the African tribes on their borders. Above all, they were forbidden to supply them with guns—a prohibition they had brought with them from the old eastern frontier. Indeed, about this time the *Volksraad* in Pretoria had laid it down that anyone found furnishing arms to African chieftains might suffer the death penalty, but in fact in the wild conditions of the border they could not enforce this law and guns were traded to the eager chiefs by unscrupulous men of their own race. Nevertheless, they were appalled to find that Livingstone had given guns to some of the Africans he lived amongst.

They would also have disputed Livingstone's accusation that they enslaved anyone—but here, although they would have been arguing with the law of the Transvaal on their side, they were arguing against the facts. The government allowed for a system of 'apprenticeship' of servants, but in fact these 'apprentices' were often young people carried off from some burning kraal they had raided, or Bushmen children whose parents had been hunted to death. The Boers felt they had good reason to distrust missionaries because of their painful experiences in the past on the old Eastern frontier where they had been hated and denounced by such evangelicals as Dr. John Philip of the London Missionary Society.

As Livingstone's fame increased, so did the revulsion of feeling in Britain grow against the Boers.

Livingstone had said he would open up the interior, and he kept his word. He found it possible to travel freely through much of Central Africa, and the chief dangers he suffered were from hardship and disease. He found poverty and ignorance, but very rarely did he meet enmity. The threat to the peace of the lands north of the Zambesi, he realized, lay in the slave trade, run chiefly by Arab half-castes, which was penetrating steadily deeper into the interior and destroying or debauching the tribes. Livingstone condemned this trafficking in human souls with an eloquent indignation that reverberated through England. The progressive demoralization of the inhabitants of the interior had to be stopped. Livingstone pondered on a method of achieving this until he arrived at a conclusion that satisfied both his religion and the state of mind that had developed in England as a result of the leaping growth of its commercial and industrial strength.

Livingstone declared of Central Africa that, 'if we can introduce commerce, an effectual blow will be struck against the slave trade,' and that, 'The capabilities of the new region lead me to hope that by the production of the raw materials of our manufacture, African and English interests will become more linked than heretofore.'[4] Commerce was to go to Africa in partnership with religion, indeed, the Bible was to be 'the Magna Charta of all the rights and privileges of modern civilization.' Livingstone pleaded for an end to the old form of colonial domination, of which Portugal with her inertia and her sketchy claims over much of the interior offered the prime example. 'Let the pathway into the interior be free to all,' he urged, 'and instead of wretched forts with scarcely an acre of land round them that can be called their own, let real colonies be made.' He wished to see 'merchants teaching the nations lessons of mutual dependence.'

As Livingstone first envisaged it, the idea was noble and philanthropic, and its combination of virtue with profit was practical enough: it promised to flatter the piety of those whom it enriched, and was thus likely to have some appeal in quarters where a purely religious plea would not have been considered. But Livingstone showed himself ignorant of the convulsions that could be expected to occur in traditional African societies with the introduction of a money economy and the profit motive. He also seems to have discounted the greed that might increasingly motivate the merchants and settlers who would find themselves so advantageously placed in relation to the majority of the inhabitants of the country. Livingstone suffered the defect of the good: he thought all men would act and respond as he did. Yet his was a solution honourably founded in the beliefs of his time.

Livingstone associated trade and religion even more closely by his words on activities proper to a missionary:

'Such a combination (as being at the same time a merchant and a missionary) would not be morally wrong, for nothing would be more fair, and apostolic, too, than that the man who devotes his time to the spiritual welfare of a people should derive temporal advantage from upright commerce.'

Thus, from the African point of view, the missionary would not only arrive a man rich in possessions, but he would set about to increase his wealth by trade. Apostolic poverty has given way, here, to apostolic shopkeeping.

Livingstone's slogan of 'Religion and Commerce' which was to gain renown as the formula by which Central Africa should be saved from barbarism and slavery, was one of the factors that helped to change the climate of public opinion in Britain during the latter half of the nineteenth century. Later, the ideas expressed in it were to be given a rather more cynical interpretation.

CHAPTER 2

The Nature of the Scramble

I n 1853, Cecil Rhodes was born. In that same year, Livingstone was an obscure missionary, making his first of many journeys into the interior of Africa. In that year, again, the British government of the day seemed to have finally decided to disengage itself, as far as possible, from the barren and expensive exercise of Imperial rule in South Africa. By the terms of the Sand River Convention of 1852 it had at last agreed to recognize the independence of the Boers of the Transvaal. The Bloemfontein Convention, to be signed early in 1854, secured the establishment of the second Boer republic, the Orange Free State. Here, as a proof of disengagement, it was prevailed upon to sign a statement which included the clause that—with the exception of Adam Kok and his Griquas—it had no treaties with native chiefs beyond the Orange and no wish or intention to enter into any such treaties which 'might be injurious or prejudicial to the interests of the Orange River government'. A plainer statement of withdrawal could not have been wished for by the Boers.

In the eyes of British statesmen such as Lord Grey, British Imperial commitments in South Africa were to be diminished with the object of 'ultimate abandonment'. The endless Kaffir wars and border disputes, the sullen opposition of the Dutch, the perpetual drain on public money without hope of return, all helped to persuade the British government that it would be foolish to follow such a thankless course any longer— particularly as the money it laid out in subjugation and pacification seemed all too often to flow as a subsidy to unscrupulous traders and to the speculators who battened on the confiscated lands of native chiefs. This was the situation in 1853.

Thirty-three years later, practically the whole coastline of Southern Africa, from the mouth of the Orange River on the west to the Mozambique border on the east, had come under British rule. The Imperial power had by then extended far beyond the Orange River, embracing Griqualand West and the gigantic arid expanse of Bechuanaland, and within the next five years it was to expand even farther, to include areas even more vast, through the agency of Rhodes's Chartered Company.

Thus, within the space of forty years, British policy had reversed itself on a truly massive scale. How did this come about? Perhaps, for the time being, it might be best for us to confine ourselves to a general review of the diplomatic bargaining that took place amongst the governments of Europe and to the economic motives that underlay such bargaining. We must begin with the mention of a preliminary act of greed on the part of the Cape Colony, which, with Britain's permission, annexed Griqualand West. This is the first note in a new theme, for Griqualand was not snatched because of its arid soil, but because of the economic wealth that lay under the ground there. When this area was declared a part of the British dominions, the Empire had taken its first step over the Orange River boundary that it had previously been so anxious to see as the terminus of its responsibilities. However, at this stage, the British government was still reluctant to increase its possessions, so it agreed to the annexation only on the understanding that funds for the administration of Griqualand West were to be found by the Cape government.

This act of political brigandage was engineered by Southey, the Colonial Secretary in the Cape Executive. It took place for only one reason: in 1870, diamond fields had been discovered within the borders of Griqualand West. These were the famous dry-diggings that were to lead to Kimberley Great Hole, De Beers, and the financial empire of Cecil Rhodes. Five years after the annexation, the British Government admitted its fault in the matter by making a paltry offer of compensation —a disgraceful £90,000—to the President of the Orange Free State.

Meanwhile governments in Europe were beginning to reflect on the information given by such explorers as Livingstone and Stanley. Livingstone had offered an ideology by whose reassuring tenets the economic exploitation and military conquest of these alluring virgin territories might be arranged. Consequently, the first scheme for African exploitation was international in character. It took the form of a conference, summoned by the Belgian king, Leopold, in Brussels in 1876, which, when it attempted to define its commercial intentions, echoed the religious and philanthropic note Livingstone had first struck.

The Nature of the Scramble

But economic realities were more bleak and did not seem to allow the luxuries of benevolence that were being voiced. The latter half of the nineteenth century had seen the erection of tarrifs in trade by most of the powerful nations of Europe and by the United States. Economic blocks were being formed and the old days of Free Trade, with Britain predominant, were clearly at an end. France had become a doctrinaire exponent of protectionist policies, and so it seemed certain that British trade would be effectively shut out of any parts of Africa that the French managed to annex. Bismarck's Imperial ambitions for Germany made him listen sympathetically to the increasing clamour from German missionaries, merchants and manufacturers, all of them anxious to see the establishment of colonies in other parts of the world, and particularly in Africa, which seemed to lie, an utterly defenceless giant, a sprawling body full of the promise of markets and mineral wealth.

Leopold found that international agreement was impossible on such a subject, so in 1879 he set up his Congo Association, emphasizing once more that his motives were philanthropic as well as commercial. In this way, despite French competition, he was successful in gaining control of the Congo basin. The uses to which he put this area, which he soon began to treat like a vast, private domain, are deservedly notorious. Perhaps the best, artistic depiction of the cruelty and moral squalor of the Congo under Leopold's administration is to be found in Conrad's *Heart of Darkness*.

To the north of the lands seized by Leopold, M. de Brazza had been busy extending the power of France. In other parts of the West Coast, the French also established their rule; in North Africa, they took Tunis. The colonial frenzy began to be felt by some of the lesser nations of Europe: the interest of Italy began to stir and Portugal revived her shadowy claims on the whole of the interior of Africa between her coastal colonies of Angola and Mozambique. Bismarck found it expedient to pursue Germany's new colonial ambitions in areas where Britain had shown some interest; gambling on her diplomatic isolation at that time, following on her embroilment in Egypt, to make her nervous of retaliation. In 1883, the German flag was raised at Angra Pequena on the coast of Namaqualand, a region on the west side of southern Africa that had always been thought to come loosely under the influence of the Cape Government, though the majority of the missionaries in the area were German, and Germans controlled most of the trade in ivory and feathers. By 1884, it had become clear that Britain and the Cape Colony would not resist the German occupation, despite their prior claim on the area, so Bismarck followed his luck by declaring a German protectorate over both Namaqualand and the adjoining territory of Damaraland. The British Government protested, but soon gave grudging recognition to this new German possession.

Many people, both in Britain and at the Cape, had become alarmed by this extension of German power. Its direction seemed particularly ominous: the vital Missionaries' Road in Bechuanaland, the only way open from the Cape into the interior, was now flanked by the Germans on the west and the Boers on the east. There were rumours that they intended to join hands, thus cutting the Missionaries' Road and with it the only British route into the interior.

The situation looked particularly dangerous because of two petty, independent Boer Republics, Stellaland and Land of Goshen, that had been set up in areas wrested from native chieftains on land athwart the Missionaries' Road. It seemed only a matter of time before they would ask to be incorporated in the Transvaal.

In 1884, Britain acted in defence of the Road. At the London Convention of that year, although she left open the question of the annexation of Bechuanaland, which was being pressed for in some quarters as the obvious counter-blow to German and Boer moves, she announced that the Road and the Republics of Stellaland and Goshen must be excluded from the Transvaal. Kruger, who was well aware of the importance of the Road, did his best to keep some power over it, even suggesting that it should be neutralized, but Britain was inflexible in this matter.

Two things led to more decisive British action before long. There was, first, the pressure put on the Government by Rhodes and his supporters, and second, the provocation it suffered from the Transvaal. Kruger had sent an emissary, du Toit, to the kraal of the African chief, Montsoia, whose lands lay in and about the Boer Republic of Goshen. Du Toit hoisted the *Vierkleur* flag in Montsoia's country and declared it annexed to the Transvaal. As this was obviously a move intended to gain control over the Road, the British Government could claim sincerely that the London Convention had been violated and that the Road was once more threatened. Britain protested to the Transvaal, and this time, feeling freer than it did under the restraints imposed by European diplomacy, followed its protest with an expeditionary force of some 5,000 men. These were sent up to Bechuanaland under the command of General Warren, an irascible Imperialist whose distrust of the Boers was inflamed to rage by the stories he heard about them from

Mackenzie, the missionary, who went with him. Mackenzie wished to see Bechuanaland come under the direct control of Britain and had been stirring up public opinion there against the Boers in a series of speeches and newspaper articles. He had won the support of such influential bodies as the Aborigines' Protection Society, and of eminent men in English public life.

Warren deliberately rode roughshod over the burghers of the little Boer Republics, and made a great show of his superior strength when conferring with Kruger at Fourteen Streams about the demarcation of the Transvaal boundary. Kruger was forced to admit that the Transvaal would not press for any further westward expansion. He had already repudiated the action of his emissary, du Toit, and the *Vierkleur* had been lowered in Land of Goshen.

As a result of all this, British Bechuanaland, in the south of the region, was made into a Crown Colony and the rest of modern Bechuanaland declared a British Protectorate. The road to the interior—'the neck of the bottle,' as Rhodes called it—had been preserved and British rule in Africa extended, though not, perhaps, in the way that Rhodes and his supporters would have liked best. Rhodes was a Colonial Imperialist, a believer in a great South African confederation under the English flag, with the Cape Colony as its nucleus and most powerful member. As he saw it, Bechuanaland should naturally have come under the influence of the Cape. Warren and Mackenzie were Imperialists of a more direct kind. They distrusted the policies of the Cape Government, particularly in its treatment of natives, and felt that any new areas annexed to Britain should be governed from Whitehall.

Although the manner of British occupation in Bechuanaland may have disappointed Rhodes and his followers, they were nevertheless relieved to see the Transvaal thwarted and the Germans given a warning that Britain did not intend to stand by and see herself excluded from the interior. By her actions Britain implied that she had designs on the lands between Limpopo and Zambesi, and perhaps beyond. This suited Rhodes very well. He knew what he wanted: his desire for 'the North' was already obsessive.

The British show of force appeared to achieve its end. At any rate, German behaviour became more placatory, and at the Berlin Conference of 1885, a sort of regularity and mutual forbearance was introduced into the pattern of rapacious actions of the colonialist Powers. Rules were laid down for the dismemberment of Africa and any other available parts of the world. 'Spheres of influence' were recognized and the doctrine of 'effective occupation' promulgated. Such occupation was to be reported to the signatory Powers, who would ratify and guarantee it.

The interior lay open to the spoilers. Lobengula, son of Mizilikazi, led the last, feared Bantu military power in southern Africa. His Matabele warriors still dominated the lands between Zambesi and Limpopo; with the Mashona tribes as his vassals or his prey. Within five years of the signing of the Berlin agreement, his territories were to be halved, and three years later to be swallowed completely by forces nominally under British control.

But the way in which they were taken was rather unusual; characteristic, however, of the methods employed by one powerful and unscrupulous man, operating within the context of those new forces of expansion: the joint stock company, the huge industrial corporation, and the world of aggressive capitalism they represented. Yet, though he knew this world well, and had been vastly enriched by his talent for manipulating it, Cecil Rhodes did not owe final allegiance to it. He refused to be confined by the timid economic nature of its valuations. He used his practical knowledge of the financier's world to help bring about his dreams. The nature of his vision and the contradictory traits that went to make up his character are worth examination, for they left their stamp upon the territories he annexed for Britain.

CHAPTER 3

Cecil Rhodes

Rhodes was big and clumsy in physical appearance, with a shambling gait. He had been plagued by a late puberty, and during his first year at the Kimberley diamond diggings, seems to have been still immature. Throughout his life, his voice remained high, and during moments of excitement would rise into a falsetto shriek. His manner of speaking was repetitive: he would hit on a phrase that pleased him and work it to death for the next few days, bringing it into all his conversations with his friends and worrying at the idea it represented until he reached some kind of conclusion, or until the idea was supplanted by some other that had excited him and which he had encapsulated in another phrase.

He was a slow thinker and, in terms of reason, a defective one, but he seems to have had the alternative gifts which make for power—intuition and persuasiveness. He could burn away men's resistance to his plans; he could lay siege to their minds and sap their rational defences; on occasion, he could set their spirits in a blaze that would never have kindled without him. He did this with his timid partner, Beit, whom he converted from his simple devotion to profit and turned into an Imperialist benefactor of the most lavish kind. He caught the imagination of Dr. Jameson, who became perhaps his greatest friend and certainly his most effective lieutenant. Jameson was a gambler by temperament, a man with a charming tongue and a cool brain, who might well have dissipated himself in trivial dangers and personal triumphs if Rhodes had not harnessed his energies to employments that were more constructive if less innocent.

Rhodes was able to gain and keep the allegiance of men as diverse as Rothschild or the younger Grey. He could charm the ear of the Prince of Wales or the Kaiser. He showed loyalty to anyone among his personal acquaintance who had trusted themselves to his leadership—though his loyalty did not always extend to those who had bought shares in his Companies. He seems to have been able to make a deep impression on ordinary men, too; from his own Pioneers, who sometimes seem to have looked on him as a godlike manipulator, to the defeated Matabele of 1896, who called him *Baba*, or Father. It was this glittering attraction, this power of the will, that explains his 'extraordinary ascendancy over men'. It was a gift that owed nothing to superior powers of reason or eloquence, for he had none. It seems to have existed in its own right, like some natural force. It could be recognized and felt by many different sorts of people, but perhaps Mark Twain caught its essence best with his remark: 'When Rhodes stands at Cape Town, his shadow falls on the Zambesi.'

It may be possible to relate the intensity of Rhodes' drive to his knowledge of his approaching death. He was a man of enormous ambitions and desires who found himself caged in a sickly body. For many years before it finally brought about his suffocation, his leaking heart had been threatening to stop, and he could not help being aware of its faltering. In the latter part of his life, any excitement would suffuse his face with blood, sending it a bloated purple, and he would watch the pulse of the thick blue veins at his wrist with fascinated attention. He used to say that he would not get past forty-five, and though in fact he survived a few years longer than that—he died at the age of forty-nine—the premonition of an early death goaded him on from his youth.

From his early days in South Africa, Rhodes was associated with the diamond-fields at Kimberley. In the end, he controlled them, and in place of the primitive scramble for individual wealth, he imposed a monopolistic corporation that disposed of 90 per cent of the world's output of diamonds. It is significant that he should emerge from such a background. The diggings at Kimberley saw the first big intrusion of a new element into the old pastoral and agricultural economy of South Africa: the heavily capitalized industrial company.

Rhodes became king of Kimberley. Most of the inhabitants of the town worked for him, and those such as shopkeepers who did not, were indirectly dependant on him. In Kimberley, a new pattern of society had emerged, a world with a few big masters and many underlings, a world greedy for labour, both black and white. It heralded that shift of power whose consummation is modern Johannesburg, established by an irony of history on the land Kruger had secured for his agrarian republic. When gold was discovered on the Witswatersrand and the magnates of Kimberley extended their activities to that region, the death of the old Transvaal was certain. It would have taken place even if the republic had not been thrown down by violence in the South African War. The Boer farmers would have been overwhelmed, in any case, and their power stripped from them by the floods of adventurers and mining employees who were drawn to the mines, and by the power of capital that called them there. The old supremacy of horse and gun was over.

The mines of Kimberley, and later the Rand, had their effect on the black man, too. Their hunger for labour produced a disruption in traditional Bantu life much more profound than any created by marauding Boers. They sucked in workers from as far away as Matabeleland, and even farther, across the Zambesi, housing them, at the inspiration of Rhodes, in great compounds: barracks of concrete and corrugated iron that were designed to cut off their inmates from the rest of the world and so prevent them from smuggling diamonds out of the diggings. The shortage of labour was always acute, despite the high wages paid, which, as Rhodes complained, were greater than he would have had to give for workmen in England at that time. Very often, the black labourers used their earnings to buy the guns they still believed held the key to power in Africa.

Not only was Rhodes a financial colossus, a symbol of the new industrial capitalism that had made its appearance in South Africa, he was also a conscious Imperialist, ready to spend vast amounts of the wealth he had gained in the support of his ideas. Unlike his partner, Beit, or his opponent, 'Buccaneer' Robinson, he had little interest in money for its own sake. He valued it chiefly as the avenue to power most naturally open to him, and used it unscrupulously to fulfil his ambitions—with such success that he came to believe that all men could be bought, or 'squared', as he would have put it. He could not understand men who were satisfied by the mere process of accumulating wealth. Stead reports him as saying of Rothschild: 'Out of 365 days, he spends 300 in turning over bits of paper and marking them. . . . Think of that man and his millions—what could he not do with them!'[1]

Rhodes was in many ways an upstart. He came to Africa as a young man of eighteen, driven there by a weakness in his chest that he hoped the dry, sunny climate would help to cure. Within a few years he was rich enough to 'send himself to Oxford'. This action on the part of a successful young Kimberley miner needs a word of explanation. Though some of Rhodes' elder brothers had gone to public school, he had been sent to the grammar school at Bishop Stortford, where he seems to have been a dull pupil, quite lacking in academic distinction. Yet Rhodes longed to go to Oxford, which he felt set the mark of 'gentleman' upon its graduates and ensured that they would be accepted among the 'class of people' with whom he felt he must associate.

As a very young man, Rhodes began to formulate certain ideas on the mission of the English race. At Oxford, he found them supported in the speeches of such men as Ruskin, and embraced them with a tenacity and fervour that suggests nothing so much as the fanatical provincial, fired by his very ignorance of the complexity of affairs. Yet it was this wild determination that carried him to success in his plans, though, it must be added, even his degree of faith would not have been enough had it not struck a responsive chord in the minds of many Englishmen of his day.

In Oxford, he heard Ruskin say: 'England must found colonies as fast and as far as she is able, formed of her most energetic and worthiest men; seizing any piece of fruitful waste ground she can set her foot on, and there teaching her colonists that their chief virtue is to be fidelity to their country and their first aim is to be to advance the power of England by land and sea.'[2]

This statement should be compared with the terms of the will Rhodes made whilst still a young man. He drew up this document in 1877, on a visit to Kimberley whilst between terms at Oxford. In it, he wrote: 'I contend that every acre added to our territory provides for more of the English race, who otherwise would not be brought into existence.' He goes on to arrange for the setting up of a secret society whose aim will be the absorption of the greater part of the world within the British Empire.

Rhodes justified his Imperial appetite by arguments based on Darwinism. His was a world in which only the fittest would survive. In this opinion, as in the racialism he picked up in South Africa, he must appear now as a precursor of those men who led twentieth-century Europe into policies of war and extermination. In Rhodes, the doctrines still have an innocent, morning air, a ring of fantasy, but to us, eighty years later, the sinister implications of such remarks as the following can hardly be disputed: 'Do you think that any part of Africa was left in perpetuity for the pygmies while a superior race stands multiplying outside? I do not believe it. Our race will never adopt the doctrines of Malthus. They will go on multiplying and probably in two hundred

years they will fill the whole world.' To Honetaux, French Minister for
Foreign Affairs, Rhodes phrased it more tactfully: 'You see, the non-
civilized races must disappear. You in France must also play your part
in Africa.'[3] To a man like Gladstone who distrusted visionary flights,
and would have regarded Rhodes' fancies with commonsense repugnance, Rhodes could give a different answer again. Gladstone had asked
what advantage England could hope to gain by annexing new territory.
Rhodes replied: 'The practical reason for the acquisition of territory is
that every Power in the world, including our kinsmen, the Americans, as
soon as they take a new territory, place hostile tariffs against British
goods. Great Britain is a very small island. Great Britain's position
depends on her trade, and if we do not take and open up the depen-
dencies of the world which are at present devoted to barbarism, we
shall shut out the world's trade.'[4] Here, Rhodes defines colonialism
as a late stage of capitalism in a way that would have delighted
Lenin!

Rhodes even managed to salvage out of the wreck of his religious
ideas—which had been particularly badly shaken by Winwoode Reade's
Martyrdom of Man—enough to justify him in his sense of mission. He
argued that, on his assessment, there was a 50 per cent chance that God
existed. Therefore, he went on, it was just as reasonable to suppose that
He existed as to reject the idea of an Almighty Power. Because he himself felt the need to see a meaning in life, he would act as though God
certainly existed, and he felt sure that in these circumstances he could
assume a divine inspiration for the mission of the English race. On this
tottering scaffolding of rationalization, Rhodes seemed able to rest
content.

Yet despite his feelings for the English race, he was always sympathetic towards the Dutch, as a people, and could, on occasion, speak of
them as 'a coming race in South Africa'. Again, when he was trying to
push through his Chartered Company in London, he coupled his talk of
commercial profit with vague philanthropic statements about the advantages it would have to the natives of the region. But this is perhaps best
seen as policy—a cynical echo of Livingstone given in order, it may be,
to touch the hearts and still the consciences of English rentiers.

As we have seen, his opinions varied with his audience, but of the
underlying appetite there can be no doubt. He wanted to see as much
of Africa as possible fall under British domination, and he preferred it
to be done by his agency, and in a way which guaranteed a private
profit to himself and his shareholders. Milner said of Rhodes: 'Men are

ruled by their foibles and his foible is size.' This certainly seems to have been one facet of his obsession. Even now, in his speeches and the reports of his conversation, you can still catch an echo of that preoccupation with size itself, with magnitude as the garment of power. Some recent commentators have hinted that personal inadequacies in Rhodes might have been the cause of this fascination. Perhaps psychological compensation played a part, but men are not so simple in their motivation as is sometimes assumed, and in any case, such ideas of expansion and domination were by no means confined to Rhodes. They were common to many people of the day; even Queen Victoria seems to have taken a stolid, rather complacent pleasure in the size of the possessions Rhodes boasted to her that he had added to her Empire.

Rhodes at his most grandiloquent could cry to Stead, 'I would annex the planets and the stars, if I could,' but this must not be taken to suggest any lack of practical capacity. In fact, Rhodes was well aware that the instrument by which he must work was money, and that without it he would accomplish nothing. He used it with thoughtful unscrupulousness in the service of his ideals. When he entered politics, for instance, he ensured that his speeches would always be reported in the press by buying a share of the *Cape Argus* large enough to be influential. Later, he extended his grip over all six newspapers of the *Argus* group in South Africa. He was notorious for his cynical belief that all men could be bought, and that they should be tempted into that kind of dishonour whenever he needed their support. But he was also renowned for his ability to inspire men with enthusiasm or wear them down by his insistence. When he had at last outmanœuvred Barney Barnato and completed his diamond monopoly at Kimberley by gaining control of Barnato's 'Kimberley Mine', he took the opportunity of framing the new Corporation trust deed for De Beers Consolidated Mines in such terms that he could call on it to help him conquer the north. Barnato was one of the four men in control of the new company, and naturally he expected it to devote itself to the production of diamonds and the reaping of profit. He objected strongly when he saw that, in the terms of the deed, money could be diverted for such eccentric objects as the raising and maintaining of a private army and the setting in motion of campaigns of conquest. But in the end he was overborne by Rhodes. Barnato is quoted as saying: 'No one else in the world could have induced me into this partnership. But Rhodes has an extraordinary ascendancy over men.' This facet of his character was as important as his cynicism or his ruthless devotion to his ideals.

Cecil Rhodes

To the end of his life, Rhodes maintained his original faith. In 1898, defeated in the Cape elections and discredited in Britain, he could still say: 'We shall not relax our efforts until by our civilization and the efforts of our people we reach the shores of the Mediterranean.' And to Stead in 1900, only two years before his death: 'Faith in religion is dwindling. Faith in race is taking its place. It is the only faith left. I believe in my race.' After his death, he tried to make provision for men out of the English-speaking world (and their German cousins) who would act as the heirs of his ideals. This, according to Jameson, was his intention in founding the Rhodes' scholarships to Oxford. He had set down that he wanted in such scholars, 'scholastic and literary attainments, success in manly sport, manhood, truth, courage, sympathy and protection of the weak, kindliness, unselfishness and fellowship; and the exhibition during school days of moral force of character and of instincts to lead.' Later, contemplating the array of virtues demanded of such paragons and perhaps realizing that neither he nor most of his friends would ever have been eligible in terms of them, he was prompted to give them in sharp, cynical—and perhaps here, saving—paraphrase to Stead as: 'Smugness, brutality, unctuous rectitude and tact.'

Though it is always difficult to assess the precise nature of Rhodes' views on a subject because of his habit of tailoring his opinions to suit his audience, it does seem that towards the end of his life he began to think in terms of 'civilization' rather than race. His famous declaration that he would like to see 'equality of rights for every civilized man south of the Zambesi' and that 'any men, provided they can write their names, place of residence and occupation, and that they are workers or possessed of some property, quite irrespective of colour, would be entitled to these rights,' does suggest a more benevolent attitude towards the African. Indeed, the statement is liberal in the highest degree and all the more surprising because it came from a man who had spent most of his life in South Africa and had been deeply involved in the politics of that country. But Rhodes himself had no time before his death to put such beliefs into practice and his successors in Rhodesia seem to have used his words rather to erect 'white civilization' as a barrier against the African than to admit the large numbers of them to the electorate that Rhodes' declaration would seem to demand.

This sums up the contradictions in Rhodes, who could often be devious, but whose deviousness had its origin in the one overmastering drive that possessed him. We must now return to the situation in 1888, when with Bechuanaland secure and the wealth of the Kimberley mines at his disposal, Rhodes was poised for the thrust into the interior that would mark the climax of his realized ambitions. He felt that by this time he was ready to extend British power (and his own)—and incidentally to introduce the Mashona and the Matabele to a new kind of world.

CHAPTER 4

The Concessions
and the Chartered Company

Rhodes would never have been able to send a private army into Mashonaland if he had not first convinced the holders of the million £1 shares issued by his Chartered Company that there was mineral wealth for the taking north of the Limpopo. He financed his Pioneers partly from his own resources, partly from the profits of his Kimberley and Johannesburg Corporations, but also to a large extent from the money his venture attracted in England. His great reputation as a financier and mining magnate helped to win the confidence of investors. If he assured them that an even bigger Rand lay to the north, it seemed probable that he would be right about that, just as he had been about the potentialities of the blue-ground at Kimberley. Besides, there were other opinions that seemed to confirm his, in this instance.

Earlier in the century, an elephant hunter by the name of Henry Hartley had been led into Mashonaland by his search for ivory. He had been stirred by what he saw there: old excavations and dumps of removed quartz that spoke unmistakeably of gold-mining operations in the past. His interest was great enough for him to persuade Karl Mauch, a young German geologist, to go with him to investigate the reefs of Mashonaland.

Mauch seems to have been very impressed with what he found. In 1867, he wrote a letter to the *Cape Argus* describing in the following terms the gold deposits he claimed to have examined:

'The vast extent and beauty of these goldfields are such that at a particular spot I stood as it were transfixed, riveted to the place, struck with amazement and wonder at the sight, and for a few minutes was unable to use the hammer. Thousands of people here might find ample room to work in this extensive field without interfering with one another.'

A description framed in terms like these was calculated to provoke a rush of prospectors from all parts of the world. The information on the new fields was given publicity in England, including several enthusiastic articles in *The Times*. The news flashed to Australia and California, where seasoned old diggers began to prick up their ears at the possibility of another 'strike'. Men began to arrive at Durban and other South African ports, and between 1868 and 1870 it seemed likely that the interior would be invaded by a mob of adventurers. But the route was a long and difficult one; the dangers considerable; the problems of transport grievous; and the evidence of the new fields of the flimsiest kind. The only kind of comparison men could make was with the mining just begun in the Tati concession, which lay in the north of Bechuanaland, adjoining the Matabele kingdom. Here the field was proving a great disappointment. The indecision of many prospectors was resolved for them by the diamond 'strike' at Kimberley in 1870. The idea of penetrating the barbarous north was abandoned and they poured instead into Griqualand West.

But the memory remained, and was to gain in power and credibility when gold was struck on the Witwatersrand in 1886. Not only that. In 1873, during further wanderings in Mashonaland. Mauch had stumbled on the stone ruins at Zimbabwe. He considered them together with the ancient gold mining he knew to have taken place in the territory and decided that he was looking at the remains of the city which the Queen of Sheba had once governed. The only other explanation that offered itself was that the ruins had been the work of the Bantu, and as with almost all men of his time, that seemed to him impossible. It was much more likely—and much more promising—that he should have stumbled on distant Ophir, which had supplied the gold for Solomon. The hypothesis was not new. It had been put forward by the Portuguese as long before as the sixteenth century, when they first heard of the kingdom of the Monomatapa. It was to remain current for many years, together with the associated theories of Phoenician or Sabaean colonists, and to be parted with by Rhodesians only with great reluctance and regret under a bombardment of archaeological evidence.

The rumour of the monuments of Sheba began to spread. It grew stronger and was endowed with romantic glamour by the publication in 1885 of Rider Haggard's novel, *King Solomon's Mines*. Haggard said of the theme of his book: 'Doubtless I heard faint rumours of these things during my sojourn in Africa, having made it my habit through life to keep my ears open; but at best they were very faint.' Faint, perhaps, but pervasive. Certainly, in England they seem to have created an atmosphere of hazy expectation, and together with the golden realities of the Rand, to have produced a climate of opinion favourable to the workings of an entrepreneur such as Rhodes, who could give little more than his word, and load the air with promises, when he spoke in London about the wealth of the interior.

Rhodes was not the only one who had begun to look beyond the Limpopo. Besides the Portuguese there were the Transvaal Boers. With the declaration of the Bechuanaland Protectorate, Boer expansion to the west had been brought to an end. In the past, they had not cared to go north because of the tsetse fly belt on the Limpopo—an accident of insect distribution that probably acted as a major safeguard in the preservation of the independent Matabele kingdom. Now some of the burghers had begun to talk of trekking to the upland pastures where Lobengula ran his gigantic herds. By this point in history, land and plunder still beckoned only in this one direction. The world was beginning to close round the trek Boer. The men who favoured such an expedition to the north had the support of Joubert, the old military Commandant of the Transvaal. Kruger preferred the idea of Boer penetration into Swaziland with the Tongaland harbour of Kosi Bay as his ultimate objective. The Transvaal was landlocked, and Kruger felt that the strategic and commercial security of his state could only be assured if he could gain a port, and a railway from it to Pretoria.

If he were to be asked to dissuade his burghers from crossing the Limpopo—as he realized might happen because of British interests in the area—Kruger would want compensation. Should he be given leave to consolidate his interests in Swaziland, he would be willing to sacrifice the north—but of course he would not do so unless he had to. Nor did he expect his reasoning to be popular with some of the nomadic farmers of the Transvaal.

Kruger could sympathize with them; he understood them because he had always been one of them. He was, indeed, a fitting President for such men; burly, devout, immensely tough and with the ugliness of an old elephant. He had come up to the Transvaal as a boy of ten in the Great Trek; a time in life by which, as he declared later, he was considered quite able to shoot and fight, and had done so in various skirmishes with native bands. The stories told about him by his countrymen, besides showing their affection, declare a good deal about the kind of qualities for which a man was most cherished and respected in Boer society. It was a primitive, Heroic measure.

The legends spoke of Kruger with a thumb which had gone gangrenous after an injury, taking out his hunting-knife and hacking it off. Kruger walking alone into the kraal of a ferocious African chieftain to hold parley. Kruger as a young man, challenging the swiftest of the African tribesmen to a day-long race on foot over the veld, and pausing on his victorious way to shoot a lion. Kruger the Dopper, adherent of the sternest and most Fundamentalist of sects in a nation of Calvinists, who turned Cecil Rhodes away from his house because this Cape politician ventured to approach him on a Sunday on a matter that was not religious. Indeed, in this dour, unpretentious old man Rhodes found an opponent he could never buy nor influence. The two were natural antagonists, each dedicated to a very different vision of life.

The scramble for concessions that began in Central Africa in the late 80's of the last century cannot be represented as a mere surge of commercial greed: it also reflects the power vacuum that existed there and the desire to dress the coming domination in the rags of legality. Although Lobengula was the ruler of a state that was both strong and warlike in African terms, he could be thrown down easily by any determined European power—and he knew it. By the rules brought into the contest at the Conference of Berlin, it was desirable to have some show of legality, if only to assuage the feelings of the other signatory powers. As Rhodes saw it, the obvious way to set about getting political control of Lobengula's country was to go by the back-door of the economic concession. Besides, if he acted in support of an economic agreement he could furnish himself with the money needed for the enterprise on the London market.

Yet, at the very beginning of the intrigue, Rhodes found his hand being forced, and the first move made was a hasty political one. In 1887 news had come to Rhodes of the signing of an agreement between Lobengula and the Transvaal Boers. Piet Grobler, their emissary, had succeeded in getting Lobengula's mark to an agreement which re-affirmed the old treaty of friendship that had existed between the Matabele and the Boers since the time of Mizilikazi. It is doubtful whether it was understood by Lobengula as anything more than a reassurance that the peace would be kept between his people and the formidable burghers south of the Limpopo—and this the anxious Matabele king would have been very glad to have. But the terms of the treaty allowed for the setting-up of a Boer Consul at Bulawayo, under whose jurisdiction and protection all Boers who came into the lands of Lobengula were to fall. They were, in fact, removed from the authority of the Matabele king even though they might be living in his territory. This might well have been the preliminary to the infiltration of the Matabele kingdom by Boers hungry for land. Rhodes interpreted the move in this way and he immediately set in motion a series of actions designed to frustrate it.

Among the many men whom Rhodes had won over to his views was Sir Sydney Shippard, Commissioner for Bechuanaland. He now used Shippard's help to persuade Sir Hercules Robinson, the Governor at the Cape, to send a British agent to Lobengula who would be empowered to challenge Grobler's treaty. If possible, the agent should also get from Lobengula an agreement that would give Great Britain the exclusive influence over his country. The man chosen for the task of agent was John Moffat, Deputy Commissioner for Bechuanaland. It was a wise choice. Moffat was a son of the famous missionary who had befriended Mizilikazi many years before. He had been known to Lobengula since the Matabele king's boyhood. Lobengula liked and trusted 'Joni' and was willing to listen to him, particularly when Moffat pointed out the sinister implications that could be read into Grobler's treaty.

Lobengula seems to have sensed by this time that the situation was critical for himself and his people. Indeed, he appears to have been carried through the next few years by a sense of fatality, aware that the Matabele were doomed, yet trying to stave off the day by a policy of hesitation, by the long inconclusive *indabas* he spun out at his place of council with various groups of white men whose rapacity shone through their flattery and their gifts. If he was overborne into making some concession, he would try to repudiate it later, or make some other grant that contradicted the first one. There was no hope of ultimate success: in the game he played delay was the only kind of victory.

His recognition of the impending fall of the Matabele nation was not shared by his young warriors, who often urged him to let them put a stop to this obsequious white vanguard of invasion by slaughtering the Europeans who flocked to his kraal with requests of one kind or another. Once, when they pressed him fiercely for his permission, he answered: 'If you want to fight the white men, you may go to Kimberley. Remain there and try to fight the white men and you will see what they will do to you.'[1] The warriors had heard about the awesome marvels of Kimberley; some of them had even been down there to work for a time as labourers on the mines. Lobengula could not make his sense of impotence any more explicit without losing their respect. He went on to say that the white men at his kraal were guests, and should be treated according to the laws of hospitality. He maintained this position honourably, right up to the final débâcle of 1893, when his armies had been swathed down like corn by the Maxims of Jameson's column, and he himself was abandoning his royal residence and preparing to flee towards the Zambesi. In the extremity of that time, he remembered the two white traders still living in Bulawayo and left them a bodyguard to ensure they were not attacked by any of his enraged warriors after he had gone.

Yet in other matters, he acted with the traditional ruthlessness of the Matabele. He could hardly do otherwise. His nation was founded on military prowess and fierce discipline. It was a predatory regime, whose nature was symbolized by the great annual raid. The mystique by which his warriors lived demanded perpetual victims, and in such matters Lobengula was a child of his people: he does not ever seem to have envisaged any other way of living. In the same vein, he could be merciless to any of his councillors who he thought had betrayed him by giving him bad advice. Later, for instance, when Rhodes had got an economic concession out of him which he afterwards recognized as an instrument of invasion, he turned on Lotje, the councillor who had advised him to sign, and 'ate him up' with the assegai in the traditional Zulu manner, sending a detachment of his warriors to destroy his kraal and wipe out his family and erase all memory of him from the Matabele nation.

And even though with one part of his mind, he recognized the inevitable advance of white power and its consequences for him, with another he seems to have remained fixed on the pursuit of traditional enmities. It was this second part that still allowed him to think in terms of beating the Barotse, even whilst he knew that those days, that whole way of life, were drawing to an end. He showed the urgent desire for firearms usual to Africans of the period—indeed, when he put his country into the hands of Rhodes, it was in exchange for the rifles and ammunition with which he hoped to defend it. He was not to know that the 1,000 rifles, 100,000 rounds of ammunition and the gunboat on the Zambesi which he was promised by the terms of the Rudd Concession would be inadequate for his purpose. To Lobengula, they must have seemed a formidable armoury, a tremendous addition to his strength. The gunboat that was (ludicrously) thrown in with the deal, illustrated Lobengula's inability to escape wholly from the conditions of the past: he thought it would break the superiority of Barotse canoe-power, which had often put his warriors at a disadvantage as they made the crossing of

9. Officials of the Chartered Company. Cecil Rhodes (*centre*), Managing Director, with (*left*) the Duke of Abercorn, President of the Company, and (*right*) Lord Grey, a director.

10. Wagons on the road, 1892.

11. An old prospector.

12. Salisbury in 1891, after one year of European occupation.

the Zambesi on their way north to raid. In fact, the gunboat was never delivered and presumably Lobengula received the cash payment stipulated as a substitute. Besides the arms, Lobengula was to receive a yearly pension of £1,300 from Rhodes and the Chartered Company. But before the Rudd Concession could be negotiated, it was necessary to bring the Matabele kingdom within the British 'sphere of influence'.

Moffat managed to get Lobengula's mark on a treaty stating that he would 'refrain from entering into any correspondence or treaty with any foreign State or Power to sell, alienate, or cede' any part of the Matabele kingdom without 'the previous knowledge and sanction of Her Majesty's High Commissioner for South Africa'. The Portuguese, when they heard of this document, issued a protest at the inclusion of Mashonaland within Lobengula's territories. The Boers ignored it. Kruger sent Grobler shortly afterwards to act as his Consul in Bulawayo, and issued a proclamation that all Boers living in the lands of the Matabele should contact their accredited representative, Piet Grobler, who had been sent to act for them 'at king Lobengula's own request'. Grobler arrived at Bulawayo and set up his Consulate, but when going back to the Transvaal on a visit a few months later, he was killed in a skirmish with some Africans. The British Government investigated the matter and came to the conclusion that Khama, African ruler in Bechuanaland must take responsibility for the killing and pay the widow of the dead man compensation. A slight odour of suspicion has always surrounded the murder of Grobler: it is not quite impossible that his death was arranged by someone in Rhodes' party.

Certainly, Grobler's death was convenient to Rhodes, removing, as it did, the agent of the Transvaal from Bulawayo and providing Kruger with an indirect warning not to interfere any more in the north. But, in any case, when Moffat gained Lobengula's mark to his treaty, he drew the Matabele kingdom within the British 'sphere of influence', according to the rules of the game laid down at Berlin, and in these circumstances she would have been hard to dislodge.

After the Moffat treaty had denied the Matabele kingdom to his political rivals, Rhodes could press forward with the legal fiction required for actual occupation. Shortly after Moffat had been sent to Lobengula's kraal, Rhodes dispatched a negotiator of his own, a man by the name of Fry, to try to get a concession for mineral rights from Lobengula. As it happened, it was the rainy season, when the climate was at its most unhealthy, and Fry was stopped by fever before he could reach Bulawayo, and trailed back to the Cape to die a little later.

In view of this failure, Rhodes felt he had to move quickly: he knew there were other companies trying to persuade Lobengula to give them concessions over his lands. This time, Rhodes sent up three men instead of one, to minimize the risk of them not arriving. They were: Rudd, who had been his partner since the early days in Kimberley; Maguire, an old Oxford friend and a Fellow of All Souls; and Thomson, a man expert in African languages and customs. This somewhat bizarre trio reached Bulawayo without accident, and after lengthy bargaining, and despite the opposition of various rivals, they succeeded in extracting from the king his mark on the document since known as the Rudd Concession. This gave Rhodes 'the complete and exclusive charge over all metals and minerals' in the lands under Lobengula's dominion and promised him the king's help in excluding all other persons 'seeking land, metals or minerals or mining rights.'[2]

Lobengula made no grant of land with this concession, and seems to have deluded himself that his own powers as a ruler would not be seriously affected by it. Later, he became alarmed at the construction he saw being put upon his agreement and claimed that he had never understood the terms of the concession properly. He insisted that, as he had envisaged it, the white men were simply coming to 'make a big hole' like the one at Kimberley.

His protests could not save him, nor the letters he sent to Queen Victoria, which seem to have been deliberately delayed by government officers who supported Rhodes, nor the two Matabele elders he dispatched to the Queen. The message they carried for her does have an ingenuous air, it must be admitted: 'Lobengula desires, if there is a Queen, to ask her to advise and help him, as he is much troubled by white men who come into his country and ask to dig gold.' It looks very much as though Lobengula was playing his usual game of setting one white authority against another, but with Rhodes he had overreached himself.

The Matabele elders were received courteously in England, and treated to such edifying spectacles as a military tattoo at Aldershot and a glimpse of the bullion chambers of the Bank of England. They were also given an audience with the Queen, who sent them back with a letter to Lobengula bidding him to be wary in his dealings with white men who came to dig for gold. The influential Aborigines' Protection Society sent a similar letter. The advice in both was good, but impossible to act upon. Meanwhile, Rhodes had his concession and was moving rapidly towards the formation of a Company to exploit the rights he had been granted in it.

The Concessions and the Chartered Company

Imperial expansion in the eighties of the last century brought about the revival of the type of Chartered Company that had been so powerful in the days of the Tudors and Stuarts. Such ancient corporations as the East India Company or the Hudson Bay Company had been granted a combination of commercial and administrative powers very similar to the kind Rhodes now coveted. Directly comparable with such old charters were those that had been granted to the British North Borneo Company in 1881 and the Royal Niger Company in 1886. When Rhodes went to London to gain a royal Charter for himself, that of the Imperial British East Africa Company was just being negotiated. With these examples before his eyes, Rhodes could feel hopeful of the success of his mission. The idea of a commercial kingdom, governed privately by his servants under the shadow of the Union Jack, was one that appealed to him very much.

To be sure of getting the royal consent, Rhodes needed as much influential support as he could muster. He spoke about the matter with the Prince of Wales, who liked him, and who was always interested in adventurous commercial ventures with the promise of good profits. The Prince proposed that his friend, the Duke of Abercorn, should be president of the Company, and that his son-in-law, the Duke of Fife, should be vice-president. Fife was to take the lesser post so that the royal connexion should not be made too apparent. With two such names at the head of his Board, Rhodes found no difficulty in recruiting eminent men for the rest of the seats he wanted filled. He even managed to win over the younger Grey, a man valuable because of his great reputation for honesty in public affairs. The Queen made no difficulties, the Charter was granted, and Rhodes became Managing Director of the Company.

The Chartered Company declared its aims to be the extension of the railway and telegraph northward to the Zambesi; the encouragement of colonization; the promotion of trade and commerce in the area; and the development of mineral and other concessions. The Company's unique claims on the territory were stressed in its advertisements; it was emphasized that, as all development would be in the hands of a single powerful organization, free from the jockeyings of rivals, rapid exploitation of the area could be expected. The Charter granted the Company great freedom of political as well as economic action. It was authorized to make treaties with native chiefs within the sphere of its operations; to keep the peace; to promulgate laws; it was entrusted with the making of roads and railways and the administering of all other public works;

it had the power to set up banks; to make grants of land; to carry on all kinds of lawful commerce; and to acquire further concessions.

Thus we arrive at that strange amalgam: an enterprise created for private profit but vested in addition with powers of government over the area in which it operates.

When the scheme was advertised in London, Livingstone's formula of commercial penetration as a vehicle for philanthropy was touched upon once more, as in this article in *The Times*, which spoke of, '. . . the formation of a new Company of British capitalists and philanthropists . . . opening up to trade and civilization certain territories in central Zambesi. . . . It is rich, fabulously rich we are told, in precious metals and half a dozen others besides. Whether the Company finds the wealth of Ophir in the mountains and rivers of Mashonaland or not, we cannot doubt that it will lay the basis of a great English-speaking Colony.'

Here the various attractions the venture might have for the investing public of the time are touched upon. Foremost, no doubt, was the hope of a dazzling profit from a monopolistic company which, it was commonly supposed, would be exploiting an area richer in gold than the Rand, and which would be free from rivals or from the interference of a hostile government. There was the reference to philanthropy, the easy belief that the natives of the region would be transformed without much trouble from their barbarism, moving upwards by a voluntary participation both in Christianity and in the forms of capitalistic business with which it would be associated. Then, the Imperial theme was sounded, and at that time the extension of the British Empire seemed a stirring, absolutely legitimate aim, which was cherished by a large number of English people. It offered new markets, prestige, all the intoxicating panoply of power. Many felt that in a world devoted to 'Progress', the British Empire was the instrument of Destiny, working itself out in Darwinian terms, so that backward races fell inevitably into the hands of 'the Fittest'. It was a comfortable doctrine for those who were temporarily the strongest.

For such reasons as these, together with the persuasive power of his own reputation, Rhodes could expect the money he needed to be subscribed. All he had to offer were unsupported promises, but these were of an irresistible kind. He himself believed the Company would be a commercial success but more than that, he hungered for the lands of the north as a first major step in 'painting the map of Africa red, British red'. As for the philanthropic aspect of his venture, he made a remark that reads like a cynical paraphrase of Livingstone's slogan of 'Religion and Commerce'. He said: 'Philanthropy is all very well in its way, but philanthropy plus 5 per cent is much better.' The phrasing of this remark is like the knell of all that Livingstone meant. Later, Rhodes was to say that he preferred 'land to niggers'. This presents a truer picture of his scale of values in this period than any talk about philanthropy. Rhodes was too much of a South African at this time, he had drawn too near to men such as his friend and political ally, Hofmeyer of the Afrikaner Bond, to think of the African in terms much other than as a source of cheap labour.

Rhodes' expectations were realized: subscriptions poured in; the shares of the Chartered Company rose to four times their nominal value. The stage was set for the organization of the Pioneer Column which would go into Mashonaland.

Whilst this was being done, and the telegraph was being taken on by the Company to Palapye in Bechuanaland and on towards Macloutsie, the base camp of the Pioneers, certain difficulties arose. A Boer of British ancestry called Bowler was gathering men in the Transvaal for a trek into Mashonaland; Lobengula was uneasy and could not be trusted to keep his warriors inactive when the Column went through his territory; and trouble had arisen over the number of men who should accompany the Pioneers as a military escort. The British officer in Bechuanaland who had been approached for an estimate gave a figure of 2,500 men, a number that would be financially crippling from the Company's point of view.

The three difficulties were solved. Bowler's trek was averted by an agreement made between Kruger and Sir Henry Loch: in return for dissuading his burghers from their trek, Kruger was to be allowed to advance his claims in Swaziland. The paramount chief of the Swazi nation had been corrupted beyond hope by concession hunters. He was willing by this time to give whatever was demanded of him so long as he was supplied with the champagne and the greyhounds for which he had developed an addiction. The difficulty presented by Lobengula's possible hostility, Rhodes solved by employing Selous, the hunter, to find for the Column a route that would skirt the lands occupied by the Matabele. Selous had been claiming before that Mashonaland was not effectively occupied by the Matabele and none of its rights could therefore be ceded by Lobengula. Rhodes offered him the post of Adviser for the Mashonaland Column at a salary of £3,000 a year, and no more was heard of the invalidity of the Rudd Concession in Mashonaland. The third obstacle that had arisen, the size of the military escort, was solved by Rhodes in a way that was unconventional but typical of much else in this conquest by public Company. One morning, Rhodes was having breakfast at the Kimberley Club, very much worried about the problem of the escort to be provided for the Column. A young man called Frank Johnson happened to come in and was invited to Rhodes' table and taken into his confidence. Johnson remarked airily at one point that he thought he could do the business much less expensively. Rhodes seized on this remark and asked Johnson to provide a detailed explanation for him of how he would carry it out. Johnson did so, and Rhodes was impressed enough to offer to put him in charge of the expedition as a servant of the Company. This did not appeal to Johnson, who reports himself as answering: 'You give me a cheque for £87,500, supply me with field and machine-guns, rifles and ammunition, and I will undertake to hand Mashonaland over to you, fit for civil government, within nine months, but I want you to remember that I am not your servant but your contractor.'[3] Rhodes agreed to all the demands of this remarkable young man, who was twenty-three years old at the time.

Thus, the invasion of Mashonaland was arranged between a public Company and a private contractor who would have charge of a column of pioneers and a small private army, the whole scheme to operate in terms of profit. The actual military command was in the hands of Colonel Pennefather of the British Army, and Dr. Jameson was to go with the force as the representative of the Company.

As well as the 'field and machine-guns, rifles and ammunition' he had specified to Rhodes, Johnson equipped the column with naval searchlights and dynamite. He hoped to overawe any Africans they might meet by demonstrating the supernatural quality of these devices: great eyes like the sun that burned at night and mighty upheavals of the earth caused by dynamite exploded at a distance from the observers.

One hundred and eighty-six men, of both Dutch and English stock, were recruited to make up the Pioneers. The mixture of races was deliberate policy. Rhodes had always stressed the need for inclusion of the Dutch in South Africa as equals under the English flag. It was the Transvaal Boers and their like that he objected to, because of their exclusive culture and Republican ideal of government, not the Dutch in general. In addition to these men, a force of 500 'police' was raised on a set contract. They were, in fact, a band of mercenaries, whose duties covered those usually performed by an army and a gendarmerie. These men went by the name of The British South Africa Police.

The Concessions and the Chartered Company

While the recruits gathered at their base on the Macloutsie river, Selous was already cutting the first part of the road the column was to follow, using some of Khama's men as his labourers. In order to skirt the land occupied by the Matabele, the road had to be taken through the low veld for a long distance. Here the ground was broken and covered with thick bush. In such country, the Matabele could have set an ambush most effectively, and the fear of this dominated the minds of the men in the column for over a month, until finally they climbed the pass that Selous had discovered—and named 'Providential' in token of his relief—and found themselves at last on the open grass lands of the high veld.

Twice Lobengula sent messages to the Pioneer Column, both of them expressing his distrust and sense of betrayal.[4] As he claimed to understand the situation, he had only given permission for miners to work in places that he appointed. Now he saw an army invading his land. His first letter asked: 'Has the king killed any white men that an *impi* is collecting on his borders? Or have the white men lost anything they are looking for?'

According to his own description, Johnson answered this enquiry by demonstrating to the Matabele elders who had come with the message the power of his Maxims and nine-pounders. He also showed them the searchlights in action, which they took to be witchcraft, as he had expected.

Lobengula wrote again. His letter said: 'From whom did the Dakatela (Doctor Jameson) hear that the king had given leave for digging in the Mashona country? Did not the Dakatela agree at Bulawayo to dig only in such places as the king might appoint? Now he wants to dig in a new place and the king will not allow it. Does he want to raid the king's country and dig by force? The Dakatela says the king showed the road, but he did not understand the king's words on that day.'

An answer was returned by Colonel Pennefather which stated that 'in obedience to the Queen's orders, I must go on,' adding the evasive and placatory clause, 'but if the Queen orders me back I will go.'

As the Pioneers rode on through the brilliant blue weather of the Rhodesian winter, they came in contact with their first Mashona. The villages of mud huts were perched on boulders and small kopjes or hidden in deep bush. Their inhabitants were timid, running away at first when the white men tried to approach them. For some time they refused to come any nearer than hailing distance and were quick to disappear if the Pioneers made any sudden movement. The white men set down their nervous shyness to long experience of raiders in the past, and although this may have been true, we must understand that the sight of the column itself would have been enough to strike terror in them. To the Mashona, it must have seemed an apparition beyond the powers of the imagination: one hundred heavy houses labouring across country, drawn miraculously forward by oxen; the great wheels on which they 'walked' churning up the dust of the road; the wagons lurching and creaking, their canvas hoods swaying monstrously against the sky. Troops of warriors, too, big white-faced men riding a strange sort of cattle, each man with a gun and a great many clothes; and over this whole witches' vision, a moving canopy of dust that revealed its passage over the land from far away. The sheer masculine power the column presented as it ground its way through the bush must have seemed like an invasion by beings of a new order of formidableness. It is easy to understand why such an aggressive image should have appalled the Mashona, and perhaps touched the hearts of the more reflective of them with a further anguished apprehension for the future. But gradually they realized that the great white *impi* meant them no harm, and were persuaded to barter with it, exchanging their grain and pumpkins and scraggy fowls for wonders such as beads and calico.

The column trundled on, the men forming laager each night, dragging their wagons into defensive squares and directing the beams of their searchlights in raking shafts into the tangled obscurity of the bush. When darkness falls in Africa, the bush becomes a sea, teeming and noisy with denizens; waves of thin, insistent stridulation lap against the ear; and now and again, there is a deeper noise, a screech or a grunt, like a predatory maw breaking the shimmering surface of the blackness. As the Pioneers lay by their camp-fires at the end of a day, they must have listened uneasily for other sounds that might disturb this ancient pattern of noise. There was always a chance that the Matabele might be stealing up to take them by surprise, and if they attacked by night in this broken terrain, the expedition might end in massacre.

But though Lobengula seemed to bow to the demands of his warriors by calling all his regiments in to Bulawayo and parading them before him in full war regalia, he knew that if he moved against the white men he would be destroying his nation. He allowed the Column to traverse the low veld and crawl unhindered up the narrow defile of Providential Pass, where there was not even room enough to form laager. Once out of the pass, the Pioneers found themselves on the open uplands, moving through plains of yellow grass, where scouts and patrols could operate with ease and every kopje offered a wide view of the surrounding country. They were out of danger and pressed forward eagerly.

Selous had chosen Mount Hampden as their destination, but in fact the column stopped a few miles from this hill and finding their camp a good one, furnished with a stream and a kopje for defence, they decided to go no farther. A wooden fort was thrown up and the place was named after Lord Salisbury. The occupation of Mashonaland had been accomplished without the loss of a single man.

Within two weeks of their arrival at Salisbury, the majority of the Pioneers were already scattering over Mashonaland, each of them anxious not to be forestalled at the rich reefs they expected to find. Rhodes had offered his recruits 7/6d. a day whilst they were on the march, but their real reward lay in the Company's permission for each man to peg out fifteen gold claims. He was also given the right to a 3,000-acre farm, but this was not so appealing. The Pioneers had not come all the weary way to Mashonaland in order to sweat at virgin bush with only raw natives as labour. They all hoped to strike it rich, as men had done at Kimberley, and again on the Rand. For a good many years, this prejudice against farming was to persist in Rhodesia, until the dreams of a fortune in gold had shrivelled in the hearts of all but the most stubborn.

CHAPTER 5

White Settlement
and the Fall of Lobengula

Once out in the bush, the earliest settlers lived in grass huts with thorn fences dragged into position round them to discourage the wild beasts that were still common in the country. The white men depended on the local Mashona to build their huts for them. To some extent, they also relied on them for food. The white men would have brought away with them from Salisbury such things as tea, sugar, bully beef, split peas, and Boer meal, but the Mashona would be asked to provide pumpkin, mealies, monkey-nuts, eggs, and fowls. The European custom of eating eggs came as a surprise to the Mashona, who regarded it as the wilful destruction of a form of natural increase to gratify an immediate pleasure, but they supplied the eggs as they supplied the other produce. In return, they were given meretricious trifles such as beads, cartridge caps, and brass curtain rings, all of which they treasured as rarities, having no notion of the position occupied by such goods in the European scale of values. Indeed, it seems quite possible that they looked on their dealings with white men as an exchange of gifts at first, rather than the driving of trade. In the same way, they may well have built the white man's hut in the spirit of the *nhimbe*, the beer-and-work party, rather than with any notion of selling their labour.

Some Mashona were thus brought into immediate contact with the Pioneers, but the majority saw little of them at first. It was the Company's policy—and, indeed, it was the only practical course at that time—to leave Africans undisturbed, as much as possible, in their traditional way of life. The qualification 'as much as possible', represents the Company's understanding that Africans would be needed to provide the labour on the mines.

The Africans were useful in other ways, too. They could be of great help to the white prospector because they knew the country and could point out the ancient mine-workings to him. The Pioneers soon realized that those who had mined Mashonaland in the past had located the paying reefs. A blanket was the usual reward given to Africans who supplied such information. Besides being used as objects of trade, blankets had other uses, or so the story goes. Rhodes had decreed that no women were to go with his column, nor to enter the new territory for the first two years after its occupation. The order was disobeyed by one or two adventurous white women—one of whom followed closely on the heels of the column, dressed as a boy—but the majority of Pioneers had either to take Mashona women or stay celibate. Some of them are reputed to have put a blanket between themselves and the body of the black woman they were using, with a gap cut in it to allow intercourse. But some began to develop a taste for the submissive Mashona girls and a few, like 'Matabele Thomson' even took African wives.

Mining was carried on by solitary white individuals or by partnerships of two or three men. They usually were short of capital and ran their smallworking by hard labour and improvization. Tools and engines were cripplingly expensive and the reef was always a gamble. Often the gamble ended in failure, and the jaunty sign the miners had painted on a spar of wood and nailed up on a tree to proclaim their hopes—'Lucky Strike' or 'Christmas Gift'—was left to go grey and rot after the claim had been abandoned. In the early days, the trunk of a tree was commonly used as a windlass, with a crooked branch to act as the handle; twisted strips of buckskin served as ropes; and buckets were made from hide stretched over a wooden framework. The pan in which the breakfast had been cooked that morning might well serve for the rest of the day to wash samples in.

The men suffered from loneliness and hope that was continually deferred. They were marooned in a sea of bush, with only the Mashona to help them, and these were 'raw natives' who had to be taught every least action in either mining or cooking. For their part, the Mashona must have felt themselves face to face with mysteries that threatened to be permanently impenetrable: almost all the actions and desires of the white man baffled them. The Pioneers were in some danger from beasts of prey, but they injured themselves more often from falling into game-pits dug by the Mashona. The paths trodden by game were often used as rides by European horsemen because of their freedom from obstacles; if they met one of these concealed pits, both horse and rider would fall headlong.

Malaria was another danger, the worst of all. At this time, the anopheles mosquito had not yet been recognized as the agent of the disease and so it could not be fought effectively. The small stocks of quinine and phenacetin carried up to Mashonaland were soon exhausted, and as the rainy season advanced, many men succumbed to the disease. Most people would have echoed Dr. Livingstone, who had written earlier: 'I have often remarked the effluvium in sickly spots and cannot help believing that it has some connexion with the fever.' Men would shun marshy areas whenever they could, but beyond that they had little or no defence against malaria.

In the winter of 1890–91, many young men could not even avoid the swamps. The success of the occupation of Mashonaland had brought a number of adventurers along the Pioneer road. When the rains came down in November, they were still struggling through the low veld, and found themselves stranded beside flooded rivers or bogged down in deep mud. Weakened by lack of food and exposed to the bite of innumerable mosquitoes, many of them died. With the dirt road turned to a channel of greasy mud, wagons carrying supplies to Salisbury could not get through and a severe shortage resulted in Mashonaland. Malaria was endemic there, too, and the country gained such a bad reputation for the disease that men began to ask whether permanent white settlement was really possible. Amongst those who answered that it was probably not was Lord Randolph Churchill, who had included Mashonaland in a South African tour he was making. He was also very sceptical of the claims made for the country as a gold-producing area. His views received publicity in England and struck the first note of doubt about the glamorous new venture.

Behind the settlers stood the Company, watching uneasily and waiting for news of the major gold strikes that would serve as justification to overseas shareholders of its large expenditures. The aim of the Company was not to develop Mashonaland for itself: the task would have been onerous and was, in any case, unnecessary. It did not wish to compete against the miners and speculators it attracted; instead, it envisaged a situation where the hard work of the settlers and the capital of exploiting companies would increase the value of its property. In part, it acted as a giant landlord, taking its cut in payments and benefiting from the increase in value to its property that followed from all improvements brought about in the country. With the first of these aims in mind, the Board declared that mines were to be developed as joint stock companies in which the Chartered Company held half the shares; they justified this move by pointing to the enormous financial risk they had undertaken in opening up the country. Ordinary settlers began to murmur that they had put their lives in jeopardy, not just their cash, and now were struggling against disease and hardship in a strange country merely to fill the pockets of a Company controlled by a Board in distant London.

Thus, the rift between the Company and the settlers opened early, and was to persist until the Company finally relinquished its governmental powers many years later. Men who toiled on meagre claims or worked as transport-riders resented the Company's policy of encouraging big concerns to come into the country and compete against them. From the Company's point of view, the large-scale land development or mining company was welcome because of the flow of capital it brought with it. To the ordinary Pioneer, the situation looked very different: he saw much land locked up in merely speculative ventures, and had to watch rich companies move in to exploit mines he and his fellows had not the capital to work. He was quick to accuse the Company of using him whilst man's work had to be done and then abandoning him once Mashonaland had been made safe.

The ambiguity of the Company's position began to show clearly. Besides the commercial revenue it drew from mining royalties, sales of land and share investment, it also had an administrative revenue, gathered by virtue of its governmental position, which came from such things as customs duties, postal revenues, fines, timber rights, and later, taxes imposed on the natives. Not for many years was there to be a surplus of revenue over expenditure; the rest of the money needed had to be made up by the Company. The state ran at a loss.

The chronic weakness of the Company's whole position lay in its original assumption that the lands it opened up would be rich in gold. It became more and more clear as time went on that this had been a miscalculation. As a result of its first assessment, the Company had invested far too heavily—as it turned out—in such enterprises as the telegraph line that reached Salisbury in the wake of the Pioneers and the railway line that was being constructed through Bechuanaland. The Company had never intended to administer the territories for more than a few years, after which time, Rhodes had hoped to see a thriving colony that could stand on its own feet and that would run its own affairs, preferably in some connexion with the Cape. The Company would then be left to reap its commercial rewards undistracted by governmental issues. This situation did not develop for a number of reasons, first amongst them the comparative poverty of the new region which did not grant the Company any return on the money it had committed. In the whole thirty-three years that it governed Southern Rhodesia, the Company did not pay a single dividend.

When Mashonaland failed to provide a new Rand, eyes began to stray in the direction of the Matabele kingdom, where Lobengula was still trying to keep his unruly warriors in check. Three years after the arrival of the Pioneer column in Salisbury, Rhodes took another step in his Imperial march. The Company had already secured great tracts of land north of the Zambesi, and the Matabele position was becoming increasingly that of an enclave of barbarism in the midst of a vast slab of territory administered by Britain or her agents. No doubt Rhodes had always intended to annex Lobengula's kingdom one day, but a new sharpness was given to his appetite by the failure of the Mashonaland goldfields.

It was generally supposed that there was gold in Matabeleland. It is noteworthy that when Jameson was signing men on for the column which was to destroy Matabele power, he offered each of them, in the Victoria Agreement, which he drew up in his position as Administrator of Mashonaland, no less than twenty gold claims each and a farm of 6,000 acres. The bids had been raised since the 1890 expedition! Moreover, to counteract the disillusion felt by those who had tried to sell their Mashonaland farms and found them practically worthless, Jameson placed a guaranteed value of £1 10s. an acre on any such land that the Company might wish to buy back for public purposes. As a final inducement, Jameson promised a share in the loot to every man who rode with him. He was referring here to Lobengula's treasure, which was popularly said to amount to many millions sterling in diamonds (smuggled from Kimberley), ivory and gold; and perhaps to the royal herds held by the Matabele king, many thousands strong.

It was not thought worthwhile to recruit Mashona for the war. Marshall Hole, private secretary to Jameson at this time, makes clear why, and incidentally gives us a clear picture of how the Pioneers regarded them: 'For the so-called Mashona . . . few entertained feelings other than contempt. . . . They were useful as hewers of wood and drawers of water; they were ready to barter their miserable produce for cheap blankets and other European trade goods, and could sometimes even be persuaded to work underground on the claims, but as fighting men they were deemed of no account.'[1]

Although Lobengula remained very quiet whilst he watched the whites take over Mashonaland and set up a government there that must have seemed to him a repudiation of his authority, he felt he could not allow his former vassals, the Mashona, to slip out of their allegiance to him unchallenged. Several times, he sent out punitive expeditions against the Mashona, and could not understand the protests he received from Jameson because, as he said, he did not intend to interfere with the white men. Of course, such intrusions were intolerable to the European settlers and became a cause of increasing friction in themselves, but there can be little doubt that Rhodes had intended to swallow the Matabele kingdom anyway, just as soon as the opportunity arose.

The reason for war was found in a Matabele raid on the Mashona that took place near the little mining settlement of Fort Victoria. Lobengula had sent out his *impi* because of the insult he considered he had received from the local Mashona, who had used some of the royal cattle they herded for him as vassals to pay a fine imposed on them by the European court, which had found them guilty of cutting and stealing a length of telegraph wire. The Matabele raiders killed and pillaged right to the outskirts of Victoria, hovering in the district for several days. The inhabitants of the little town prepared their defences and telegraphed for assistance to Jameson in Salisbury. He decided to go down there personally and have a look at the state of affairs. The Matabele were still roaming the countryside when he arrived. An arrangement was made to speak with the *induna* in charge of the war-party, and Jameson gave him warning that if he did not withdraw his warriors towards the border, the troopers would drive them to it. The *induna* asked what Jameson meant by 'the border', implying that Lobengula had never defined one in his agreement with the Company; then he rose to go. The Matabele forces began to pull out slowly; too slowly to save them from being fired on by a troop of police and volunteers under the command of Captain Lendy. In explaining the matter, Lendy said that the Matabele were deliberately dawdling and had fired another village as they went. This may have been so, but Lendy was an unsavoury and cruel man who would have been quick to imagine himself affronted by the least sign of insolence in an African. He had recently been severely censured by the Imperial Government for torturing a Mashona chief to death in an attempt to recover some stolen property.

The incident at Fort Victoria roused white opinion throughout

Mashonaland. The settlers, perhaps with hidden collusion or encouragement by the Company, decided to petition the Administrator, Dr.
Jameson, for an end to the threat of the Matabele. Whether or not the
Company was directly involved in the petition, it took advantage of the
opportunity it presented: volunteers were enrolled by Jameson and the
strategy of the campaign planned. One column was to make a thrust
from Mashonaland along the high veld, whilst a second column was to
advance, by way of diversion, from Tuli in the south. Both columns
were to be equipped with Maxims on galloping carriages. Rhodes, at
this time Prime Minister of the Cape, urgently sent up supplies and
remounts for this new expedition and placed £50,000 out of his private
funds at the disposal of Jameson to help finance the campaign. He was
anxious to keep the Imperial Government out of the affair, fearing that
its ministers might demand a voice in the terms of settlement and insist
on leniencies that would not suit the Company. Lord Ripon, Secretary
of State for the Colonies, had become notorious for the tender heart he
showed towards subjugated peoples.

After exacting the permission of the High Commissioner for South
Africa by long range from Cape Town, Jameson led his column into
Matabeleland. It was first attacked as it lay in laager, after fording the
Shangani river. The battle began by night and went on well into the
next day. The pattern by which it was fought was extremely simple: the
Matabele tried to rush the laager in the darkness; they were driven off
so they tried again by daylight. The Maxim guns mowed them down
with ease. Later in the day, they mustered for a third attack, their
depleted ranks stiffened by the arrival of the Insukamini regiment, but
before this assault could develop, whilst, in fact, the Matabele were still
massing, some accurate fire from the Hotchkiss guns and seven-pounders
scattered them and put them into panicky retreat. They had never before
come under artillery fire and were seen to be firing their rifles frenziedly
at the flashes of the exploding shells. Such repeated and deadly witchcraft unnerved them and they were soon in full flight, harassed by bands
of white horsemen who now sallied out of the laager. The Matabele
lost several hundred men in this encounter. European casualties were
one man killed and five wounded. War of this kind was only a little more
dangerous to the Europeans than hunting. Given open terrain, their
supremacy in weapons was so great it made them not only invincible
but almost invulnerable.

The final battle was fought at the Imbembesi river a few days later
and was a repetition of the fight at Shangani, though with heavier losses

13. The Pioneers often had to improvise. Above is Tulloch's water-wheel on the Umtali river. It was made from whiskey cases and used for crushing ore from the Liverpool mine (1898).

14. Third Street, Salisbury, in 1902, after twelve years of European occupation.

15. The same view of Third Street, taken in 1959.

on both sides. The Matabele were gunned and sprayed to such good effect that the Imbezu alone—one of the three Matabele regiments engaged—suffered about 500 casualties. The total number of dead and wounded was estimated to be 'very heavy' though the Matabele habit of removing their casualties from the battlefield made precise calculation impossible. The Pioneer losses this time were four men killed and seven wounded.

After the rout at Imbembesi, the way lay open to Bulawayo, but as the men of the column neared it, they saw great clouds of smoke rising into the air and heard a big explosion. Lobengula had fired his great kraal in despair and blown up the boxes of ammunition sent to him by the Company under the terms of the Rudd Concession. The advance guard of the invaders rode into a ruined and deserted town; the only people about were the two white traders whose lives Lobengula had protected. The Matabele king had fled north towards the Zambesi and was to die miserably there of smallpox before many months were out. Thus Lobengula, 'that anachronism', as it was fashionable—and correct—to call him among the more educated Pioneers, was destroyed and the military brigandage of his nation rooted out. The whole of Southern Rhodesia was now in the hands of the Company.

Lord Ripon had tried to intervene before the battle of Shangani was fought, ordering that any peace negotiations were to be carried out between Lobengula and the High Commissioner of South Africa. This was an attempt to exclude the Company, just as Rhodes had feared. But London was far away and the Imperial Government powerless to act. Besides, as Rhodes pointed out in a telegraphed conversation from Salisbury, the Company felt entitled to take charge in Matabeleland; there had been no request to the Imperial Government for assistance; the Company had used its own troops to subdue the Matabele; and he himself had furnished much of the money for the campaign.

Dr. Jameson, *de facto* ruler of Matabeleland, set about the pacification of the country. He began to impound large numbers of the royal cattle and he issued an edict stating that only those Matabele who gave in their rifles and assegais would be allowed back to their villages to take advantage of the rainy season and plant their crops. The demand for weapons was a wise one, but to demand their surrender on the condition of starvation was too severe a move for Lord Ripon. He sent a telegram to the High Commissioner asking whether it was true, as newspapers had reported, that Jameson was marking out townships in Matabeleland, including one in the Bulawayo kraal of Lobengula; whether patrols were seizing large numbers of native cattle; and whether the Matabele were being prevented from sowing until they had given up their arms. He laid it down that Her Majesty's Government would not countenance such conduct against a people who had ceased to offer any organized resistance. On the advice of the High Commissioner, Jameson called a reluctant halt to the forced disarmament of the Matabele. But, after setting aside a few areas for the Africans, the rest of Matabeleland was converted, at Rhodes' instance, into public land, and the men of the column were given first choice of farms. 'It is your right,' Rhodes assured them, 'for you have conquered the country.'

CHAPTER 6

Raid and Rebellion

The period between 1893 and 1895 saw Rhodes at the height of his power, drunk with success, and heading swiftly for disaster. During that time, he combined political office with great financial influence: it gave him the complex, tangled variety of powers that he best liked to wield, and which he felt would allow him to unlock the continent of Africa, let it swing open like a door to permit the entry of his pioneers and mercenaries. Besides being Prime Minister of Cape Colony, he was Managing Director of the Chartered Company which controlled a vast northern hinterland. He was also in control of the world's output of diamonds and was the economic dictator of Kimberley; lastly, he was a power on the Rand, though in the gold-mining industry he could not claim to be more than one magnate acting with his peers.

The ease with which the Matabele had been crushed swelled his reputation after the event. Financial circles in London were buzzing with reports of the new gold reefs discovered in Matabeleland. Within a couple of years of the annexation, over 200 companies and syndicates had been formed, mostly with English money, to exploit the new fields. Bulawayo turned into a sprawling boom town, thronged with company directors and land speculators. Twelve hotels had been thrown up; there were three banks and no less than three printed newspapers. The population of the town climbed until it had passed the 2,000 mark. And all this had happened without the production of a single ounce of gold. The nature of the deposits meant that until the arrival of milling machinery, none could be extracted, but hopes were high again and the tide of greed ran strongly after the mining successes of the past twenty years in southern Africa. Matabeleland floated up on a bubble of speculation in which prices were inflated even higher by the cost of dragging up commodities of all kinds by ox-wagon from the railhead at Mafeking.

Rhodes' plans appeared to be succeeding, and during these years he went on working to increase their scope. He pressed for the annexation of the Crown Colony of Bechuanaland to the Cape, and for the inclusion of the much bigger Bechuanaland Protectorate within the lands administered by his Chartered Company. At the time, he seemed likely to succeed in both objects. His eyes had wandered as far north as Uganda, which he offered to run for the British Government. The Congo Free State had been induced to cede a railway strip linking Lake Tanganyika with Uganda, and for a brief while it looked as if the way might be open for Rhodes' Cape-to-Cairo railway scheme. But, later, Leopold repudiated the cession under pressure from the French and German Governments, and Rhodes had to shelve this part of his dream for the time being. On the other hand, the Natal Government seemed willing to operate within a Customs Union, and, all in all, Rhodes must have felt that his vision of a federation of African states under the Union Jack was coming much nearer.

The Transvaal was the major obstacle. It sat like an obdurate growth on the body of Rhodes' plans, sullenly refusing to respond to any kind of treatment, either persuasion or pressure. If the removal of Lobengula, that 'fat, naked savage', could be justified by calling him an anachronism, the same argument could be logically extended to Kruger and his Republican farmers. But though they might be obsolescent in terms of the new industrial economy, they were by no means feeble, nor yet so overwhelmed by the number of *Uitlanders* drawn to the Rand as to make resistance impossible.

If Kruger, on his part, had pushed logic to its extreme, he would have forbidden the hordes of foreigners to come within his borders, even if this meant doing without the flow of revenue his government received from the mines. He would, in fact, have left the Rand unexploited. Such a conclusion was unimaginable in the South Africa of his day. In any case, the Transvaal had been poor in the past, from its very nature; now it found itself rich, and riches once acquired are not easy to give up. The burghers themselves found this: though they might complain at the invasion of their land by foreigners, they were anxious enough to get into their hands some of the money the foreigners brought with them. Because of the perennial emptiness of the Transvaal exchequer, Kruger had welcomed the trickle of foreigners who entered the country in 1884 when gold was first discovered on the Rand. Ten years later, the trickle had become a threatening flood. The new city of Johannesburg, a monster of corrugated iron and utilitarian brick, quite overshadowed the Boer capital at Pretoria, only thirty miles away.

With the proving of the deep levels at about this time, it became certain that this was no transitory invasion. The mines, with their alien population and way of life, were there to stay for as long as it took to exploit the vast formation of 'banket', spreading thirty miles on either side of Johannesburg and descending some 3,000 feet below the surface of the land. The gold was deposited thinly but in a uniform way, so that expenses and profits could be easily calculated. Immense amounts of quartz would have to be mined and crushed to gain the gold; the Rand was no place for the smallworker, but to the big mining companies it was a lucrative proposition, particularly as nearby coal deposits removed the fuel problem.

Faced with this dilemma, the Transvaal Government acted in a predictable, contradictory, and very human fashion. It milked the mines of a good deal of revenue—though its imposts never approached the crippling 50 per cent tax on profits that Rhodes had set on mines operating in the territories of his Chartered Company. It also set heavy customs duties on supplies that entered the Republic by railway and it turned the importing of dynamite—essential to the mines—into a monopoly. Thus, the Transvaal Government set about to enrich itself from the mines whose presence it detested, and with the money that flowed into its treasury, it began to buy arms. At the same time that it made itself economically dependent, and by means of that dependence, it sought to reinforce its political independence. The Boers saw that this was vital if they were to maintain the integrity of their state. Hence, over the years, they passed an increasingly stringent series of franchise laws whose effect was to strip the *Uitlanders* of the vote for the foreseeable future. With the same kind of end in view, they refused a grant to any school that did not use Dutch as its medium for teaching, with the result that about half the children in Johannesburg did not go to school at all, whilst others were sent to dubious private institutions.

The pattern we observe here is similar to that in South Africa today, where increasing economic dependence on the African has been accompanied by restrictive legislation designed to prevent him ever gaining a shred of political power.

But it is always dangerous to put heavy taxes on people who have no voice in the government. The *Uitlanders* knew how great their contribution was to the wealth of the Transvaal, yet they were left without representation and treated in some respects like an inferior group. They showed resentment, but this only served to deepen the Boer sense of insecurity, and by 1894, insurrection was being discussed as the solution to the problem by the more hot-headed Englishmen on the Rand.

Rhodes had recently received the ominous verdict of Hays Hammond, an American mining engineer, that the gold he hoped to find in the Chartered territories would never amount to much. He turned his attention to the Rand, where he also had large interests, anxious to provoke the *Uitlanders* to revolt and draw the Transvaal in its new form into economic federation with Charterland and the Cape. His hope seems to have been that ultimately a political association would follow.

An organization calling itself the National Union had been set up in Johannesburg to agitate for reform; it was led by a solicitor and it drew its members chiefly from amongst the professional men and artisans of the town. Rhodes decided to use this as his instrument of insurrection. The interests of the capitalists were represented on it by Phillips, chairman of the Johannesburg Chamber of Mines. Amongst the agents Rhodes planted in Johannesburg to help fan the flames was his own brother Frank.

The *Uitlanders* began to show rebellious insolence towards the Government of the Transvaal: men drilled in the streets of Johannesburg; rifle clubs were formed; some Englishmen sent their wives and children away to the safety of the Cape. De Beers received instructions from Rhodes to forward contraband arms from Kimberley to Johannesburg: Maxims, rifles, and ammunition, were hidden in packing-cases, stowed in sacks or oildrums or buried under loads of coke and consigned to the sidings of the Rand.

Rhodes was at pains to implicate Chamberlain, in England, and Sir Hercules Robinson, the South African High Commissioner, in his plans for the overthrow of the Transvaal Government. He also arranged for 500 Chartered police, many of them withdrawn from Bulawayo, to gather at Pitsani, a little place in Bechuanaland that had been recently ceded to the Company in connexion with their rail project. He set Dr. Jameson, conqueror of Matabeleland, at the head of his police, as his expert in military raiding.

As it was originally planned, the insurrection was to take the form of a 'spontaneous' rising in Johannesburg aided by Jameson's flying column, which would thrust in from the border and help divert the attention of the Boers during the first crucial days. But revolutions are impossible to stage unless grievances are felt to be intolerable. Although the *Uitlanders* considered themselves slighted by their treatment at the hands of Kruger and his *Raad*, they did not suffer either in the pocket or the belly, the two most potent centres of revolutionary agitation. Indeed, Johannesburg was a boom town and its inhabitants did not suffer any but political restrictions. Though they felt the necessity to protest and bluster in order to preserve their honour, it is doubtful if they wanted to go so far as to kill and be killed for it. The Boers were redoubtable marksmen and they had already challenged an English petitioner in the *Raad* to fight for his privileges if he wanted them. The situation was not one where the ordinary man could be easily provoked to revolt. Despite the contraband arms and the gifts of money, despite the various manipulations of public sentiment arranged by Rhodes and his followers, many people in Johannesburg remained tepid. The plot had the smell of a capitalists' *coup d'état*, and the more Rhodes intervened, the stronger the smell became.

In the end, whilst the leaders in Johannesburg were still dithering, Jameson decided to force their hand. He took his column over the border and invaded the Transvaal. He did not have Rhodes' permission for this action, but he knew that success on his part would still all accusations, and he gambled on it. When the mutineers of Johannesburg heard the news, they acted belatedly and indecisively. They were not much trouble to the Transvaal Government, which let them sit in Johannesburg under the *Vierkleur* they had nervously hoisted as their flag of insurrection. Jameson pushed on, but meanwhile his action had been repudiated by the South African High Commissioner and he was left with no more status than that of an outlaw, leader of a band of brigands.

The raid ended in disaster. Cronje, the old Boer general, led out a commando which mauled Jameson's column and forced him to surrender at Doornkop. The consequences of failure were great. Rhodes was pulled down by Jameson's impetuosity; his conspiracies were brought into the open and he fell from office, discredited and humiliated. Jameson was turned over by Kruger to be judged in England, and he passed through Wormwood Scrubs before returning to a position of power in Rhodes' entourage in South Africa.

The Transvaal Boers had won the first round. Their defence of their way of life appeared to be successful, but the industrial capital of Johannesburg continued to flourish and grow monstrously in the midst of their pastoral Republic. It had at its command forces greater than they could muster. However crude its power and however forbidding its disciplines appeared to the Boer farmers, it was, as Rhodes correctly saw, the shape of the future, the representative of a new kind of life. Next time the clash came it would be heralded by Milner's dispatch to Britain which spoke of: '. . . the spectacle of thousands of British subjects kept permanently in the position of helots, constantly chafing under undoubted grievances and calling vainly to Her Majesty's Government for redress.' And it would bring all the forces of the British Empire to the task of dismantling the old Boer Republics, where power was based on land and the gun. The pastoral stock farmer was fated to go down before the new industrial world no less certainly than the tribal African. Both had to face, not mere defeat, but the long agony of supercession until a new pattern formed.

As well as stripping Rhodes of office, the Jameson Raid had one other immediate consequence: it showed the Matabele that their conquerors were by no means invincible. Jameson had withdrawn most of the Matabeleland police to help fill his column; now they were lying in jail at Pretoria or had been shipped back to England for trial. It was not so much the removal of the police—the Matabele understood all about the nature of raiding—but their total defeat that seemed significant. The white *impi* would not come riding back to revenge any deeds that had been done by the Matabele in their absence.

The Matabele had other reasons for rebelling, beyond the natural resistance of a warrior people to defeat and the ensuing disruptions in their traditional way of life. An attempt had been made to thrust many of them into two barren Reserves, which could not house their numbers and which were on the wrong kind of soil. Like their kinsmen the Zulus, the Matabele liked to cultivate heavy loam soils; the Mashona, on the other hand, preferred the light, sandy, granitic soil. This worked against the Matabele: the loams of Matabeleland covered the gold reefs and this land was quickly alienated and pegged for claims by white men. Many of their cattle had also been confiscated because they were thought to form part of Lobengula's vast royal herds, and those which had been returned to them could be taken back at the Company's discretion—a state of affairs that turned them into herd boys. Like the Mashona, the Matabele used cattle to make the *lobola* payments necessary to a marriage; but in addition, the Matabele were great eaters of beef and had supplied their wants in the past by raiding. Beef was a symbol of their warrior status and they felt its curtailment for more reasons than those of appetite. Again, they were now in the power of native police, some of whom bullied them; and they were subjected to forced labour.

Two natural catastrophes at this time seemed to come like promptings from a god of wrath. First, rinderpest broke out amongst their herds—it had been brought by the oxen of a Boer transport-rider from north of the Zambesi—and spread rapidly. The Company attempted to stamp out the disease by slaughtering entire herds where one beast had been infected, a policy looked on with bitter lack of understanding by Africans. In addition, there was a plague of locusts. Their cattle slaughtered and their crops ravaged, the Matabele were ready to react violently. Their formless anger and resentment was given shape by pronouncements from the *Mulumo*, officer of the *Mwari* cult in the Matopos hills. The god was reported to have put the blame for the scourges which had fallen on the land on the presence of the white man, who must be killed or driven out. The Matabele knew now that he was not invincible. The insurrection that followed was, in fact, the last desperate movement of the old order, an infuriated attempt to fling the usurping white man off their backs and go back to their traditional way of life.

The Matabele acted ruthlessly and were answered with equal ruthlessness. They had gained experience of the power of the shell and the Maxim gun, so this time they operated as guerillas, gathering in armed bands throughout the country and falling by surprise on the miners and traders scattered unsuspectingly about the land. Some of the native police defected to the rebels and were welcomed as valuable recruits who had guns and knew how to use them.

The rebellion opened in the last week of March, 1896, and by the end of the first seven days, 130 white people had been killed, all of them in isolated settlements; chopped down and afterwards mutilated by roaming gangs. Every white man who could, raced for the safety of Bulawayo, where a big laager had been set up round the Market Hall, its defensive outworks strengthened by emplacements for Maxim guns and field-pieces. Volunteers from the able-bodied men organized themselves into a defence force and patrols were sent into the surrounding country to try to rescue any white people who might still be holding out there.

But there were not enough men to engage the bands of armed Matabele swarming everywhere in the countryside, and the situation was made worse by the lack of horses and rifles. Bulawayo could do little more than rest in a state of semi-siege until help arrived. There was every hope that help would come, for although the Matabele could have cut the road to the south, they had chosen to leave it open, apparently as a hint to the white men to escape along it and leave the country to them. As soon as this was realized in Bulawayo, patrols were sent out to scour along the road and thus discourage any later attempt to cut it: a series of little stockades was even built at intervals along it.

Meanwhile, a body of 150 horse was on its way from Salisbury, and the British Government had sanctioned the raising of 750 volunteers in South Africa, to be led by General Plumer, an Imperial officer. When it seemed certain that the troops already dispatched would not be strong enough to quell the rising, the British Government insisted on sending a force of regular soldiers and placing the whole direction of the Matabeleland campaign into the hands of a British general officer. Rhodes was not at all happy about this intervention in Company territories; he felt that it might lead to demands by the British Government for a voice in the settlement that would follow the pacification of the Matabele. Nor did he much like the conditions on which the British Government had forced its troops upon him: the demand that all expenses should be met by the Company seemed like an acknowledgement of the Company's ineptitude in allowing such a state of affairs to develop.

Even with the arrival of these large reinforcements, the Matabele could not be subdued, though they were driven back into the Matopos hills, from where they carried on a guerilla war. Detachments of troops sent to 'sweep' the Matabele suffered heavy casualties as they clambered and stumbled amongst the hills, which were composed of tumbled and fissured granite, with many caves and boulders that the Matabele used as cover.

The only reasonable military solution seemed to be that of starving the Matabele into submission, but this would be a long and costly operation, with the Company bearing all expenses. Driven by thoughts such as these, Rhodes, who was by this time in Bulawayo, solved the problem by an act of personal daring. He had never been accounted a very brave man in terms of physical courage, but now he gambled with his life by going unarmed into the Matopos to seek an *indaba*, or council, with the rebel leaders. After much persuasion, in a series of talks that went on for two months, Rhodes managed to convince the Matabele *indunas* that they could hope for nothing except starvation by carrying on the fight. He offered comparatively liberal terms and promised to help them with food over the coming year if they would surrender. When they did so, he was as good as his word, and sent large amounts of maize from the south to help hold off the famine that threatened them. But if Rhodes could afford magnaminity, many of the ordinary settlers could not. They felt they had been victims of treachery on a massive scale; most of them had lost friends or relatives in the original week of slaughter; their houses had been burnt and their lives disrupted. The rather callous indifference towards the native that is often found amongst white South Africans, even in normal circumstances, hardened into distrust and hatred.

To make matters worse, the despised Mashona, who were not thought sufficiently manly to indulge in war, had risen in the rear of the column sent to help Bulawayo. In the first few days a similar pattern of violence asserted itself, with 120 deaths amongst outlying Europeans who had been taken by surprise at their mines or trading posts. Laager was formed at Salisbury and patrols rode out to rescue those who might still survive in the country districts.

If the Matabele rising came as a surprise, that of the Mashona seemed an affront against Nature: it ran absolutely counter to all previous views on Shona mentality. The tribes had been so stirred to revolt by the ancestral guardian spirits speaking through their mediums, the *mhondoros*. Kagubi, wrongly referred to at the time as the 'lion-god' of western Mashonaland was one of the chief instigators of the rebellion; and with him another *mhondoro*, Nyanda, described by Marshall Hole as 'the notorious witch of Mazoe'. They were able to give their words the force of religious sanction; but the Mashona would be ready to listen, in any case, if they felt, as they are reported to have done, that 'the Matabele oppressed us some of the time but the white man oppresses us all the time'. There seems no doubt that the officers of *Mwari* (*Mlimo*) in his Matopos stronghold were in touch with the *mhondoro* mediums of Mashonaland and that it was they who were responsible for the timing of the revolt, which caught the Mashonaland settlers at the moment when many of their men had ridden off to help in Bulawayo.

This time there could be no quick solution. The Matabele were a single nation still subject to central control, but there was no authority amongst the Mashona powerful enough to compel individual chiefs to lay down their arms once the fighting had begun. Each tribal leader would fight on independently until he was defeated or saw fit to surrender. The struggle against the Mashona dragged on long after the rebellion in Matabeleland was over. The rebels were hunted and driven, cornered on rocky hillsides, brought to bay in caves. Though they had few modern rifles, the Mashona owned a variety of old trade-guns, for like all Africans, they had come to recognize the gun as the symbol of power in an encroaching white world. Muskets had even taken the place of cattle, sometimes, in *lobola* agreements amongst them. Their weapons were mostly muzzle-loaders and blunderbusses that had filtered into the interior from the East Coast; guns that were useless for fighting at a distance, but terrifying when discharged at short range from inside the mouth of a cave or from behind a boulder. The Mashona were short of ammunition so they used whatever they could lay their hands on: bits of telegraph wire, nails, jagged fragments of metal, the glass balls from the tops of old soda-water bottles. If a white trooper received the contents of such a gun as he clambered up a kopje or tried to force his way into a cave, it was like being hit by a hail of shrapnel; the wounds were ragged, with flesh scooped away in dreadful mutilations. The white soldiers replied by dynamiting any kopjes where they thought Mashona insurgents might be skulking, killing some of those hidden in the caves and burying others alive with the falls of rock that blocked the entrances. They 'drove' the country, and rather than go into a village where they might be fired on out of some dark doorway, they turned their Maxims on it. The straw huts offered no protection, and anyone inside—man, woman or child—was at the mercy of the ripping bullets. Afterwards, the kraal might be fired.

Of all the kinds of war in which men can engage, guerilla fighting and the repression that follows it are perhaps the most corrupting. The constant danger leads men into savagery. The indiscriminate slaughter performed by one gang leads to reprisals against an entire neighbourhood. Men are driven to fury by the killing of their women and children; and as there is no visible enemy for much of the time, everyone becomes suspect within the widest definition possible—in this case, all those with skins of the opposing colour.

Selous took part in the operations against the rebels, and the hatred kindled in him by what he saw, may be taken to be a usual response. He writes: 'It may be that I have here and there shown a very strong racial feeling against the black man, but it must be remembered that my story has been written in the midst of all the horrors of a native rebellion, that I have seen many gruesome sights and have with my own hands collected together the broken skulls of murdered women and children —Dutch and English—in order to give them Christian burial.'[1]

But the Africans were not without champions amongst the English and South African radicals of the day. It seemed to them that the treachery—as they would have put it—of the Jameson raid, and the Native Rebellions which were its indirect consequence, were all to be explained by the ruthless greed of Rhodes and his Chartered Company. In their eyes, he appeared as a man degraded by lust for land and money until he had become a monster. Such an old opponent as Labouchere, editor of the radical magazine, *Truth*, attacked Rhodes sharply and contemptuously. Labouchere had looked upon the operations of the Chartered Company from the beginning as a cynical exercise in pillage and murder. His comment on the column that Jameson led against Lobengula had been:

'That the present war was provoked by the Chartered Company, no one I suppose who is neither employed by the Company nor interested in it financially, doubts. Equally certain is it that Lobengula and his people, although by no means desirable neighbours, have had a war forced upon them because Mashonaland is not a paying property and the Chartered Company hopes that if it can get hold of Matabeleland, it will, whether it be really so auriferous as it is stated or not, get British investors to believe that it is.'[2]

This shrewd interpretation of events was followed by invective much less impressive because of its wild note of harangue; 'Mr. Rhodes . . . the head of a gang of shady financiers who forced on a war . . . conducted it on the principle that "godless heathen" ought to be mowed down with Maxim guns if they happen to inhabit a country where there may be gold and their envoys murdered in order that a rotten Company might be saved from immediate bankruptcy.'

His reaction to the way in which the 1896 rebellions were put down was to speak of 'border riff-raff . . . shooting natives with as little qualm as an English squire shoots a partridge,' and he claimed to have received reports of the execution in cold blood of captured insurgents, including wounded men. Whatever the truth of these remarks, their censorious bitterness was deeply resented in Rhodesia, where it was felt that the true nature of events had not been understood in England, or that men like Labouchere were motivated by blind malice.

Perhaps a more significant opponent of Rhodes' actions was Olive Schreiner, the South African authoress. In earlier days she had been a great supporter of his, almost a worshipper, at the time before the Chartered Company began its operations. Now, in her disillusionment, she wrote a short novel called *Trooper Peter Halket of Mashonaland*, which had some success in England. It was, among other things, a bitter attack on Rhodes and the principles he employed in life, however, the book fails to stir in the reader the force of indignation that had shaken Miss Schreiner, probably because she wished it to do so above all else and let her emotion rob it of all literary merit. Nevertheless, the book gives a picture of events that indisputably occurred during the Mashona revolt and which may help to give us a picture of the nature of its suppression. Peter Halket, a simple country boy from England, is bringing to mind incidents that he has taken part in. In his imagination, he sees: '. . . the fires they made to burn the natives' grain by, and they were throwing in all they could not carry away. . . . Then he seemed to see his huts where he had lived with the prospectors and the native women who used to live with him. . . . Then, he saw the skull of an old Mashona blown off at the top, the hands still moving. He heard the loud cry of the native women and children as they turned the Maxims on the kraal; then he heard the dynamite explode that blew up a cave. . . . Then he thought suddenly of a black woman he and another man caught alone in the bush, her baby on her back but young and pretty. Well, they didn't shoot her!'

So it goes on, a recital of slaughter and rapine. There is a revolting example of a public hanging at Bulawayo, of which a photograph was taken; Miss Schreiner used it as the frontispiece of her book. Here is her trooper's description of it, which followed contemporary accounts: 'I wasn't there myself but a fellow who was told me they made the niggers jump from the tree and hang themselves; one fellow wouldn't bally jump till they gave him a charge of buckshot in the back: and then he caught hold of a branch with his hands and they had to shoot 'em loose. . . . I saw a photograph of the niggers hanging and our fellows standing round smoking.'

Miss Schreiner's indignation at the man she felt had brought about such a state of affairs was ferocious. It is a bitter comment on our own day that, after the succession of revolutions and civil wars that has convulsed the world in the last fifty years, it is the absence of atrocities that would be more likely to excite comment.

The rebellions had two lasting results. First, there emerged out of them a slow-burning hatred and distrust of the African in European hearts, a feeling of repugnance, instinctual in its depth, that can still sometimes be met with in Rhodesia; a picture of the African was fixed in the white consciousness which showed him as 'a treacherous black ape', less than human, cruel and untrustworthy. It has been said that before one man enslaves or exploits another, he must first create an image of his victim that will justify the conduct he metes out to him. The rebellions helped such an image to be formed and thrust it deeply and painfully in the minds of the white population. The second result was the distrust of radicals abroad, or indeed of all who set themselves up as critics and moralists, inveighing against the actions of the settlers when they did not 'know the country' and 'the local conditions'. The fierce anger that Selous shows in his writings against Labouchere, is very similar to the rage and contempt provoked by such a 'meddler' as John Stonehouse, who Rhodesians felt had used their hospitality to betray them. The Labour Party as a whole is disliked and Rhodesians dread the idea of it returning to power. But any overseas politician who offers criticism is likely to evoke the same hurt and angry response.

Interference was liked no more in Selous's day, and, then as now, the peculiarities of 'local conditions' were used to ward off investigation or criticism. Here is Selous writing after the rebellions when there was fear that Britain might intervene in the Chartered territories: 'Should this territory be converted into a Crown Colony and governed from Downing Street on hard-and-fast lines, some of them not at all applicable to local requirements, with an Administrator very likely ignorant of his local surroundings and possibly out of sympathy with the settlers—Dutch and English—who have made the country their home, nothing but disaster is to be expected.'[3]

There is an element of truth in this argument, of course, but it is all too often used as a weapon to bludgeon opponents and stifle controversy. It is, after all, an unanswerable contention, and even people who have lived in the country for several years may find themselves refused the qualification that allows a man to speak, should their views not follow the popular direction.

CHAPTER 7

Capital and Labour
and Company Rule

By September, 1897, the last desperate flicker of resistance had been stamped out amongst the Mashona. The *mhondoros*, Kagubi and Nyanda, surrendered themselves to the authorities and were executed early in the next year; the tribes they had led were prostrate. Both the Mashona and their old masters, the Matabele, learnt in the hard school of military defeat that they were powerless to resist the white man's world and must therefore accept European domination as inevitable and try to adjust themselves to the conditions this strange new world imposed on them.

To the settlers and the Company, the Jameson Raid and the rebellions that followed it had brought the threat of Imperial intervention. Company rule had been shown to be irresponsible and many people feared that the British Government might bring the territory under its colonial administration. In fact, this was not done: it would have been unpopular in Rhodesia and in business circles in London, and besides, the British Government was reluctant to abrogate a Charter it had so recently granted, but more than that, it did not want to incur any unnecessary expense. In the end, the only curb that was set upon the Company's powers was an order forbidding it to keep its own military police. A Resident Commissioner was appointed, responsible to the High Commissioner in Cape Town, and command over any military forces raised was vested in him. But apart from this one restriction, which lasted in its original form only until 1898, when a separate Commandant General was created, the Company remained supreme, and although the challenge to its authority began in 1898, with the granting of settler representation on the Legislative Council set up in that year, a very long time was to elapse before white Rhodesians wrested political power out of its hands.

For some years, the Company still hoped to draw its profits from enterprises working the minerals of the country and the crippling 50 per cent tax that had been fastened on all mining profits went on, to the indignation of the settlers. Because of its policy, the Company showed a particular tenderness towards any big land development or mining companies that cared to bring their capital into the country, and inevitably, the 'small man' moved into opposition. He regarded himself as exploited—which he seems to have been—and cried out that he was at the mercy of a monopolistic group carrying on operations from London Wall. If Rhodes had been alive, he said, things would have been different, but Rhodes was dead, and the present Directors of the Company had no interest in the country beyond that of screwing a profit from it.

The truth was that the Company was snared; its behaviour was dictated by that original false assumption, held by everyone from Rhodes to the least shareholder, that the lands between Limpopo and Zambesi would be rich in gold. Unless this were true, the Company had no real commercial foundation. There had to be gold; without it, the Company's rule could show no real benevolence, nor was there the possibility of it relinquishing its political power as quickly as had been hoped. But gold was sparse, and there was no mineral substitute precious enough to fill the gap.

Perhaps this situation would not have worried Rhodes so much as it did his successors: to him, the commercial nature of the conquest was a suitable expedient, but he was less interested in profit than in empire. During the period of Rhodes' life—he died in March, 1902—there still seemed to be some, lingering hope that the territory might prove profitable. A thorough exploration of its resources had been set back by the disturbances of the early years: the Matabele war, the Raid, the rebellions, and finally the South African War. The Company was slow to accept that Southern Rhodesia was not a commercial proposition.

Disillusion was only admitted as late as 1907, by a change in Company policy. Farming was to be deliberately encouraged for the first time, with the hope of bringing in greater revenues and increasing the value of the land. The Company based its right to the land on a document known as the Lippert Concession, which had been signed by Lobengula after the occupation of Mashonaland by the Pioneers. It seems to have been a last desperate attempt on the part of the Matabele king to frustrate the white men by offering them contradictory concessions. Under the terms of the agreement, Lippert was given the sole right 'to lay out, grant, or lease' land in the whole of Lobengula's possessions for a period of 100 years. The Company had already been carving up Mashonaland into farms but it had no legal title to the land. Rhodes solved the problem by buying up the Lippert Concession. Arguing from this authority (and also, in Matabeleland, from the right of conquest) the Company assumed the right to fix arbitrary rates for the price of land. It sought to wring a maximum profit by laying heavy charges on land where stores, hotels, or houses were to be built, and on land near the railway line.

In 1903, the Company had been forced by the facts to make a retreat from its original vision of itself as the beneficiary of great gold-mining companies and had given some belated encouragement to the small-workers in the industry by introducing a system of royalty payments less onerous than the 50 per cent tax, though still heavy enough to stir resentment. Now, under its new policy, it began to encourage immigration seriously; it set up an Agricultural College (1911) to help train new farmers; and it became a model landowner itself, farming its big estates for profit and branching out into cattle ranching. Thus it moved away from its old position as landlord and entered into competition with its subjects.

But, overall, the realization by the Company that there was no great mineral wealth to be looked for was bound to lead to a more benevolent attitude towards the ordinary settlers. Only by the industry of the 'small men' could there be any improvement in the prosperity of the country, any increase in its real wealth. But though they adopted this policy, the Directors, in the words of one of them, were already looking for 'a good get-out'; one in which they might gain some recompense for the money they had laid out, and perhaps be able to influence the course of events in Southern Africa in a manner they approved. Over the years that followed, they came more and more to favour the inclusion of Southern Rhodesia in the Union of South Africa, where the predominantly British background and loyalties of the Rhodesians would help to keep out Hertzog and the resurgent Boer nationalists who seemed likely to be a threat to British interests and capital there.

The image of the Company as a great octopus whose tentacles embraced the state and whose power intruded into every kind of activity a man might want to follow, became a favourite one amongst Rhodesian settlers. They clamoured for an end to the suffocating rule of the Company. Meanwhile, the Company, a commercial undertaking which had never succeeded in paying a dividend, and was never to do so throughout the period of its rule, found that its commercial failure influenced it in the sphere of government. If dissatisfaction amongst the ruled is the mark of governmental failure, then the Company had demonstrably failed in this respect, too. It was forced into predatory measures against its citizens just because it was not a commercial proposition and could not produce a dividend with which to placate its shareholders. Inevitably, in these circumstances, it became disliked, even hated, by those it ruled. The administrative revenue it raised for purposes of government was supposedly separate from its commercial revenues, but in fact no clear distinction of expenditure was made, and almost everything spent by the Company seems to have been set down to its administrative account. This kind of financial juggling did not increase its popularity.

Thus, for the first thirty years after the occupation of Southern Rhodesia, one of the main objectives of the white settlers was to bring Company rule to an end. It filled their minds and dominated their politics. Such leaders amongst them as Coghlan called on the traditions of British democracy to support them in their fight. He and his followers felt themselves to be oppressed. Coghlan was fond of making such statements as, 'I shall go on unflinchingly with the object of getting from the B.S.A. Company a due recognition of the rights of the people.' And, 'The people made the country and have a right to say that they shall have a share, one and all, in the shaping of its destiny. It is for the people of Rhodesia, who are under the harrow, to say what they will do with their own future.'[1]

In this and similar statements when 'the people' are invoked, the word must be understood in only a limited sense. Coghlan did not mean this term to be extended to anyone beyond the white community, nor would there have been the least danger of anyone in his audience misunderstanding him. 'The people' did not include the black men; that was taken for granted. Hence, Coghlan could use that term, so powerfully charged by history with political emotion, to stir his hearers against the Company; use it in all sincerity and go through life like a crusading knight with words like 'freedom' and 'justice' forever on his lips, without appearing to feel the dangerous incongruity of such a cry when it applied only to a few thousand Europeans under whose power lay a great, black anonymous multitude.

Coghlan's behaviour demonstrates one of the foremost truths of Rhodesian society, one which is only slowly being undermined today:

that the black man is, quite seriously, beneath consideration. In the past, he was often spoken of as though he were a natural—if intractable —resource; something to be exploited in the same way that one exploited the land or the minerals beneath it. He was 'labour', and very unsatisfactory labour at that: a crop that men found it hard to grow successfully; an ore that had to be mined, but with only an uncertain prospect of profit. This was one important facet of a more complex image of the African that grew up in European minds. Besides being dumb 'labour', he became increasingly associated with danger. It was not so much that Africans had rebelled in the past and might again, it was more the impression of them as a dull, impercipient, threat: a brutish flood that threatened to swamp the white enclave; a bog that might suck white men down into its barbarism. The African was also regarded as a 'black peril', lusting after white women and intent on their rape. He was feckless in the manner of an animal, as you could see by his insistence on breeding large numbers of children when he could barely even keep them in their rags. He was also a creature whose very apathy could sometimes stir guilt in his exploiter, although often guilt was transformed into hatred when it was socially expressed. In personal terms, he could be a childish, lovable rogue or even an inferior kind of friend, but above all, in the mass, he was 'labour'.

The white men who had come to Rhodesia brought with them the South African belief that, on the whole, it is below the dignity of the European to work with his hands. Hence, from the first, there was a strong demand for pliable Africans who might be taught simple manual skills in the mines, the fields, or the kitchens. But neither the Mashona nor the Matabele were anxious to leave their kraals in any great number and submit to the new status of labourer. When they did come, it was usually for a few months at the most, after which they would drift back to their customary life in the villages, leaving their exasperated employer to begin teaching some 'raw' boy all over again.

Methods of forcing the African out for his master had to be found. Selous had already admitted, in 1896, the absolute necessity of the African to the European economy: 'From the black man's point of view, the white man is probably not necessary as a factor in the prosperity of the country. He could get along very well without him. Unfortunately, we cannot manage without the black man; he is absolutely necessary for the development of the country on the white man's lines.'[2] Thus, from the start, he seems to have been envisaged as the proletarian of the future, though the inevitable consequences of forcing him into this role have been consistently evaded. At first, Europeans adopted the easy fiction that the African would never change. Later, when it became apparent that he was changing, the Southern Rhodesian legislature did its best to pen him in, control his movements, strip him of bargaining power, and remove him (when not at work) from the neighbourhood if all white people.

The first legal means of coercion adopted to increase the supply of labour was a hut-tax of ten shillings, originally imposed in 1896. Besides forcing male Africans out to work, this had the advantage of swelling the Company's administrative revenues. When the tax failed to provide enough men, the obvious answer was to continue the earlier policy of using forced labour. Though this came under strong disapproval from the Imperial Government, nevertheless, the Company sometimes resorted to it. Sir Richard Martin, in a report to the South African High Commissioner about this time, remarked that: 'Compulsory labour undoubtedly exists in Matabeleland, if not in Mashonaland . . . procured by various Native Commissioners for the various requirements of the Government (the Company) and private persons . . . a labour system synonymous with slavery.'[3]

In 1901, because of the Company's behaviour in this matter, the Colonial Office threatened to deprive it of its administrative powers. It asked that the recruitment of Africans should be privately arranged between free and willing parties. In response to this request, the Company set up a Native Labour Bureau in 1903, and did everything it could to give the Bureau a monopoly of recruiting in Northern and Southern Rhodesia. The saving grace of this scheme was that it did offer some legal protection for those recruited, though it is doubtful how far their rights in the matter were explained to them. But this new monopoly had the effect of holding African wages stable at their very low existing level by preventing competition between rival employers or agencies. Thus, the African was manœuvred out of the one asset he held: the ability to sell his labour to the highest bidder. The Bureau made uniform charges to employers and laid down rigid rates of pay that gave little or no recognition to the amount of skill needed to do any particular job. There was no reward for enterprise, and, as might be expected, the Africans would not tackle the harder jobs if they could avoid them. It was a state of affairs likely to encourage indolence and discourage the gaining of skills.

Africans remained slow and ignorant, said the whites. They did not want to settle permanently in a job, and they performed the repetitive, unexplained actions their employers imposed on them without much verve. Often their repugnance for the work was increased by the beatings and generally bad treatment they were given by incensed employers. In view of all this, from very early on, the Europeans had begun to cast about for some alternative supply of labour. In the 1890's, the Southern Rhodesia Chamber of Mines was already petitioning the Company to provide regular and diligent workers to supplant the untrustworthy natives. Such labour was clearly not to be found indigenously, so it would have to be imported. This was not a very novel idea in South Africa, which had a long record of importing, first slaves, and later indentured labour.

During the South African War, Chamberlain granted the Company's request to bring in Chinese coolies, but he hedged his permission round with a good many protective regulations. Chamberlain wanted the Rhodesian Chinese to be brought in together with a contingent destined for the mines on the Rand; he would have liked to associate the two importations because the Chartered Company had gained such a bad reputation in England for its treatment of natives that he did not care to enter into an agreement with it alone. The Rand was hungry for more labour: the natives employed there were being ravaged by lung complaints and new recruits were increasingly hard to get. The mining authorities had already tried to find men in Uganda, the Gold Coast, and Nigeria, but without success. In 1904, the first Chinese were brought to the Rand, but none were introduced into Rhodesia: the restraints were too numerous for the Company. Between 1900 and 1905, the Company had sent its agents to Aden, Abyssinia and India, as well as China, in its hunt for labour, but in the end it dropped the scheme.

One outcome of the employment of the Chinese on the Rand is worth mentioning for the light it throws on contemporary attitudes. By 1906, about 50,000 coolies had been imported into the Transvaal. During that year, Milner was severely attacked in the House of Commons for authorizing the use of the lash on Chinese workers in the mines there. Public opinion in Rhodesia, as well as South Africa, was indignant that Milner's decision should be questioned. Coghlan spoke feelingly about 'the necessity for keeping law and order in an inferior population' and stressed that ways and means must be left to the 'men on the spot' who had guided Milner. His words unintentionally define the nature of his appeals to 'freedom' and his vision of 'the people'.

Yet Coghlan was regarded by most Rhodesians as a just and moderate man and his view on 'lesser breeds' were those of his day. The contemporary liberal has to take an imaginative backward leap if he is to understand the attitudes of white men of the period. The frequent arrogance, the failure of human sympathy, the assumption of racial superiority, were by no means confined to men in Southern Africa—but they have survived there to this day, whereas the events of the past fifty years have burnt them out of the minds of most thinking people in Europe. Such traits must be understood if the attitude of white settlers to the Africans amongst whom they lived is to be grasped. They must be felt to run so deep that it was hardly ever necessary to argue about them or defend them; to be self-evident and immutable.

Men existing in the environment of such beliefs were authorized to commit thoughtless little acts of contempt every day of their lives; they were freed from the need for consideration in their dealings with the 'inferior' races and allowed to perpetuate, with an easy conscience, a niggling assault on human dignity, persistent rather than harsh in many cases, but falling on the despised like an endless drizzle of misery. But such men were often upright and pleasant amongst their own, they had no sense of performing evil, quite the contrary, very often. They were the heirs to a tradition brought up with them from South Africa by the Pioneers; a way of living and being far older than they were themselves. The practical amongst them never questioned it; those more intellectually inclined could throw up a barricade of rationalizations against any doubt that might threaten them, resting their proofs ultimately on their 'civilization', by which they usually meant their technological excellence.

The next step taken to bring the Africans out of their kraals and into the labour market took the form of a request to the Imperial Government: the Company asked for permission to raise the current 10/- hut-tax to an amount similar to that levied in the Transvaal: £2. This was a sum it might take unskilled labourers several months to earn at the existing low rates of pay. The British Government rejected this levy, but the Company successfully introduced an alternative tax in 1904. The old hut-tax, they argued, had not been sufficiently compulsive and male Africans had learnt to evade its full force by living several together in one hut and clubbing-up to find the ten shillings required. Now a poll-tax of £1 was substituted, with an additional payment of 10/- for each polygamous wife a man might have.

Still the complaints kept coming from white employers. There seems to have been great resentment amongst them at the way in which the African continued to reject the profit motive. If he came to work, he would only do so, very often, for just so long as it took him to pay his tax and save enough to buy some object he coveted. He still thought of himself as living in his village: his excursions into the white areas were an imposition or at best a curious interlude. As soon as he felt like it, the African would head back for his kraal; and he lived there, said white men, in unashamed sloth, basking in the sun or gossiping in the *dare* whilst his women toiled for him in the fields. There was talk amongst Europeans of forcing African husbands to pay their wives wages for the work they did 'to teach them the value of money'. This scheme would have been impossible to put into operation but it serves to illustrate the exasperation of the settler. Later he was to come to accept the casual, migrant labour of the African and to try to build on it a system for the exclusion of settled Africans from the white half of the country, but here again he would be thwarted because long contact with an industrial economy was gradually creating the urban African. The tides of migrant labour left a sediment of Africans in the towns—men who had lost contact with their villages and had become willing to be absorbed into the European economy. By about 1920, clusters of them were to be found in the towns. The Europeans then realized that such people constituted a danger, as we shall see.

The appetite for labour was constant. It was never really satiated, despite the sucking in of many Africans from Northern Rhodesia, Nyasaland and Mozambique. Even today, when new steps have been taken to ensure a supply and the towns have become crowded with dispossessed peasants, the European farmer still finds it hard to recruit enough labourers. And with this constant preoccupation of the white man, like the can tied to the dog's tail, went the endless talk about the ineptitude of the African once he had been successfully gathered into employment.

It is true that the African is often a poor worker, but it is just as true that he has shown himself the equal of a white operative when the rewards have been even reasonably adequate. On the whole, he has had nothing by way of reward sufficient to induce him to work hard. From the early days of the Native Labour Bureau his wages have been maintained at an artificially low level. There has been no economic spur, and outside the economic field, there have been many grievances of other kinds. Colin Leys recently estimated the position as follows: 'The distribution of the increased national income (of Southern Rhodesia) is so uneven, with over 92 per cent of the population receiving only about a quarter of it, that it is difficult to say with confidence that the real incomes of the majority of the population have appreciably risen during the fifty years of contact with the European economy.'[4]

Inefficiency and deliberate laziness are bound to be bred by such a state of affairs, and it may be asked why the various governments of Southern Rhodesia have never taken steps to ensure a more equitable spread of wealth throughout the population, if only in the interests of good business. The answer lies in the European fear of the African that we have already touched upon. It is a motif that has been growing stronger in recent years. To the dread of being swamped as a race has been added an uneasy apprehension of the treatment that the black man might mete out in his turn, should he gain political power. But at the deepest level it often remains racial and is likely to provoke a rising of the gorge, a physical disgust, such as might be felt at the idea of men being subject to animals. It is a reflex of horror and dismay whose strength is not often realized in British evaluations of the Rhodesian or South African scene; one which will be hard to eradicate. Commercial exploitation of the African has been used as an instrument of political bondage; one thing has been used to justify another; and at the foundation of this structure is a traditional detestation that often descends to the darkest and most irrational regions of the mind.

Since the early days, white settlers have always seen their defence against the African danger in massive immigration. Fifty years and more ago, men such as Coghlan were already stressing that part of Rhodes' policy which envisaged Rhodesia as a great white Dominion, a refuge for the superfluous population of industrial England. In this spirit, they challenged the Company's right to the land. The exclusive mineral rights held by the Company might be galling, but its legal position in respect of them seemed unassailable. In the even more important matter of the land, they fought the Company for years, demanding that 'land that has not already been alienated should belong to the people of the country and should be disposed of for their benefit.'

In 1914, the opposing arguments were placed before the Privy Council. Claims were lodged on behalf of four parties: the Company, the People, the Crown, and—at the insistence of a few philanthropists— the Natives. In 1917, a decision was come to. The Privy Council rejected the Company's claim to ownership of the land, and with it those of the People and the Natives: judgement was given in favour of the Crown. The settlers regarded this as a victory against the Company, for the new ruling meant that the land would belong to any fresh government set up under the Crown. They had already been struggling for years to gain responsible government and felt confident that they would succeed before long.

This ruling by the Privy Council can also be taken to mark the point when the Company definitely decided to give up the administration as soon as it could do so on terms reasonably favourable to itself.

When responsible government arrived, its policy would be to encourage as many new immigrants as the land could support in an attempt to build a strong bastion against the black flood. This policy has been determinedly followed ever since. Because of it, any improvement in real wealth has been channelled away from the black majority and devoted to the encouragement of immigration and the maintenance of a great gap between the levels of material prosperity enjoyed by the European and the African. White men have to be induced to enter the country and are bribed to stay. Thus, the whole of the European population exists on a high, deliberately contrived financial plateau. This gives white rule the look of a plutocratic conspiracy but in fact, as I have tried to indicate, it contains other drives than the simple one of economic exploitation.

It was uneasiness at the idea of taking on further swarms of black men that prompted the elected (settler) members of the Southern Rhodesian Legislative Assembly to reject a scheme put forward by Jameson in 1915, when he was President of the Company. He had asked for an amalgamation of Northern and Southern Rhodesia, which would have lightened the administrative burden for the two territories, both of which were under Company rule. But the idea was unattractive to the settlers. The north was a huge, backward area with very few whites to balance against the large numbers of black men it held. At that time, no way had been found of working the vast copper deposits on the Katanga border, and there seemed no reason to endanger the position of the white man in Southern Rhodesia. The proposed amalgamation was dropped.

Fears of increasing African influence had already led to defensive legal action some years previously in Southern Rhodesia. The country had inherited a Common Roll from the Cape, but by 1912, steps had already been taken to restrict the number of Africans who could get on to it by the simple device of raising the qualifications required. The ascending qualification was to be used again for the same purpose in 1951, when Huggins put through the Electoral Amendment Act in the Southern Rhodesian House, claiming that it would be 'almost as much as closing the Roll for fifteen years' against the greater numbers of

Africans who were becoming eligible for the vote. Thus whenever the Africans came near to jumping the gate in any numbers, it was thought prudent to add another bar to it.

Another aspect of European fears about the black majority is revealed by their abhorrence of the Poor White. Their distaste had its foundation in the inbred feeling that no white man should live in poverty like an African nor labour with his hands at an unskilled job. A Poor White illustrated the form of damnation that Europeans most dreaded: he was a man who, so it seemed, had been corrupted by the force of African example. He had, in moral wilfulness, stripped himself of the advantages of his civilization and now lived 'no better than a Kaffir'.

So, though white immigrants were always wanted, Poor Whites from the union or unskilled labourers from Europe were not welcome. A Poor White was a blemish on the European ideology of domination, a walking paradox that the system could scarcely tolerate, dangerous in practical terms because he demonstrated to Africans that white men could live in poverty like their own. He was capable of doing severe damage to the image which Europeans habitually held up to Africans as a true reflection of themselves.

The wish to stop poor Europeans from entering the country fought in men's minds with the desire to strengthen the white position by immigration. In the early days, regulations could not afford to be too severe, and though the Afrikaner *bywoner* and the Jewish and Greek pedlars were frowned upon, they were admitted. Many of the Jews and Greeks have since moved beyond reproach in this respect: the sons and grandsons of the original immigrants have become rich through trade, much of it Kaffir truck, and now form influential communities in the major cities of Southern Rhodesia. In more recent years, immigration laws have seen to it that no person without either a skill or a good deal of capital shall enter the country.

Fear of an influx of Poor Whites helped to persuade the settlers of Southern Rhodesia to set up their own government when the Company relinquished its administrative powers, rather than become another Province of the Union. Rhodes had always believed that his north would one day link itself in federation with other states in southern Africa to form a single great Dominion under the Union Jack. When a National Convention met in 1908 to decide the nature of the South African Union, it was recognized by all the delegates present that one day the Union should include the Chartered territories. Most Rhodesians would have agreed as a matter of course at that time, but as the years passed, the desire to enter the Union faded. There were a number of reasons that helped to bring about this change of mind, besides the fear of opening the door to the Poor Whites of the south.

Rhodesians felt themselves to be exponents of the direct Imperial tradition, they were fiercely loyal to the Crown, partly no doubt because they felt the need for powerful connexions in a dangerous world, but also with an unquestioning emotional allegiance which they demonstrated by their wholehearted support of Britain in both World Wars, and which is still strong today. By 1922, when the British Government had decided on a referendum to decide the future of the country, Rhodesians saw much they disliked in the Union of South Africa. Afrikaner nationalism was strong and seemed likely to grow stronger: Afrikaners cherished their old resentments and took pains to cultivate them whenever they seemed likely to wilt from the passage of the years. They were excellent haters, with the stubborn memories of an unlettered people. Now they were set on the long road of revenge, seeking redress for the defeats and humiliations of the South African War, the concentration camps in which so many of their women and children had died, and the dismantling of their republics. Hertzog and his extremists were powerful; there was the fear of bilingualism, which was already part of Afrikaner policy—the demand that every schoolchild be compelled to learn Afrikaans as well as English—and which seemed an effrontery to many Englishmen. There was the fear that the perennial scarcity of native labour might be made worse, with many Rhodesian Africans drawn off to the Rand by the lure of higher wages. There was also the sense of a possible diversion in the economic policies of the two countries. Southern Rhodesia was a primary producer who hoped to gain world markets, and so she favoured low import duties, low taxes, low prices for manufactured goods—a state of affairs she hoped would also help to attract increasing numbers of immigrants. But in the Union, the raising of a tariff barrier was being urged by powerful groups. A last reason was the Rhodesians' desire to govern themselves, for a while at least, until they should become more numerous and their country more powerful, so that they could talk with South Africa on more equal terms should they later decide to enter the Union.

The interests of the Directors of the Chartered Company extended beyond Rhodesia. They supported the idea of immediate inclusion in the Union to strengthen Smuts' position against the Nationalists. They and their supporters pointed to the origins of the Rhodesian settlers, most of whom had come from the Union. The system of law in both countries, they went on, was fundamentally the same, and the majority of Rhodesian trade was carried on with her southern neighbour. To join it, they urged, was merely to acknowledge political reality: Rhodes had known this and had always looked forward to the day of the federation of southern Africa; he had even provided the two territories with a continuous railways system. Smuts badly wanted the English vote and offered Rhodesia terms of representation that were generous to the point of bribery: she would be given, he said, ten seats in the House of Assembly, a number that would have been very flattering to the small European electorate of Rhodesia and very helpful to Smuts.

Despite all this, the Company and the Union Association it supported were unsuccessful. Their policy was rejected by the electors of Southern Rhodesia in a referendum held in 1922, and the Responsible Government Association, headed by Coghlan, was given a decisive victory: 8,744 votes were cast for independence and 5,989 for inclusion in the Union. Southern Rhodesia was declared a self-governing colony in the next year and Sir Charles Coghlan became its first Prime Minister.

CHAPTER 8

Since 1923

Southern Rhodesian independence was not absolute. There were certain reserved clauses in the constitution offered by the British Government which were intended to act as a safeguar for the African population. By their terms, any legislation that differentiated between African and European had to receive the consent of the British Secretary of State before it could be enacted.

But, of course, once Southern Rhodesia was, in all other respects, an independent member of the Commonwealth, the British Government was very unwilling to interfere in her domestic affairs. This weapon which the British Government kept in its hands was never used. Gale, an apologist for the Southern Rhodesian mode of government was able to write in 1950 that 'so far no objection has been raised to any law discriminating against Africans.'[1] It was a triumphant claim in the curcumstances, for by that time most of the laws intended to segregate the African and perpetuate his inferiority had already been passed. The British Government seems to have maintained its record of passivity in the decade that has gone by since Gale reported, though it is possible that it may have used the threat of the reserved clauses to influence Southern Rhodesian leaders in private. Certainly, Rhodesians have shown a frantic anxiety in recent years to see them removed before it is too late.

At the time of Rhodesian independence, there had been little legislation aimed directly against the African. His inferior status had been conferred by custom rather than law. When his labour was not wanted, most white people wished only to forget that he existed, so far as that was possible. More adequate reserves had been set up for tribesmen on the recommendation of an Order in Council of 1898. By 1902 the shape of the new Reserves was fixed. They had been created rather arbitrarily,

on the often inexpert advice of Native Commissioners, but they had
certain things in common. They tended to be in the less fertile and more
remote districts of the country, a long way from the white settlements
and the line of rail. This seemed common sense to the settlers at the
time—those who lived the tribal life had no need of railways and were a
nuisance near the white areas—but it was to cause much resentment
later. In the Reserves, the African might live out a parody of the kind of
traditional life he had followed before the European came, provided
that he obeyed the Native Commissioner set over him and came to
work on the mines or farms when required. Reserves were a necessity
when two such different modes of life had to exist side by side and the
one was not strong enough to absorb the other. There was no alternative
to them. The only criticism that might have been made of them
originally was that the allocation of land was rather mean, but it is not
usually in the nature of conquerors to be generous to a people they
despise. It was only later that the Reserves were made part of a deliberate
mechanism of exclusion.

In the early days, it was generally felt by Europeans that the African
was safest when least disturbed: so long as he preserved his initial
barbarism he could not present any new threat to white rule. Missionaries who went into the Reserves to convert and educate Africans were
therefore often looked on with suspicion. Some people found their
grudging respect for these men of God turning into anger and distrust
when faced with the products of their teaching. It soon became fashionable to decry the 'mission boy' as a conceited half-educated nuisance—
not always without reason—and to state a preference for 'the old type of
native'. The stresses set up by missionaries were, of course, nothing
new in South Africa, where religious evangelists had often been accused
of working to subvert white authority. But, on the whole, little thought
was given to Africans by the white population except in terms of labour.
The threat of their numbers, though understood, seemed as yet comparatively remote, and it was still possible to believe in remedies such as
massive immigration.

The strongest dissentient note that can be heard in the first twenty-
five years of European settlement in Rhodesia is perhaps that of a
Native Affairs Commission which reported in 1911. It gave a picture of
increasing breakdown in the Reserves, with the life of the villages sapped
by the frequent absence of the young men who went as migrant labourers.
On their return, these new sophisticates often flouted custom and
challenged the authority of chiefs and headmen, whose influence was

in serious decline now that they were seen to be no more than the mouthpieces of the Native Commissioner. Missionaries were said to aid the process of disintegration, sometimes, by attacking African traditional religion without understanding its true nature nor the intimate part it played in tribal life. When the missionaries made a convert of a man who was polygamous, they forced him to turn away his excess wives, thus creating a situation that had no precedent in African life. The Commission also spoke of the black man's bewilderment under the rain of injunctions and prohibitions he encountered under white laws; often such matters made no sense to him, were quite different from the modes of behaviour he had learnt from childhood in the kraal, and were rarely thought to be worth explaining. The report commented sharply on the prevalent white views that African men were lazy, that in traditional life they made drudges of their women, and that as a corrective they should be made to pay them wages. These views, said the Commission, were false. In village life, work was shared between a man and his wives, with the man playing the more arduous role.

The report of the Commission was ignored. Industry and farming were hungry for labour and could not afford to pay attention to descriptions of the breakdown their demands were causing in the Reserves. Similarly, traditional opinions on the male African in his natural state remained popular amongst Europeans, who thought them proven beyond all doubt by the African's poor performance as a labourer.

In its later period, the Company had come down heavily in favour of the settlers. Milton, the creator of the Civil Service in Southern Rhodesia, had been trained at the Cape and his system aimed at the kind of objectives regarded there as right. When the Company handed over to Coghlan in 1923, it bequeathed him an administration geared to the protection and furthering of white interests. Now, with a free hand, matters looked promising for the Europeans. The economic position of the country was improved by the introduction, in 1925, of Imperial Preference, which gave Rhodesian farmers a new cash crop in tobacco, which they could sell on the English market. Immigrants were coming into the country steadily, and between 1924 and 1931, the white population rose from 35,000 to nearly 50,000. Though the production of gold remained rather disappointing, it was an important export; there were also big deposits of base minerals in the earth and although development of mining schemes designed to exploit them was slow at the moment, there was always the hope of increased world demand in the future.

The new government set out to entrench the privileged position of the Europeans by incorporating African disabilities in new laws. Only a few years before, in 1920, there had been a rearrangement in the Reserves which had reduced them slightly in extent. In 1925, the government appointed the Morris Carter Commission to enquire into a permanent division of the land between African and European. The report it made was used as the basis of the Land Apportionment Act of 1930. Perhaps Gale should be called on to explain the purposes behind this measure; he was a supporter of the system and so can be expected to put it in its best light. 'The Land Apportionment Act,' he writes, 'is the basis of our whole Native policy. It enables the Africans to develop in their own areas along their own lines, retaining the best in their own traditions and building up their own economy according to their own interests. It also sets aside areas known as European areas, in which the interests of the European are the first concern, but while Europeans may not work in Native Areas unless they benefit the African, Africans are allowed in the European areas to assist in the developing of the country as workers in mines, on farms, in industry and domestic service.'[2]

It is worth remarking that Gale apparently considers all 'developing of the country' is likely to take place in the European areas. He had good reason for this supposition. Under the terms of the Act, Europeans were granted more than half of all assigned land, and that the most fertile and the nearest to the line of rail. Every town in Southern Rhodesia was designated as a white area, and obviously these places where industry was already established and had been equipped with the necessary facilities were the ones which would attract new industry. Nobody was likely to try to establish a factory in the middle of the Reserves, where there were no main services, no railways and only dirt roads. Gale uses the delicate word 'allow' to describe the entry of black workers into white areas. In fact, as we have seen, white settlers had always been dependent on black labour and could not have survived without it. In his enthusiastic description of the Reserves as places where the African can 'develop along their own lines', Gale strikes a note heard more commonly nowadays amongst the adherents of *apartheid* anxious to impress the outside world with the wisdom and philanthropy implicit in the concept of the 'Bantustan'. And indeed, the kind of arrangement laid down in Southern Rhodesia by law in 1930 was a form of *apartheid*, based on white supremacy and ownership of all the more valuable land and property. It converted the fact of cheap migrant labour into a principle of government, used it as the instrument of an indefinite exclusion. Though it can be explained in terms of racial entrenchment, and even perhaps as the harsh means by which an industrial revolution could be pushed through most quickly, in terms of social justice it is indefensible.

The effects of the Land Apportionment Act were to seal off more than half the country from Africans and gradually to move those who were 'squatting' in European portions of it, by force if necessary, to places of resettlement in their own areas; to prevent any African from owning property in the towns, or living near them except on sufferance; and to stop Africans buying land in European farming areas—as a few had begun to do—where they might compete on the open market with anything like an equal chance of success. Those Africans who could prove that they were in full-time employment were allowed to live in 'locations' and 'compounds' near the towns. These became the pullulating dormitories of a shifting proletariat. Because labour was migrant, and should continue to be so, little or no provision was made at first for married people. Men lived, crowded six or eight to a room in squalid barrack-blocks where there was often little in the way of sanitation and a stand-tap in the yard provided the only supply of water. Their cooking had to be done over braziers or open fires. Brother crowded in with brother in these verminous hovels, and soon young women began to follow the young men to the towns, and they too shared the same room with perhaps seven or eight men. They slept on the floor or, if they were lucky, on straw palliasses, and to gain some remnant of privacy they often hung up curtains of sacking round their beds or across corners of the room. The private compounds of industrial firms were often the worst: here the employees might live in shacks of corrugated iron or structures they had put up themselves, crazy huts of wood, cardboard, asbestos strips, sacking; the detritus of urban life. Many Africans, wandering in this chaotic underworld, had to camp out where they could at night: sleeping in ditches or on building sites, anywhere that offered some protection from the cold that comes with darkness on the plateau. Municipalities put up rather more reasonable housing, but much too slowly to cope with the situation. The bleak blocks of rooms they offered were subject to the same kind of overcrowding. Life was a fierce, anguished scramble for the urban African, but Europeans could dismiss the extremity of his situation by pointing out that he was only a migrant, lodging in land that was not his and going back after a year or two to his real home in the Reserves. This was repeated long after it ceased to be true for all Africans, though even now, a vast amount of labour is still migrant, much of it coming from the old reservoirs of men in Nyasaland, Northern Rhodesia and Mozambique.

With the Land Apportionment Act, the Southern Rhodesian Government defined itself to Africans as an instrument of white domination rather than a body seeking the good of the whole country. Africans felt themselves relegated to an inferior position for ever and their response, dim and feeble at first but growing stronger over the years, was to repudiate the government. Their opposition could, in the nature of the situation, only take an unconstitutional form, because they were denied any voice in the government and could therefore only see it as an oppressive organ of the white man.

Actions taken against Africans in the depressed period of the thirties can only have helped to confirm this view. When times became hard for the European farmer, Africans who produced beef or maize were penalized by being forced to sell at a lower price than their white competitors. Africans who tried to prospect were refused licences. The pass laws were enforced more rigidly and given a new use: they were the mechanism employed to shut African street traders into the locations, where they could not offer direct competition to white retailers in the towns. The development of the pass system gives an interesting glimpse of the way in which a simple device could be elaborated into an instrument of oppression. Africans had been forced to carry passes since the early days of the Company. The original pass, or *situpa*, was intended as a means of identification and a document on which a contract of service could be shown. It also served as a place where the receipt of taxes could be written down conveniently. Given the circumstances of the occupation, it was probably necessary to insist on each African carrying a *situpa*, though these vital bits of paper were always disliked by Africans, who went in fear of losing them. In 1936, Godfrey Huggins, later Lord Malvern, who was by this time Prime Minister of Southern Rhodesia, introduced an Act which extended the pass system and made use of it to impose segregation more rigorously in the towns. Under the new regulations, the African did not only have to be able to produce a *situpa* if challenged by the police to do so; he had, as well, to be carrying about with him either a pass to seek work in the town, or a certificate of employment, or a certificate from a Native Commissioner which stated that he was earning his living in the town by lawful means, or, if he was employed out of town, a visiting-pass written by his white master. If he did not have the correct passes, he would be arrested should the police happen to ask him to produce them.

Huggins had been pursuing a policy of segregation since he came to power in 1933. He described his aims as the 'gradual differential treatment of the natives'.[3] He talked of their 'childishness' and the lack amongst them of 'some regular form of religion' to justify actions which were segregationalist, though in a limited way paternal. Where African needs did not conflict with those of the European, he would help them, as he did over the matters of overstocking and erosion in the Reserves. He was also anxious to buttress the power of the chiefs, but these figureheads could not longer inspire men with their dignity, even when they were decked out in red dress robes and white pith helmets, such as they wore on formal occasions. Nor could their chain of office with its brass crescent proclaiming their rank stir much respect. In the twenties, Bullock had already noted that, 'Today you may see natives passing their chiefs with little or no formal salutation. When reproved, they will say, "Where is the land?" That is to say—"The whites are now owners of the land. Why should we salute a landless man?" '[4] The chiefs acknowledged their new servile status by referring to themselves, when speaking with officials, as the 'dogs' or 'women' of the government. It will be remembered that under the customary system, the chief had not been the individual owner of the land but the bailiff for his tribe. The land had belonged to them all. Now they saw their old lands taken, some of their people deprived of their heritage, and the chiefs apparently conniving at this and acting as the agents of the European. No doubt they realized the chief had little alternative, but they also knew him to be the fee'd servant of the government: there were no grounds left for respect.

In 1936, Huggins also took steps to improve the medical facilities in the Reserves after the Medical Director had warned that they were 'reservoirs of infection' from which, again and again, diseases could be taken into the white areas. African orderlies were trained and set in charge of sub-clinics in the Reserves; a scheme which proved most effective.

Huggins wanted to direct the forms of African trade so that they did not 'undermine the economic structure of the white race' and was only prepared to assist amongst Africans a type of farming 'on lines supplementary to and not competitive with that of the European'.[5]

But the chief move Huggins made against the African appeared in disguise: coming in an apparently innocuous bill in 1934 which purported to be creating an instrument for the settlement of industrial disputes. It followed on a strike of European employees in the building industry and provided for the setting-up of councils of employers' and workers' representatives to gain agreement by modern methods of conciliation on disputes concerning rates of pay and working conditions. But by explicitly excluding the African from its definition of 'an employee', the Act refused him the power to negotiate. As the wage-rates decided upon by the Industrial Councils could be enforced in any skilled job, the African found himself shut out of all occupations of that kind. No employer would be willing to pay an African at the inflated European rates. Nor was it only a question of whether or not he could do the job: an African paid at European rates would have been a menace. One must always keep in mind the solidarity of white with white; all Europeans were aware that basically their interests were the same; that if the privileged position of any one section of them were threatened, ultimately they were all threatened. A philanthropic employer who defied public opinion in such a matter would have suffered social ostracism, public contempt, trade boycott and the withdrawal of white labour.

The Industrial Councils were also given the power to regulate the conditions of apprenticeship, and assumed that Africans were outside its scope as they could not be regarded as 'employees'. Thus by the Industrial Conciliation Act, Africans were prevented from bargaining or from learning industrial skills. In the hands of white trade unionists, the Act was used to enforce a colour-bar in industry and keep off the threat to 'the white standard of life' offered by Africans ready to work at lower wages. It was welcomed jubilantly by the Southern Rhodesian Labour Party, which in the hard times of the thirties was preoccupied above all else with defending the living standard of the white artisan. This party advocated a white Rhodesia—as it had to, from the nature of its following—at all levels of labour except the lowest.

On these two Acts, the contemporary pattern of privilege in Southern Rhodesia was legally founded. One of them deprived the African of more than half of the best land in the country and forbade him to own a business or property in any of the urban centres. The other prevented him from rising in the industrial scale. His role was defined as that of the unskilled proletarian. He was cheap labour and had no other social value, and he carried the mark of his servitude where it could not be hidden: in the colour of his face.

More recently, the Southern Rhodesian Government has passed another Act to which many Africans also point with hostility. The official argument is that some re-adjustment of African society had to come in the modern world; that under present-day conditions communal land-

holding and subsistence farming are wasteful anachronisms that will
have to disappear. There is a good deal to be said for this argument. In
1951, the Land Husbandry Act was passed with the intention of transforming the system of land tenure from a communal to an individual
one. The government envisaged the rise of a contented black peasantry
husbanding its land efficiently and fulfilling what has been a European
dream for some time now: a conservative community of petty farmers
which might act as a counterpoise to the more volatile proletarians in
the towns. What the government refused to consider was that the old
system was much more than a method of holding land; it was a way of
life that ensured a high degree of security and a share in the fruits of the
earth.

The Act sets up African farmers on individual holdings, but these are
very small, no more than six acres on the average, and asks them to
wring a living from them. Highly intensive farming would be the only
way to gain a measure of prosperity in these conditions, but scarcely any
Africans have the capital needed: what most of them get is a very bare
living. Garfield Todd summed up the defects of the Bill when it was
discussed in the Legislative Assembly. The government, he said, was
'all out for a system of small peasant farming which will give the native
nothing more than a subsistence, however good his ideas.' He went on
to say that 'we do not want native peasants' and proceeded to give his
own solution which entailed absorbing something like another half a
million Africans into the European areas, and settling them, as families,
in places where they would have security of tenure, and could serve as
additions to the urban labour force. Of those who were left in the
Reserves, he would then be able to 'give each family 150 or 200 acres on
a ninety-nine year lease.'⁶ As other members of the House pointed out,
his plan would smash the provisions of the Land Apportionment Act
and thus destroy the fundamental policy of segregation. It was dismissed.

African criticism of the Land Husbandry Act took two forms. Many
Africans mourned the passing of the tribal areas, in which a man could
still feel a sense of belonging, and recognized sadly that they were wit-
nessing the end of a way of life. Others felt that the Act was not bad in
itself; indeed, saw that despite the upheaval it would cause, it was
necessary, but they hated it because it had been made to work within
the framework of the Land Apportionment Act. The African farmer
was to be confined to six acres yet he knew that no European was advised, or even permitted to take a farm of less than 750 acres, that the

average European farm was about 2,000 acres, and that many were much bigger still. The astonishing position was sometimes reached where the big white farmer, who could gain a rich living off a few hundred acres of tobacco, cultivated nothing else, leaving all the rest of his 10,000 acres idle. Each year he would put his tobacco seedlings in a different part of his land and work round the more fertile areas in a cycle, operating a system of shifting agriculture such as the tribal African once followed but which, as his descendants have had dinned into them, is primitive and wasteful. Faced with this kind of comparison, the bitterness of the African grew.

Those Africans forced off the land are expected to form the new industrial working-class, living permanently in their locations and townships on the fringes of the cities. It can be seen that the doctrinaire assumptions of segregation have been abandoned of recent years; migrant labour is no longer to be the sole source of supply and the improbable fiction of the Africans 'developing in their own areas along their own lines' has been dropped. But all the advantages gained under the Land Apportionment Act have been retained for Europeans.

Few provisions have been made for these new urban Africans which would compensate them for the loss of their traditional security in tribal life. Now that great numbers of Africans are being cut off from the Reserves, such benefits as pensions for old age or help in sickness must be given. In the past, help was always available from the branches of the family; nowadays, for many landless town labourers, any kind of personal misfortune, including the natural process of growing old, can only lead to destitution. The effect of this 'enclosure' system on those driven into the towns can be seen in the terms of the Vagrancy Act of 1960, which is aimed at 'the beggar . . . any person who is unable to show that he is living by honest means, any person unable to show he is in employment, any person lodging in a verandah, outhouse, shed, unoccupied building, park garden, open trench, culvert or drain.' The degree of want and misery these words imply needs no elaboration. The welfare the government is offering to such people at the moment is to arrest them and send them to a 're-establishment centre' for as long as three years.

It will be realized from this that, in recent years, and partly as a result of government legislation, the supply of labour in the towns has at last come to exceed the demand. Africans with no land under the new system face pauperdom unless they can keep in work. African leaders point bitterly to the vast areas of land alienated for Europeans, of which no more than 4 per cent is ever in cultivation. The Land Husbandry Act, they say, has deliberately set about to destroy their old way of life without offering them a decent alternative. They are given the choice between a hard life of toil on a small allotment and a precarious existence in the teeming native townships, stripped of the welfare of the tribal system provided. Their position, I suppose, is not unlike that of the English operative in the early years of the nineteenth century: men whose past lay with the soil but who could not go back to the country any longer because of the enclosures and so were thrown into the chaos of the labour market in the new industrial towns. No doubt the enclosure of land was necessary by some arrangement or other, but one questions the necessity of the form it took. Critics of Rhodesia's conversion of itself into an industrial nation might echo that sentiment: no doubt, with the old African life falling apart and vast numbers of people groping towards a new one, there was bound to be hardship and upset, but the unavoidable harshness of change has been exacerbated by racial legislation.

The Rhodesian towns themselves have altered greatly over the years. The pole and mud huts of the early Pioneers soon gave way to structures of wood and corrugated iron. The primitive severity of the early buildings was softened as brick came into use, and many builders compensated for past structural nakedness by going to the opposite extreme of senseless elaboration. This echoed the contemporary mood in Britain, of course, and was therefore desirable. Under this influence, even the metal pillars that supported the shop awnings burst into floral mouldings and decorative scolls. In those days, houses were built with deep verandahs, netted against mosquitoes; the ceilings were high to provide coolness and the interiors shadowy. Some such houses can still be found today, hidden behind tall hedges of hibiscus in avenues where *jacarandas* and *flamboyants*, planted fifty years ago, still flower in season. The rooms were made big enough to house the cumbersome furniture that was fashionable; the carved sideboards, the *chaises-longues* in buttoned green plush, the intricate gilt mirrors. Often the plaster of the ceilings seemed to be moulded into formal designs, though in fact this effect was created by using sheets of stamped metal. Fireplaces were ornate with mantels big enough to hold the many trinkets and photographs in soft silver frames that it was thought *chic* to display. The dining-room was large and importantly furnished; its table could seat twelve without trouble; it might even sport a bad painting in oils over the serving-table. The kitchen beyond it at the back of the house was also big: heavy tables and meat-safes like cages left enough room for two or three servants to work in it together. At the bottom of the garden, hidden if possible behind a shrubbery, were the living-quarters of the servants, and here there was less amplitude and no elaboration. A little brick box, with perhaps a tiny window, was 'what they were used to'.

The description may sound vaguely familiar to many people. It should bring back nostalgic memories to the old, for these houses with their heavy furniture and velvet curtains, their obsequious servants and lumbering pursuit of elegance were created in accordance with the canons of the late Victorian world. They were the villa: the desirable residence of the professional man. But in Africa this image had become rather distorted: above the fancy gabling the roof was corrugated iron; the cook, scullion, nursemaid and gardener were black and bemused; the road beyond the garden hedge was thick red dust in winter, and in summer when the rains came it turned into sticky mud; many of the flowers and trees in the garden were strange, and not far away the bush began.

This was the early ideal, and it can still be used to illustrate two important facets of white Rhodesian thinking. First, there is the sense of Rhodesia as an extension of England as she was in her final Imperialistic period. Rhodesians remain very conscious of the flag and the Crown; the old image of setting wider the bounds of empire, of being part of the greatest power on earth, was naturally adopted by them. These early houses bear the stamp of a way of life, the warrant of Imperial authority. Rhodesians have gone on thinking of themselves in this vein, whilst in England such ideas have been discarded over the past half century. Rhodesians find themselves a tenacious outpost of an empire that no longer exists; that the mother country has resigned from. This goes a long way to explain their bewilderment at Britain's more recent behaviour towards them, their vague sense of betrayal and their deep insecurity. The only heritage they have is an abandoned hypothesis.

Second, though over the years the style of Rhodesian building has changed, certain values implicit in the old ideal have remained constant. There is still the demand for servants and a high degree of comfort, and that demand continues to be satisfied. Even on big estates of European bungalows, each house should have its half-acre of garden, at the least; and each house will have its own little brick box at the bottom of the garden providing quarters for the gardener and the cook-boy. The rooms in the house will be furnished in a style that is luxurious if often tasteless and there will very likely be two cars in the garage. This kind of social demand has led to gigantic urban sprawl: it is as far across modern Salisbury as it is across Greater London, though only 70,000 Europeans live in the Rhodesian capital.

In the centres of the two major cities, the stores of corrugated iron and brick have long ago given place to big department stores and towering blocks of offices. The need to make a display of wealth has led, particularly in Salisbury, to façades of glittering white stone, mosaic pillars and murals, and marble entrance halls equipped with bronze statues and playing fountains. Big companies vie with each other in ostentation, and in some of the old avenues, skyscrapers are tall enough to cut off the sun. Behind plate glass are displayed luxuries imported from all over the world. The smell of money is strong in Salisbury; at first it is exhilarating to the newcomer, but later depressing, when the squalid foundations of this mart for conspicuous consumption are glimpsed.

Federation with Northern Rhodesia and Nyasaland increased the flow of capital into the country for a time. Salisbury benefited most markedly, but a discussion of Federation as a whole is outside the scope of this book. It is enough to say that so far it has brought little improvement to the mass of the population, that the pledge of 'partnership' which induced the British Government to agree to the formation of this new political unit has not been carried out. As a consequence, African support has not been won, distrust has hardened into hatred —particularly in the northern territories—and it looks very much as though the Federation must be broken up, or changed out of all recognition.

Where has power habitually lain in Southern Rhodesia and how has it been influenced? Officially, of course, it lay in the hands of the government, but there was always a strong feeling of solidarity between the European population and the government whose members were themselves white and who were all elected by it; their rule often had the appearance of collusion to maintain white privilege. But the settlers have never merely expressed themselves as an electorate. In a country like Southern Rhodesia, where the dominant community is small in numbers and politicians are personally known to many leading citizens, there has always been scope for pressure in the office and persuasion in the clubs. If such groups as the Rhodesia National Farmers' Union or the Federated Chambers of Commerce exercised pressure, the government was usually ready to pay attention. More powerful still are the Corporations, which exist like great magnates with a voice in affairs almost as authoritative as that of the king. The British South Africa Company has been joined in this role by the two big copper corporations, Anglo-American and Rhodesian Selection Trust, both of which now have their main offices in Salisbury. Colin Leys has said of them in relation to the Federation that 'their role in the economy is itself decisive'. They supply 10 per cent of the gross national investment each year, and they also indulge in direct loans to the government to the order of millions of pounds.

Despite the existence of the many controls which restrict the economic and political liberty of the African, most Europeans readily declare themselves in favour of Free Enterprise and the capitalist system, as does the government which has been the author of such a mass of restrictive legislation. White Rhodesians remain convinced that they are living in an open society dedicated to *laissez faire*. It is true that they indulge in competition amongst themselves, but this is carried on behind a barricade of Acts meant to protect them from the African challenge. A kind of double-think is habitually employed at all levels of white Rhodesian society, right down to the artisan who proclaims the virtues of the open market but at the same time forms unions against employers and erects fences to keep Africans out of skilled manual work. The artisan's success in this respect has led to an endless, completely artificial scarcity of men in skilled trades; he can therefore demand and get very high rates of pay and his ranks can only be augmented at present by further European immigration. In all this, the artisan had to have the connivance of the government, which accepted such manœuvres as part of the general entrenchment of white privilege. Government became an apparatus for racial defence rather than of economic expansion in realistic terms.

Yet it is almost impossible to convince most white Rhodesians that their society is an oligarchic conspiracy, that it has chosen deliberately to confine the majority of the population in want rather than allow them the freedom to display enterprise, should they have it. In this respect, the Rhodesian sense of virtue seems unshakeable, and from the top of his racial stockade the European displays the banners of Free Enterprise and the Capitalist System and would be not so much indignant as incredulous of anyone who questioned his right to do so.

Meanwhile, the Africans go on existing. The old ways in the country are slowly being changed, but it is in the towns where the huge locations have grown up, that we find the apex of African advance, amongst the urban proletariat. Life there is a fierce struggle for most, carried on in an environment that smacks of a new deprived sort of poverty, quite different from the egalitarian lack of possessions found in village life. Poverty is the constant companion of nearly all town Africans, and has been since their conditions were first investigated. Before the 1940's, no kinds of record were kept; the government seems to have had no knowledge of the quality of life enjoyed by urban Africans and no desire to impose any kind of policy that might affect their circumstances. The first investigation was carried out by a clergyman, the secretary of the Native Welfare Society, in 1942. He saw much evidence of malnutrition and reported desperate living conditions amongst town Africans. About the same time, the government set up the Howman Commission to enquire into conditions amongst black workers in the towns. The Commission found evidence of poverty so widespread and deep that many people were living below the line estimated as the bare minimum for subsistence. They were caught in the trap of static wages and rising costs. In 1944, a social survey undertaken in Salisbury by Professor Bateson of Cape Town revealed an even worse state of affairs. The government shelved the Howman Commission report and made no constructive attempt to alleviate African poverty. The same story was still being told as recently as 1958, when the Plewman Commission reported on urban Africans that 'The overall picture is one of extreme poverty'. It went on to describe the kind of upbringing received by the new kind of African child, those born into locations and reared in the teeming 'urban areas' that fringe the white towns: 'The majority of the children in the sample are being brought up under conditions of extreme poverty and in want of the essentials of life. . . . Children were found to be an active cause of poverty and also of a greater degree of poverty. The majority of children were living in acute poverty.'

In less official language, all too often this means rickets, legs like splints, tapeworm, tuberculosis, ophthalmia, a range of deficiency diseases, general dirt and persistent hunger. Nobody who has lived for very long in Southern Rhodesia needs to be informed by a Commission of the prevalence of poverty among the great mass of the African workers.

In the towns, bonds of custom and relationship are being broken and amongst many Africans there must be a consequent sense of loss. The old religion of *mudzimu* and *mhondoro*, born of a reverence for the family and tribe and closely associated with the land and its fruits, is fading into a memory. It no longer has any relevance under modern conditions. But witchcraft has survived, as might be expected, for it is the child of insecurity and the new world of the African is full of dangerous and inexplicable things.

Some of the sufferings of the Africans would have taken place even under the most benevolent government. They are being made to break with the immemorial customs of the past, forsaking the limited attempt at order their forefathers constructed and being plunged instead into the whirlpool of an industrial society still largely unregulated except for measures intended to keep them at a disadvantage. At this point in history, the severe hardships that are known to occur in the initial period of industrial accumulation might have been avoided, at least to some extent. A government which felt itself responsible for the welfare of the whole of the people would have tried to ease the transition, but the politicians of Southern Rhodesia have, with some honourable and far-seeing exceptions, largely chosen to regard themselves in the past as committed to a very different kind of policy.

Yet, above all things, the African is resilient; new sorts of power are being born amongst the urban proletariat; unions and political parties pledged to the destruction of the present system. By creating an industrial working-class amongst the Africans, there seems little doubt that the Europeans have fashioned the instrument which will bring about the end of their own privilege.

PART THREE

A Personal View

A Personal View

I arrived at Cape Town one morning in early May, 1955. My first day on the African continent gave me a glimpse of the terms of the dilemma there. On a trip up Table Mountain, I saw the sparkling white villas that climb its slopes. Later, as my train left Cape Town on its way north, I looked out at the hovels of the coloured population. At their worst, these heaps of wood, asbestos, cardboard and flattened tins give the impression of having been created by some animal that lives in symbiotic gratitude on the litter, the industrial dung of the cities. Such creatures seemed defined by their habitat as less than men.

The train wound its way through the mountains in the north of Cape Province. The country became increasingly dry, the towns smaller and dustier until they shrank out of existence and all that we saw were rare, utilitarian houses built along the trackside by the railway authorities. They looked ugly in their isolation and rather lost, set against a background of faded scrub. The whole of the land seemed bleached by drought. Only the sky remained vivid: there were no clouds and the glare of the sun fell in a bright deluge.

This was Bechuanaland in winter. It looked a barren wilderness. You did not expect to see people there, but whenever the train stopped to refuel, they appeared: Africans with carvings, baskets, pokerwork, beads, and karosses to sell, or to make the pretext for begging. There were others whose disfigurement was their only ware: some had grotesque buds of flesh where a limb had never developed; some were blind and led along by small boys on the end of a stick, tin cups tied round their necks to receive any coppers they might be offered. The most horrifying of them—partly because of their energy—were those with withered or deformed legs. They slithered along in the dust, propelled by rowing movements of their hands. To protect their trailing legs and the palms of their hands, they had fastened shields of leather or cardboard on to them, so that with each lurch forward they scraped and grated on the dry earth with a dreadful susurrus. There were children with hardly any flesh on their limbs amongst the crowd of hawkers and beggars.

This, of course, was poverty and crippledom on display for money. I was never to see its like again in terms of public degradation. It was as though, at the outset, Africa was stating in its most extreme terms the problem that afflicts it. As I was to realize later, the poverty of the Rhodesian African, though widespread, is more reticent. You do not see such dramatic evidence paraded on street-corners in Salisbury or Bula-wayo, but there are plenty of poor people about.

I glanced at some of the other people who had travelled with me from England to see how they had reacted to this abject display. They seemed uneasy. Those accustomed to Africa carried it off with a less troubled air, however, and for the first time I heard the remark that 'Kaffirs are used to it. They haven't ever known anything else. It's not the same for them as it would be for you.'

I was to hear this conviction of an innate disparity between African and European voiced often enough later and it never failed to awake in me a particularly sharp anxiety. Here was a hypothesis I had met before. I happen to have been born into a poor family in northern England and as a small boy in the thirties, many of my schoolmates were the sons of the unemployed. They wore patched and torn clothes; their noses often ran unhindered; sometimes their boots were plugged with brown paper to keep out the wet; many of them existed from one year to the next in a single frayed and greasy jersey. They would come to school with 'sleep' in their eyes and hair that had never seen a comb. In the winter months, when it was too cold to wash much under a cold tap, their hands would be ingrained with dirt.

I suppose to prosperous outsiders they must have seemed irreclaim-able; it was a comfortable doctrine that made them 'different'. I learnt in later years of the traditional arguments aimed by the middle-classes against the poor: 'They've never known any better. They don't really feel it as we should. Give them better houses and they'll only turn them into slums, too. They keep coals in the bath.'

Fortunately, a more understanding view of human nature prevailed in England and nowadays the 'irreclaimable' urchins who shared my elementary school days have turned into respectable citizens with a share in the general prosperity. But here in Africa I was to be often asked to subscribe to theories that would have condemned them all, theories that were frequently offered with an air of authority by people who, from their own experience, should have known better.

I am thinking particularly of the immigrant artisans. After a short time in the country, they would refuse with angry vehemence to see any connexion between their own past and the black labourers who worked beside them for less than a twentieth of their weekly pay. No doubt they had to do so, if they were to go on living equably with themselves: they had been gathered by the circumstances of Rhodesian society into the ranks of the privileged and, in common with many others, had to justify their elevation as best they could. At the same time, they were the ones who would be threatened first by any African advance, and they knew it; the knowledge turned them into some of the most strident and bigoted opponents of African advancement. Few if any groups give up their advantages without a struggle, and I suppose it was foolish to expect these English carpenters and bricklayers to provide an exception. Yet, for all that, it was saddening to hear in their mouths the same terms that had been used to condemn their fathers and grandfathers to poverty. On the other hand, they could not allow themselves to see the truth nakedly without shattering their vision of themselves as just and reasonable men—which they were, in all matters that did not involve their privilege.

Every white person in Rhodesia lives within the tension caused by this struggle between interest and social justice. Many would deny that they do, but the marks of it can be seen even in the stoniest supremacists, emerging in stray actions and remarks, just as a suppressed neurosis may betray itself in the uncontrollable *tic* or stammer. From a distance, in England, it may seem easy to condemn such people; but many of those who do so would, I think, have reacted no differently had they been placed in a similar position and offered the temptation of great material prosperity.

The last lap of my journey was an overnight trip from Bulawayo to Salisbury. I was up early in the morning and went into the corridor to get a good look at the country I had come to. It lay under the golden early-morning light of winter: the yellow plains were tufted and flecked with bushes, and dark green kopjes floated there like hulks. It was an untouched land. Only occasionally was there a sign of life or cultivation: a white farmhouse seen for a moment through a gap in a curtain of gum trees; an area of cleared ground; a field of exhausted maize stems; and sometimes, a group of mud huts crouching in the lee of a hill. But most of the land seemed empty and the distance was very great before it met the curve of the horizon.

I had been joined by a young man in Air Force uniform. We looked out in silence for a while at the landscape sliding past, and then he said abruptly, as though the scene had provoked him into uttering his thoughts: 'I'm on my way back from England. I was there on a course—and you can keep it, man! This is the best country God ever made. Just look at it.'

He nodded his head towards the window. Staring out again, I felt I understood what he meant. In the gentle morning light the land had a size and freshness that stirred a vague rejoicing, even in me, who was a stranger to it. England seemed small and cluttered by comparison, a place soiled by the mistakes and defilements of the past, which lay upon it with a weight that a living man could hardly hope to shift. This looked new and bright; all the decisions on it had still to be taken; it looked unmarked. For a moment, I glimpsed, in a dim way, the kind of excitement that must have stirred in the hearts of the Pioneers as they sat their horses; each man wondering, with a kind of primitive riches, which way in all this wilderness to turn his mount's head.

I remarked that I had expected to see more African villages about. 'No,' he said. 'Not near the line of rail. But there are plenty of them up and down the place. We'd be better off without them. Still. . . .' He smiled and realizing by my remark that I was an immigrant, he added, 'But you'll soon get used to them. They won't bother you. After a while, you know, you'll stop seeing them. It's just as though they weren't there.'

As the sun rose higher, it stripped the glamour from the land. The light became more harsh and the parched vegetation looked drab in the glare. A wind whipped up particles of earth that went twisting off across country in a dark spout. The vision of the early morning had gone: only the emptiness remained and that seemed more hostile.

The Air Force man seemed to read my thoughts. 'Of course, it's winter,' he said a shade defensively. 'No rain now till November, at the earliest. Everything gets dried up.' I nodded. The note of devotion had not left his voice; if anything, he seemed more tender at having to point out a blemish in his country. So I learned very early on of the love that many white Rhodesians feel for the land. It is not really surprising but it is sometimes a forgotten factor, and Europeans are depicted as little more than exploiters of its natural wealth.

The train drew into Salisbury. The platform was crowded with people waiting to welcome travellers back and as soon as the train stopped there were tears, embraces, handshakes. I felt rather lost but was rescued by an announcement over a loudspeaker asking all new Civil Servants to gather by the kiosk. An official met us there and we were taken to a reception-camp for government employees. It lay twelve miles out of the city and had been an R.A.F. aerodrome during the last war, where young airmen were brought under the Dominion Training Scheme. The corrugated iron hutments had grown shabby with age. The camp had lost its original military polish—the chilling gleam of brass and whitewash—and nothing much had been put in its place. It had a neglected air; the plantations of euphorbia and frangipani were poorly tended; and what had once been flowerbeds were now for the most part trampled earth.

Yet though the quarters were poor, some aspects of our living were to prove luxurious. We ate in a communal dining-hall with an African waiter to every table and our rather monkish rooms were cleaned and our beds made by a discreet African servant. We were immediately within the area of privilege: it was shown to us like a promised land on whose outskirts we stood. Of course, it was very pleasant to have all the menial tasks taken out of one's hands, particularly as we were asked very little in the way of money for these services: the government subsidized us to ensure that from the start we enjoyed the accepted European standards.

All the same, the camp was a forlorn place and I was anxious to leave it, though not everybody thought as I did. Some immigrants had gone on living at the camp for years, squatting on the very frontier of the good life, and this despite the official description of the place. Anyone who found it possible to ignore the tired squalor of iron hutments and poky rooms could enjoy a moneyed existence and free servants—you could see big American cars parked outside some of the doors.

A journey into Salisbury gave a glimpse of what you might aspire to if you chose to live more graciously. The bungalows that lined suburban roads were not architecturally exciting, perhaps, but they were big and looked affluent. White paint shone on their woodwork; their tiled roofs glittered in the sun. Immaculate drives led to gabled garages, and by their side ran big lawns, kept green, even in winter, by the circling swish of a water sprinkler. Often, there were large patrician dogs loose in the garden, and there would probably be a black man, his clothes the colour of the soil, crouched somewhere in the flowerbeds, turning the earth. You might catch a glimpse, too, of cane chairs on a red verandah, with sometimes a barbecue grate let into one of its walls; it spoke of chicken legs and savoury sausages eaten in the open as the dusk fell and bottles and glasses on the table reflected the afterglow.

The same sense of plenty, of a rich surfeit of physical well-being, emanated from the pavilions and groomed turf of the sports clubs that play such an important part in white Rhodesian life. The inside of such clubs might vary from the fronded elegance of the more exclusive establishments to the roisterous men's bars where sawdust was still strewn piously on the floor and the walls carried jokes in pokerwork about the golfer who lost his balls or whimsical cartoons celebrating 'la différance'. But in all of them drink would be cheap, cigarettes even cheaper, servants plentiful, and a spirit of noisy camaraderie not difficult to establish by practised bonhomists after the game of tennis or bowls or rugby football.

This was the kind of environment where easy prejudices flourished, a good place to hear the jokes against the African which were commonly used to affirm white superiority and ward off uneasiness. A few of the classic ones are worth a brief examination because of the attitudes they display. The story was often told of the farmer who taught a baboon to drive a tractor. He sent the baboon off to plough a field and, later in the morning, went to have a look how it was getting on. The baboon had made a good job of the ploughing except that in one place, where a boulder stuck out of the ground, the furrows swerved round it. 'Look,' said the farmer, 'you can't leave that rock there. You're spoiling the field with it. Get down from the tractor and shift it.' 'What!' shouted the baboon. 'What do you think I am? A bloody munt?'

This illustrates succinctly the white contempt for physical labour and those who perform it. Even a baboon would rebel from 'Kaffir's work'. It is echoed in other stories such as that of the South African who visited London for the first time. On his return, he was asked what he thought of England. 'Christ, man!' he said in amazement. 'What a place! What a place! Why, even the Kaffirs are white.' The bitter joke that Swift made against mankind at the end of *Gulliver's Travels* when he reported that the Houyhnhnms were thinking of discarding the Yahoos for some more efficient and less unreliable form of labour can be heard in the Rhodesian setting as: 'They're thinking of getting rid of the munts and bringing in baboons instead.' The baboon figures once more in a cartoon I remember seeing pinned to the woodwork of a club bar. In this case, it is retreating out of a room with a tray in its hands and it has on the typical servant's uniform. Two Europeans are watching it go, and one is saying to the other: 'Looks a bit odd, I know, but he's the best house-boy we've ever had.'

There are many house-boy jokes, most of them celebrating his complete ineptitude, but here is one of a different kind: In one of the disturbances of recent years, the rumour ran round the white population that on a certain date their servants would attack and kill them all. Mrs. Smith, as the story goes, was most distressed by this news. She felt that she had always 'done well by her boys' and was incredulous at the idea that she, who had acted so maternally towards her servants, might be rewarded in this way. She called her house-boy in and said gently, 'Sixpence, you wouldn't kill your Missus, would you, who's done so much for you?' Sixpence smiled brightly. 'No, Missus. Me go nex' door, kill that Missus. Boy nex' door, he come kill you.' This joke says a good deal: about European beliefs on the nature of African reasoning; about the constant white uneasiness; and the knowledge that Europeans are very vulnerable to assault because of the number of servants they employ about their houses.

The African tendency to ape European ways is another common theme. When certain of the Northern Rhodesian bars were opened to Africans, inane stories like this one appeared:

A European walked into a bar and ordered a gin and vermouth, 'Oh,' he said, 'and put a cherry in it, please.' A gawking African who had followed him in thought he would show himself as good as the white man. 'Gimme a pint of beer,' he shouted. 'An' put a *paw-paw* in it.' A *paw-paw* is a big, soft, pulpy fruit.

Perhaps we might end this little survey with a joke whose implications are more complex. It concerns Federation. As the story goes, Sir Roy Welensky, or some such white politician, was touring the tribal areas to try to persuade the rural Africans there to support Federation. 'Yes,' he said in his speech to them, 'with Federation you will be able to go into all the white restaurants and shops.' The African crowd clapped their hands politely and murmured '*Zoruba, zoruba.*' 'You will be able to vote and you will earn money like the white man.' '*Zoruba, zoruba,*' the Africans replied. 'With Federation we shall all be partners together.' '*Zoruba, zoruba,*' came the respectful murmur again.

After the speech was over, the chief insisted on making Sir Roy the gift of a bull in token of his admiration. They all went down to the cattle-kraal together to inspect the beasts. 'There's the one I'd like,' said Sir Roy, moving forward into the kraal to point out a white bull. 'Careful, baas,' said the chief quickly. 'You step in the *zoruba.*'

Here European cynicism about the 'partnership' promised by Federation is reflected through the African. In the terms of the story, the African is supposed to recognize the fraudulence of the promises and, in a way, to accept the situation: he and his white master are in a kind of collusion and the only ones really hoodwinked are the men in Whitehall. This was a common attitude towards the pledges made in the preamble to the Federal constitution. Promises were made in order to gain certain ends but their implementation, it was felt, could be indefinitely delayed. In this way, British idealism could be soothed without any real transfer of power. Expediency and manipulation have always been strong forces in Rhodesian politics. Concessions have been made in the past with the intention of shoring up white power as far as possible, not on any liberal principle. No doubt they will be so again. The real flash point will come, not at the enfranchising of an African minority or the opening of post-offices or restaurants, but at the moment when political power has to be relinquished and the entrenched position of the European becomes vulnerable to sweeping legislation by African members of the House of Assembly.

I was to find out all this sort of thing later. My first glimpse of the bungalows and sports pavilions showed them bathed in a vibrant light, a brightness that seemed like a physical manifestation of innocence—what people refer to always as 'the climate', giving it as one of the strongest of reasons why they could never go back to England to live.

The centre of the city developed the same theme: buildings unsullied by dirt; high façades sparkling in the sun; palm trees and flowering avenues. The air of prosperity was heartening. The only exceptions—with a shabbiness that seemed almost wilful—were the Africans, those of them, that is, who were not dressed in the khaki uniform of the messenger, the sweeper or the tea-boy.

After a little while, you began to notice the Africans more. You saw how they stepped aside with swift deference should you meet one on the pavements; how they crowded into the cheap department stores where the trade they brought was valuable enough to secure their admittance; how the women still suckled their babies in the streets, often squatting down on the edge of the gutter to take advantage of the shade cast by a parked car. You saw how eagerly they eyed the children's garments in the shops, despite the fact that most of the prices on the tags were far out of their reach, and the gentleness with which they treated their own piccaninns.

It was obvious that they were very poor, and equally obvious that

216

most of them were nervous. Twenty years before, if they had been found walking on the pavements, they would have been shouldered off into the gutter: the towns were the white man's place. This feeling had been enshrined in an Act of 1906 which forbade any African to use the footpaths or pavements in a municipality. It was no longer enforced, but the Africans did not seem to have forgotten that the pavement was a privilege their fathers had not shared. They were still under the threat of many other kinds of humiliation. They might be ordered out of a store by any pert white shop-girl or kept waiting by her indefinitely whilst she attended to later European arrivals. They were open to bullying and demonstrations of contempt from white adolescents, and there was nothing they could do about it. Indeed, their whole position was one which gave great scope to the petty tyrant that lurks in many people.

The tyranny was not always petty. During my first few months in Rhodesia, a white farmer whipped one of his African employees to death with fencing wire in punishment for a trivial theft. He was brought to court and found guilty of 'culpable homicide' which entailed for him a prison sentence of surprising brevity. Perhaps that one incident illustrates the dangers in which the African felt himself to walk. It is an extreme example but it reflected a common white sentiment: Africans were of little value compared with Europeans. They had to be 'kept in their place' and not allowed to become too 'cheeky'.

But when I first walked round the city, such matters were not obvious. The Africans were unobtrusive despite their great numbers. I was puzzled to know where they might possibly live. I noticed that they swept out of the city each night after work ended in a great stream of buses and cyclists. In the evening there was hardly one to be seen in the town centre. Later, I was to find out where they lived and to walk round amongst the long dreary lines of shacks and cottages, and the tall blocks that are the vertical barracks of the single men, who still predominate.

It was not the housing of the Africans itself that was unbearable, though much of it was squalid. Some of the big blocks were show-pieces and had been the cause of resentment amongst many Europeans who said they were 'too good for munts'. But if such critics had taken a look at the institutional nature of these buildings, the utterly functional rooms where men are housed three and four together, they might have revised their opinion. Still, despite their bleak air, such buildings are sound and weatherproof; in terms of protection they are a decided advance on the leaking mud huts of the Reserves. It was not so much the kind of housing that mattered, I felt. It was something even more fundamental: the rejection implicit in the siting of the locations; the banishment of Africans to places miles outside the cities. They were in social quarantine, like the carriers of some loathed disease.

It was not long before I met the battery of arguments offered by the ordinary European to justify his treatment of the African. I had been given an introduction whilst still in England to a Salisbury family, and after a few days I decided to act upon it. The woman of the house turned out to be a widow who lived with her unmarried daughter. The house itself was typically suburban and very comfortable. I was made welcome, not only for the sake of hospitality but also because I was an immigrant, a new brick added to the height of the white dam, and in those days many people still cherished the hope that a defeating bulwark of whites could be erected against the African. After 'sundowners' we ate an excellent meal served by a rather apprehensive African, and towards him, I noticed, the natural courtesy of these women failed. Their voices became taut and clipped and they seemed to wish to remind him of their authority with every word they spoke. Of course, they were women living alone and probably felt they could not afford to relax in any way towards their black servant. But the mood was one I was to meet again: the note of impatience or even disgust that came into the voices of European women when they had to talk to 'Natives'.

Philip Mason has speculated on the causes for this apparent distaste that seems so prevalent amongst them. He refers it to an underlying attraction, not for the black man himself, but for the primitive freedom he represents, the lack of sexual restraint with which he is often credited. Most Europeans would tell you that the African was licentious by nature. They would point to the promiscuity found in the locations; the nurse-maids they have employed who were 'invariably' half-crown whores on the side; the 'spares' or 'wives of the pots' who went from man to man amongst the migrant labourers; the high incidence of syphilis. Most of them know little or nothing of African customary life or marital institutions and are unwilling to accept that the sexual license and general breakdown they can see in the locations are the result of the system their own government has imposed on the African.

European men often adopt a rather different tone amongst themselves. They are more likely to speak of the African's virility or the size of his members, mingling a faint yet discernible envy with the disparaging remarks they make about his animal nature and his inability to understand the meaning of the word 'love'.

A Personal View

I steered the conversation on to the Africans and my hostess's daughter told me they were really nothing more than 'black apes'. You had only to look at their faces to see it. They were incredibly primitive, she said, and had not even invented the wheel when the Pioneers arrived on the scene. They were 'different' from white men. I asked in what way they were different and was told that they were savages and consequently had to be held in check. I pressed the point a little further, seeking a definition of their difference, and was told that they lacked the 'two thousand years of civilization' that all white men inherited, with the further implication that it would take them a similar time to develop to 'our' present standard. Such arguments may seem crude but, as I was to find out, they were the declared basis of the ordinary man's opposition to the African. Anyone who has lived in Rhodesia will have heard them voiced a thousand times, often by people whose own quite recent ancestors were in all likelihood unlettered peasants, or illiterates penned in some urban slum of industrial England.

The daughter made another criticism, one commonly levelled against Africans, and made to carry a surprising weight of proof: 'They smell,' she said. 'They're dirty and they smell.' At first, I was inclined to put this down to poverty and overcrowding, but later I came to realize that the African does have a distinctive odour, particularly if he is excited or nervous. But it is simply a smell unlike that of European sweat; it does not conjure up visions of the monkey-house or the fold-yard, as is often implied.

People conscious of divisions of class or caste always seem to have made a great play with the olfactory sense. Orwell discussed it as a strong factor in the old middle-class shrinking dislike of the proletariat in England, and described how he himself had some trouble mastering a prejudice bred in him from childhood, as this one was.

The daughter offered one last remark: 'Even when they're educated, you know, they always revert. If they get drunk or excited, they revert.' This opinion, too, was commonly held and could be used to demolish the pretensions of the few educated Africans who had made their appearance on the Southern Rhodesian scene. They were no longer mere 'primitives'; they were 'primitives' with degrees and diplomas. Their sophistication was only a 'veneer': scratch it and you revealed the old barbarism underneath. Any evidence in support of this contention could always be expected to gain a warm welcome from many Europeans. Such an item as this one, printed in the national Sunday newspaper, would be quoted as proof that the African was still primitive at heart: 'I know one African, distinguished though he is in his personal career, who after a few drinks reverts to the tribal habit of squatting on the floor, and will even roll back the carpet to do so.'¹ Trivia of this kind were retailed in all seriousness and with a note of refined sensibility that could infuriate.

Flimsy though these arguments seemed, I was to realize that, in using them, the young woman had displayed for me all the usual debating points and rationalizations in vogue amongst ordinary Europeans. On such frail evidence, a whole people was consigned to an inferiority that was not relative and remediable but innate. Of course, behind this crazy façade lurked the much more substantial figure of self-interest, and with it, fear.

Perhaps it might be worth saying a word on the way Rhodesians are created out of immigrants. From the moment the Englishman arrives in the country, he becomes part of white society, subject to many pressures, all of them urging him to conform, by law if necessary. Though he may disapprove privately, he will find himself forced to adopt the *mores* of the country. Should he be married, with a wife and children, his entanglement will be more quickly complete. In the days when immigration was considerable, there was always a great shortage of houses and flats to let. He might put up for a time in a transit camp, in poky quarters made of corrugated iron and hardboard, but before long the place would begin to get on his nerves to the point where he would think of buying a house. He would already have had to buy a car in order to get about a city where distances are great and the bus services rare and erratic. He would take advantage of a housing loan from the government or a building society and fill his house with furniture on hire-purchase—and in that way, he would find himself netted. His property, his whole existence, would begin to seem bound up with the continuation of the present system. The various instalments had to be paid; certain standards maintained; the new, precarious prosperity enjoyed and made more secure. The threat to all these things seemed to lie in the African, who could be seen clamouring increasingly for a share in the government and an entry into all those occupations from which he was barred.

It was this kind of mixture of pressure and privilege that regularly turned quite liberal immigrants into advocates of white supremacy. They were bludgeoned into it by the terms on which their livelihood depended. Also, Rhodesia, like America, was a land of debtors; a country where it always seemed necessary to buy the next thing before the last one had been paid for. Like America, too, it was a country obsessed by symbols of material wealth. There was no other definition of status available—or acceptable—except the size of your house or your car, the nature of your furnishings, the lavishness of your hospitality. All levels of white society were drawn into this kind of continual conspicuous expenditure and as a result, most people never had enough money to do all they wanted. Their suburban splendour was compounded with debt and envy; though their salaries were high, they were never high enough.

That, roughly, was the way Rhodesians were made. Pressure was brought to bear on them in such various ways that, sooner or later, they began to conform with the expected conventions of behaviour, and in understandable human weakness, they accepted not only the privilege but the ideology that went with it. By its aid, they could find comfort and security and a sense of solidarity with the rest of the white population; they were provided with arguments that could be used to repulse any doubts about the fairness of the system that might visit them. It was a process from which visiting professors and journalists were immune—they had their own kind of additional privilege in that respect—and one which they could condemn more absolutely than I, who lived in the midst of it and was part of it. The more thoughtful of us were quite aware that the system was a pernicious one, but could see no method by which we might alter it. It seems likely that only pressure from below, from the mass of the African population, will be strong enough to convince the government that sweeping changes must be made immediately. It is a task beyond the capacity of European liberals.

I have said some harsh things in this book about white Rhodesian attitude to Africans, and I must, in justice, add now that many of them were very kind to individual Africans. But it was usually a paternal kindness, a rewarding of the faithful retainer. It rarely had any smack of equality about it. For the rest, the average European remains surprisingly ignorant both of the African past and the present conditions of life of the town worker.

However, the lives of the urban poor have a melancholy similarity everywhere: they hinge on dull labour, overcrowded quarters, lack of money, and such pleasures as prostitutes and strong drink—in this case the forbidden 'skokiaan'. A day in the life of an average town labourer would begin when he rolled off his straw mattress, sluiced himself under the cold water tap in the yard, had a drink of water and a slice or two of bread and went off to work. If he could, he would go on foot or by bike,

even over a longish distance, because the cost of bus fares out of his
small wage is crippling. He would work from 7.30 or 8 a.m. until perhaps 12.30, with no formal break. At lunch-time, if he were under an
enlightened employer, he might get an 'industrial dinner'—a hunk of
sadza porridge with gravy and some scraps of vegetable for relish served
up in a tin dixie. Otherwise, he would buy a bun or some bread from
one of the kiosks that are scattered about the industrial areas and eat it
squatting on the ground. There is no canteen that I know of in any
factory or industrial concern in Salisbury. If he was in funds, he might
treat himself to some chips or a meat pie, or a bottle of fizzy green
water. He has been criticized for such extravagances by European
dieticians, who point out that African malnutrition is aggravated by
'foolish buying' of this kind. The same accusation was made against the
English poor in the thirties; Orwell discussed it in *The Road to Wigan
Pier*. He pointed out—I think rightly—that people who live most of the
time on a meagre and inadequate diet can be expected, when the chance
arises, to tempt their dulled palates with something 'tasty' rather than
make sensible purchases. A bun and a bottle of mineral water are their
luxuries—and luxuries are indulged in to refresh the spirit, not to keep
the body alive, except indirectly. In any case, a *regimen* which achieves a
balance of protein with starch, fat with carbohydrate, is the result of
voluntary abstention and is indulged in by the prosperous. It is unlikely to occur amongst those who regularly lack enough food of any
kind and who seem likely to go on doing so for the rest of their lives.

The African will plod through the rest of his working day and then
walk home to get his main meal of the day ready. It is not likely to be
much different from his 'industrial dinner', if he had one, and often it
has to be prepared under very difficult conditions and with few or no
facilities. His 'home' is the room he sleeps in, probably with as many as
four or five other men, and possibly with women and children, too. In
some of the compounds, it may be an old, dirty place, its walls alive
with cockroaches. Privacy is usually impossible. So he goes on, one bit
of the wrack of tribal life, floating in a sea of urban poverty, caught in a
repetitive dream of labour with no hope of escaping into anything better.
Yet for all that, he still keeps alive what Livingstone spoke of as 'the
loud laughter of joy'. He shows an inextinguishable appetite for life
and a great thirst for Western knowledge.

Many town Africans are only half unloosed from the past; they still
retain many of the customary virtues. It is unlikely that they will see
anyone starve whilst they have food to offer, or will let a 'brother' sleep

in the ditches if they can spare him a bit of the floor in their cramped quarters. Lost as they must feel in a strange and dangerous world, they have kept alive, very often, their belief in witchcraft and with it their faith in the *nganga* or diviner, who is one of the few men who still gains prestige from carrying on an occupation born of the old Africa.

But the *nganga* has changed very much, and perhaps his metamorphosis might be taken as an example of the inter-action of the old with the new. Professor Mitchell, the anthropologist at the Federal University in Salisbury, gave this description of an urban *nganga* he investigated in 1959: The *nganga* had an office, tricked out in some respects like a doctor's surgery with desk and filing cabinet and typewriter. He wore a white smock and appeared, looking brusque and professional, in the doorway of his waiting-room to call in his next 'patient'. On shelves round the walls of his room there were dried herbs, shells, mummified pangolin, all the paraphernalia of his trade. He published a brochure—in rather wild English—that listed his successes in cases where white doctors had failed before him. Yet he was willing to admit the supremacy of the white doctor in some kinds of treatment, although he maintained that they were not his equal when it came to making protective magic, to arranging that examinations should be easy or white employers amenable, to ensuring love and cajoling fortune and turning away the evil of others. This *nganga* was a member of a professional association intended to protect the interests of all who followed his calling. He had grown comparatively rich from his trade and was thoroughly urbanized, so that now he never went back to the Reserves except to gather herbs and occasionally to visit relatives. Most fantastic of all, he was a practising Christian who never missed church on a Sunday morning.

This is a bizarre reflection of the Western influence that can be found shaping the lives of urban Africans more and more. They cannot resist the glamour of the cheap wrist watch, the horn-rimmed spectacles they do not need, the gaudy sweatshirt, the inappropriate face-powder, the cheap suit. They will literally starve themselves in order to scrape together enough money to buy these emblems of the new world. It is the only form of acceptance that has been offered to them by the European. Traders have been quick to exploit their weakness in this direction, after a fashion that we have already been accustomed to for a long time in Europe. African newspapers are full of advertisements telling their readers that if they drink a certain beer or smoke a certain cigarette they will be attaining an unusual sophistication which will make them 'smarter' than others. They are tempted by brazen exhortations to buy deodorants and hair-straighteners in the hope of improving their social position.

We appear to be at the threshold of a new form of commercial exploitation in Central Africa: the professional persuaders have begun to manipulate the very values by which men live, here as elsewhere. No doubt, in commercial terms, all this can be explained as an attempt to develop an internal mass market in Rhodesia, but it seems to involve the debauching of a naïve people and is a poor exchange for the values of village life, aiming as it does to set Africans on the same race as that which occupies so many Europeans, but at their own abject level. At the moment, in their emotional and cultural nakedness, they are particularly vulnerable to such blandishments, confused as these are with their wholesome and legitimate demand for more of the material pleasures of life.

Breaches have been made in recent years in the wall of segregation, but on the whole they appear to have been reluctant responses to pressure or sops to assuage British opinion, not part of a sincere and consistent liberalizing policy. An African has been able for some years to attend the multi-racial university in Salisbury. An African may also buy a sweep-ticket in the national lottery nowadays. But to an African who combined these two extremes of good fortune, a University degree and the first prize of £30,000 in the lottery, the following disabilities would still have applied as late as 1960, when I left Rhodesia:

Such a man could not buy a house or business in a European area; he could not travel in a 'European' coach in a train, use the lift in most of the office buildings in Salisbury or consult a professional man by the usual entrance. He could not get in to see a European cinema-show; he could not visit a 'white' restaurant or dance-hall and very few hotels would tolerate his presence. The only capacity in which he could join a sports club would be as a waiter. He could not try on a garment in a European shop—if he could get served at all. He could not buy a bottle of whisky or any other spirit. He would have great difficulty in taking out a comprehensive insurance for the new car he might buy. He could not go into a European swimming bath. He would be frowned on if he went into the main part of the bank that held his money. He could only use a second-class taxi. His children could not play on the swings in the public parks, nor, until recently, could he sit on some of the benches there. He would be segregated in a bus—if he boarded one on a route where he was admitted at all. He could not go to a hairdresser or chiropodist or masseur in the European area; nor to a doctor unless he chose to run a special African surgery. He could not send his son to any private school, should he wish to, nor to any of the government schools set aside for Europeans. He could not reserve a bed in a private nursing home if his wife was expecting a baby. Under no circumstances could he make use of a 'European' public lavatory. If he made an act of protest and were sent to prison, he would still find himself segregated from all whites and given inferior treatment. If he went mad—as well he might— he would be sent to an asylum run on a basis of segregation. No matter how much money he offered, he could not buy a plot in a European cemetery to provide for his death. It was a state of affairs where neither intelligence nor wealth could save him from daily humiliation.

As time goes on, all these indignities will be removed, and with them the Acts which are the foundation of white privilege. African pressure is bound to open industry and unlock the land. The African has seen that his salvation will be political and we can expect to see him wrest more and more of the control of public affairs into his own hands. Further concessions have recently been made by a nervous white government, but Europeans will delude themselves, I think, if they imagine that they can permanently satisfy the mass of the population by offers which still leave the white minority in political control.

The Southern Rhodesian Government has recently proposed, reluctantly and under pressure, to widen the franchise, though only for a separate African Roll, and to admit a minority of African members to the House of Assembly. Power will still rest in white hands, even if these proposals are successfully enacted, and the government may be cherishing once more the old hope that by this gesture it can create an African middle-class vote which will find its interests linked to those of the European and act as a buffer against the African masses. I think any such hope is bound to be disappointed.

Over the next few years, it seems inevitable that the Europeans will be driven steadily nearer to that dangerous watershed: the moment when power passes out of their hands and into those of the Africans. With each step, each new offer, each concession, they are likely to ask, 'Is that enough?' and always receive the same answer. At any point in that progress, they may strike out in their desperation, or the African may be goaded into violence by his impatience. Whatever happens, nothing seems likely to stop the movement until it has enfranchised the masses and reduced European power and influence to that which is proper for a small minority. If the white government could recognize this and willingly assist at the dismantling of European privilege within a reasonable time, much frustration and bitterness might be avoided and many old wounds soothed. This is to ask a great deal of the Europeans in Southern Rhodesia, but it would surely be better—and wiser— to give freely now than to be forced along the same path, fighting each step. What is to be demanded from the Africans is no less difficult; magnanimity towards their old masters when at last they find they have become their equals. But no other solution appears possible to either side, if hatred and bloodshed are to be avoided.

Looked at in the perspective of history, what will probably strike scholars of the twenty-first century is the brevity of the period of European domination in Southern Rhodesia and the fewness of the settlers, in face of what they accomplished. They will be able to assume a corresponding ruthlessness. White rule will be seen as a brief interlude, lasting less than 100 years from first to last. But it will surely be regarded as a crucial period, too; one in which the immemorial ways of African customary life were broken and discarded and the new industrial system was successfully imposed—with all that must come to mean in terms of the eventual prosperity of the entire population of the country. This, taking the long view, is surely the importance of the European intrusion into Central Africa, and may be offered as its justification.

The settlers did not act from philanthropy; for a good many 為 they enjoyed an improbable dream of endless domination, whereas their real role was the fugitive if essential one of the catalyst, transforming the material in which it works. The settlers succeeded, but not in what they set out to do. That is often the way history works. They were the agents of an industrial revolution; the bringers of a new world; often harsh exploiters and yet ultimately benefactors to mankind in this part of Africa.

Books and Articles
Principally Consulted

This list does not aim at being a bibliography.

History of Southern Africa. E. A. Walker. Longmans (1957), 3rd edition.

History and Ethnography of Africa South of the Zambesi before 1795. (Vol. 1 chiefly used.) G. M. Theal. Sonnenschein (1910).

Races of Africa. C. G. Seligmann. O.U.P. (1957), 3rd edition.

The Harmless People. E. Marshall Thomas. Secker & Warburg (1959).

The Lost World of the Kalahari. L. Van der Post. Hogarth Press (1958).

The Mashona. C. Bullock. Juta, Cape Town (1927).

Shona Customary Law. J. F. Holleman. O.U.P. for the Rhodes-Livingstone Institute (1952).

African Interlude. J. F. Holleman. Cape Town, Bloemfontein, Johannesburg Nasionale Boekhandel Beperk (1958).

Seven Tribes of Central Africa. (Shona Section, by J. F. Holleman). Manchester U.P. for the Rhodes-Livingstone Institute (1959), 2nd impression.

Medicine and Magic of the Mashona. M. Gelfand. Juta, Cape Town (1956).

Shona Ritual, with Special Reference to the Chaminuka Cult. M. Gelfand. Juta, Cape Town (1959).

Custom and Conflict in Africa. M. Gluckman. Blackwell, Oxford (1955).

Witchcraft, Oracles and Magic among the Azande. E. E. Evans-Pritchard. Oxford, Clarendon Press (1937).

Witchcraft. G. Parrinder. Pelican Books.

Books and Articles Principally Consulted

Mlimo' and 'Mwari'. Notes on a Native Religion in Southern Rhodesia. J. Blake Thompson and R. Summers. N.A.D.A. Vol. 33 (1956).

Some Notes on African Ritual Sacrifice. J. Blake Thompson. N.A.D.A. Vol. 34 (1957).

Names of Vashona. S. K. Jackson. N.A.D.A. Vol 34 (1957).

Shona Riddles. N. Hunt. N.A.D.A. Vol. 34 (1957).

Shaka Zulu: The Rise of the Zulu Empire. E. A. Ritter, Longmans (1955).

Prehistoric Rhodesia. R. N. Hall. Unwin (1909). Included as a representative of the literature repudiating the idea that Zimbabwe could have been African work.

The Zimbabwe Culture: Ruins and Reactions. G. Caton-Thompson. O.U.P. (1931).

Old Africa Rediscovered. Parts on Zimbabwe. Basil Davidson. Gollancz (1960).

Missionary Travels and Researches in South Africa. D. Livingstone (1857).

A Hunter's Wanderings in Africa. F. C. Selous. Richard Bentley (1895), 4th edition.

Sunshine and Storm in Rhodesia. F. C. Selous. Rowland Ward (1896).

Extracts from Francis Owen's Diaries, taken from *Settlers*. Ed. John Hale. Faber (1950).

The Making of Rhodesia. H. M. Hole. Macmillan (1926).

Great Days. (Early chapters) F. Johnson. Bell (1940).

Trooper Peter Halket of Mashonaland. O. Schreiner. T. Fisher Unwin (1897).

Cecil Rhodes. B. Williams. Constable (1921).

Cecil Rhodes. S. G. Millin. Chatto and Windus (1933).

Rhodes of Africa. Felix Gross. Cassell (1957).

Cecil Rhodes: His Political Life and Speeches. 'Vindex', Chapman (1900)

The Last Will and Testament of Cecil J. Rhodes. W. T. Stead. London (1902).

Heritage of Rhodes. W. D. Gale. O.U.P. (1950).

The Birth of a Plural Society, Northern Rhodesia, 1894–1914. Many references to S. Rhodesia throughout. L. H. Gann. Manchester U.P. (1958).

One Man's Hand: The Story of Sir Charles Coghlan and the Liberation of Southern Rhodesia. J. P. R. Wallis. Longmans (1950).

An Essay in Racial Tension. P. Mason. Royal Institute for International Affairs (1954).

Books and Articles Principally Consulted

The Birth of a Dilemma. P. Mason. O.U.P. for Institute of Race Relations (1958).

Dawn in Nyasaland. Chapters on S. Rhodesia. G. Clutton-Brock. Hodder & Stoughton (1959).

The Anatomy of Partnership. T. R. M. Creighton. Faber (1960).

The Two Nations. R. Gray. O.U.P. for Institute of Race Relations (1960).

European Politics in Southern Rhodesia. C. Leys. O.U.P. (1959).

Notes

PART ONE

Chapter 1
1. This and the extracts immediately following are taken from Theal: *History and Ethnography of Africa South of the Zambesi before 1795.*
2. Seligmann: *The Races of Africa.*

Chapter 2.
1. For a full account of these legends, see Ritter's *Chaka Zulu.*
2. Selous: *Sunshine and Storm in Southern Rhodesia.*
3. *Ibid.*
4. J. S. Moffat. *Correspondence.*

Chapter 4.
1. Bullock: *The Mashona.*

Chapter 5.
1. Freud: *Totem and Taboo.*

Chapter 6.
1. Livingstone: *Missionary Travels and Researches in South Africa.*
2. For a more extended account of *mutupo* and *chidawo* see Hollemann: *Shona Customary Law,* and Bullock: *The Mashona.*
3. Given by Dr. Gelfand: *Medicine and Magic of the Mashona.* This book and *Shona Ritual* by the same author have been widely used in this and other chapters.

Chapter 10
1. Quoted by Dr. Hollemann: *Shona Customary Law.* Much of the material in this chapter is derived from his work on the subject.
2. Livingstone: *Missionary Travels.*

Chapter 11.
1. Theal: *Ethnography.*

Notes

Chapter *14.*
1. See *Shona Riddles.* N. Hunt. N.A.D.A. (1957).

PART TWO

Chapter *1.*
1. Extract from Francis Owen's Diaries: see *Settlers,* edited by J. Hale.
2. Livingstone: *Missionary Travels.*
3. Owen's Diaries: *Settlers.*
4. This and all succeeding quotations from Livingstone in this chapter taken from *Missionary Travels.*

Chapter *3.*
1. Stead. This and succeeding references to Stead taken from: *The Last Will and Testament of Cecil J. Rhodes.*
2. Ruskin: *Inaugural Lecture,* Oxford. Quoted by Basil Williams in *Cecil Rhodes.*
3. Quoted by André Maurois: *Cecil Rhodes.*
4. See 'Vindex': *Cecil Rhodes, His Political Life and Speeches.*

Chapter *4.*
1. See Hole: *The Making of Rhodesia.*
2. Hole, in *The Making of Rhodesia,* has a facsimile reproduction of the vital portions of the Rudd Concession.
3. Johnson: *Great Days.*
4. The text of Lobengula's messages to the Pioneer Column and that of Pennefather's reply are taken from Hole: *The Making of Rhodesia.*

Chapter *5.*
1. Hole: *The Making of Rhodesia.*

Chapter *6.*
1. Selous: *Sunshine and Storm.*
2. Quotations from Labouchere in this chapter taken from Hole: *Making of Rhodesia.*
3. Selous: *Sunshine and Storm.*

Chapter *7.*
1. Extracts from Coghlan's speeches in this chapter are taken from: *One Man's Hand. The Story of Sir Charles Coghlan and the Liberation of Southern Rhodesia.*
2. Selous: *Sunshine and Storm.*
3. See Gross: *Rhodes of Africa.*
4. Leys: *European Politics in Southern Rhodesia.*

Chapter *8.*
1. Gale: *Heritage of Rhodes.*

Notes

2. *Ibid.*

3. These remarks occur in a letter to *The Times*, 31st October 1934. See Gray: *The Two Nations.*

4. Bullock: *The Mashona.*

5. See Walker: *A History of Southern Africa.*

6. S. R. Debates, 1951. See Gray: *The Two Nations* for a more extended account.

PART THREE

1. Part of letter in *Sunday Mail*, 4th October 1959.

Index

Index

Index

235

Index

Index

Index